Language
and Dialect
in Hawaii

Language and Dialec┆

A Sociolinguistic Histor┆

BY *John E. Reinecke*
EDITED BY *Stanley M. Tsuzaki*

n Hawaii

o 1935

University of Hawaii Press

HONOLULU   1969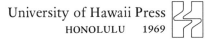

CONTENTS

TABLES

MAPS

EDITOR'S PREFACE

Language and Dialect in Hawaii is a minimally revised version of an M.A. thesis of the same title written at the University of Hawaii in 1935 by John E. Reinecke. While my interest in seeing this work published dates back many years to when I first read it, it was about two years ago that I first discussed this matter with the author. At that time we agreed that if the work was going to be revised at all for publication, I would have to assume the major part of the responsibility because of other commitments that the author had. In the two years or so that have elapsed since our initial talks, I have worked in consultation with Dr. Reinecke on several different versions of the revision. The present version is a revision containing minimal changes, with the substance of the original work consequently remaining virtually unaltered. It is a version which, however, both the author and I find quite acceptable.

Of the departures from the original, only the following need to be mentioned:

1. Deletion of peripheral material — e.g., marginal footnotes or parts of footnotes (particularly in the more lengthy ones) and non-essential references in the bibliography; several readily

available maps indicating the provenience of some of the immigrants to Hawaii—i.e., one map each of the Kwangtung region of China, of the Philippines, and of Japan and Korea; two appendices (i.e., "Appendix B: The Creole Dialect of Mauritius" and "Appendix C: Labor and Language Conditions in Jamaica"); and those few references mentioned by Reinecke in passing which I was not able to document.

2. Addition of editorial material—viz., editorial notes, which are clearly labeled and/or are set off in brackets to differentiate them from the notes in the original work. Emendations to incomplete references in the original were simply supplied (whenever possible) and are not marked in any special way.

3. Rearrangement of sections—viz., the original order of the bibliography and appendix was reversed; the section on communications, which formed part of the original bibliography, was set off as a separate section and placed after the bibliography; two appendices (i.e., supplementary sections) to Chapter 3 were incorporated into the main body of the chapter as "The Composition of the Language Groups of Hawaii" and "Statistical Material Relating to the Schools of Hawaii"; and a number of footnotes were similarly placed in the text, with the entire note affected in some cases and only part of the note in other cases.

4. Changes in the format of the maps and some of the tables, to facilitate reproduction, and in the arrangement of the bibliography, to facilitate the checking of references. The original graphs were deleted.

The publication of a work such as this, written over three decades ago, requires more than the usual kind of justification. Fortunately, this task is made relatively simple by the nature and quality of the original thesis. In the first place, it is unquestionably the best sociolinguistic history (i.e., sociology of language) of Hawaii ever written. For more than thirty years, it has served as an indispensable reference on Hawaiian "pidgin" and will undoubtedly continue to be so used. Secondly, I think it ranks among the better sociolinguistic histories written for any part of the world and may be compared favorably with such works as Leo Pap's *Portuguese-American Speech* and perhaps even with Einar Haugen's *The Norwegian Language in*

America (esp. Vol. I). Thirdly, its scope is broad enough to make this work of interest not only to those in the fields of languages and linguistics but also to those in anthropology, education, history, psychology, sociology, and possibly economics. Fourthly, in spite of more recent developments in this general area (as exemplified in the works of such scholars as Joshua A. Fishman, Robert A. Hall, Jr., Einar Haugen, and the late Uriel Weinreich), this work still stands as one of the clearest and most readable treatises on the subject, especially as restricted to a particular area of the world. While a few parts may seem a bit dated, most of the work is as valid and sound now as it was when it was written. Finally, I think that publication at this late date is justified by the increased interest shown in recent years, by professional linguists, sociologists, and others, in the fields of pidgin and creole languages as well as sociolinguistics. Not only have a greater number of publications dealing with these topics appeared (see, for example, the bibliography in R. A. Hall, Jr., *Pidgin and Creole Languages*), but specialized conferences also attest to this new interest (e.g., the UCLA Sociolinguistics Conference held on May 11-13, 1964, on the Los Angeles campus and at the University Conference Center, Lake Arrowhead;[1] and the Conference on Pidginization and Creolization of Languages held on April 9-12, 1968, at the University of the West Indies in Kingston, Jamaica). The appearance of this work at the present time seems to be particularly propitious in view of certain issues which specialists have been preoccupied with in recent years (e.g., the controversy pertaining to the origin of pidgin and creole languages), for Reinecke takes definite positions on these issues and, in my opinion, defends them ably.

Other pertinent works on language by Reinecke are listed in the Bibliography. They demonstrate clearly his long-standing interest in pidgins, creoles, and related areas—an interest which has not gone unnoticed by other scholars in the field. For example, R. A. Hall says in *Pidgin and Creole Languages*:

A full bibliography and an extensive discussion of the social nature and function of pidgins and creoles are given in Reinecke, 1937 [i.e., his Ph.D. dissertation, for which see "Marginal Languages" in the Biblio-

[1] For the proceedings of this conference, see William Bright (ed.), *Sociolinguistics*.

graphy]. . . . I am especially indebted to Dr. Reinecke for permission to utilize material from his bibliography in the preparation of this book and in many of my earlier studies on pidgins and creoles. (P. viii, n. 2.)

Also Dell Hymes has recently reprinted a summary of Reinecke's Ph.D. dissertation (see "Trade Jargons and Creole Dialects as Marginal Languages" in the Bibliography) in a reader in linguistics and anthropology: *Language in Culture and Society,* pp. 534-542.

Contentwise, the two introductory chapters of this work deal with the problem of "makeshift languages" and "regional dialects," the first being a treatment restricted to Hawaii and the second being a more generalized discussion of the topic. The ensuing chapters present the historical background of (makeshift) language and (regional) dialect in Hawaii, including sociocultural information pertaining to the language groups found in Hawaii and statistical information relating to the schools of Hawaii; the origin and functions of the creole dialect of Hawaii; the question of why the immigrant languages of Hawaii have persisted and have not been displaced, as in some other plantation areas of the world; the development of the colonial dialect from the creole dialect, principally in terms of educational and economic factors; and the nature, functions, and future of the colonial dialect. The last chapter contains theoretical as well as historical conclusions and selected topics for further investigation. The reference section at the end is comprised of an appendix containing examples of makeshift and dialectal English in Hawaii, a partially annotated bibliography, and a list of communications.

At this point it may be worthwhile to caution the reader about two problems. The first, which is relatively minor, pertains to Reinecke's use of the terms "creole" and "pidgin" in this study. From the standpoint of current technical usage (see, for example, Hall, *op. cit.,* pp. xi-xv), there is some confusion in their use in the present work, in the sense that they are not always clearly differentiated—a confusion which, incidentally, was cleared up in Reinecke's Ph.D. dissertation. This is only a potential problem, however (much of which this preliminary note of caution should preclude), because the context usually makes it clear which of the two is in fact intended.

The second problem, which is more serious, concerns the updating of references. Because of the proliferation of literature in the last thirty years or so in the various topics treated in this work, any systematic attempt in this direction would have required considerably more time and space than were allocated to this revision. Though it might have been more consistent to exclude new information altogether, the solution that was finally selected consisted of adding only those new sources that the author and/or I felt ought to be included for special reasons (e.g., so as not to mislead the reader). Practically all of these new references postdate the writing of the original work and deal with Hawaii. For additional references on Hawaii, the reader should consult the following bibliographies: (1) S. M. Tsuzaki and J. E. Reinecke, *English in Hawaii*, for post-1935 references on English in Hawaii; (2) Bernhard L. Hormann, *Selected Bibliography on Social Research in Hawaii by Sources*, for related references on Hawaii in general; (3) Mitsugu Matsuda, *The Japanese in Hawaii, 1868-1967*, for references relating to the Japanese in Hawaii.

I hope it will be borne in mind that my main concern in revising and publishing this work was to make it more accessible to professional as well as lay students of language in various disciplines and to make the information contained in it more public. Because of the demands of the task, editorial oversights may remain. For these I take full responsibility and can only hope that they do not detract too seriously from the reading of the work.

Many people have contributed in one way or another toward the completion of this work. Because several versions of the revision were involved, the number of persons to whom I am indebted is great. To all of them I express my sincerest thanks, and I hope that they will not find this blanket form of acknowledgment too difficult to accept. To the author, however, I need to convey a very special note of thanks for the helpfulness and patience shown in consultations, without which it would have been extremely difficult for me to have brought the editorial work to a conclusion.

Stanley M. Tsuzaki

HONOLULU, HAWAII   AUGUST 1968

AUTHOR'S PREFACE

This study of certain developments of language in Hawaii was begun in September, 1932, at the suggestion of Robert E. Park of the University of Chicago, who was at that time visiting professor of sociology at the University of Hawaii. Dr. Park had become interested in the formation of makeshift languages as one aspect of the contact between peoples of different cultures and suggested that I follow the development and functions of the plantation "pidgin" of Hawaii. As a teacher in the intermediate schools of Hawaii, I had adequate opportunity to observe the variety of English spoken and written by young people, and I was already interested in the purely linguistic aspects of what—thanks to T. T. Waterman of Honolulu—I already knew should be called the *dialect* of Hawaii. Inasmuch as this speech also bears the epithet of "pidgin," I soon found myself involved in establishing the connection between the two forms of speech.

The gathering of material and its digestion occupied my summer vacations and leisure time until the close of August, 1934, and thereafter I was engaged in rewriting earlier drafts of the chapters of this study.

Theoretical material dealing with the nature, functions, and formation of makeshift languages I found to be limited, whether linguistic or sociological in its point of view. The studies of creole dialects by H. Schuchardt and A. Coelho are not at present available in Hawaii. My theoretical basis in the discussion of makeshift languages rests almost wholly on the work of Joseph Vendryes and Otto Jespersen, while in appreciation of the social functions of language I owe much to Edward Sapir.[1]

The conception of makeshift or minimum languages I owe to Jespersen; that of creole languages or dialects I owe to Vendryes; for that of pidgin I am chiefly indebted to Jespersen; but the distinction between pidgin and creole is my own. As for the distinction between "pidgin" (i.e., creole dialect) and the present colloquial dialect of Hawaii, I am indebted to Waterman for certain basic ideas, but I claim whatever credit there may be for working out in some detail the differences and the connection between the two.

The ideal student of language in Hawaii would be trained in linguistics, especially in phonetics; he would be acquainted at least with Hawaiian, Japanese, Chinese, and Portuguese in addition to English; he would have a grasp of Hawaiian history and of Hawaiian social and educational conditions; he would also have a firm grounding in sociology. In the very probable absence of such a scholar, it is highly desirable that trained students should work on individual problems of linguistic development in these Islands, and that someone with a good grasp of linguistic and sociological theory should synthesize these contributions. I have received a thorough training in none of the disciplines named above, least of all in linguistics and the languages. Because of my limitations, therefore, my own study cannot be claimed as authoritative; nevertheless, I offer it as a beginning in one part of the field of linguistic development in Hawaii, and hope that it will raise questions which students better qualified than I shall answer.

---

[1]It might be helpful for the reader to bear in mind that at the time this work was done, there was a scarcity both of general information on pidgin and creole languages and of comparative data available in Hawaii.—*Ed.*

Such a study as this, dealing with makeshift language and colloquial dialect, must depend essentially upon the writer's own observations and upon the observations of those who are in a position to know something of the rapidly changing texture of the common speech of uneducated Islanders. These observations are only rarely recorded in print; they are likely to be unscientific, biased, and the result of imperfect knowledge and imperfect memory. When I have sought to elicit information through correspondence, several persons have not had the time or the interest to reply to my letters, and it has been hard to frame questions which would bring valuable replies. Interviews have been only partially satisfactory, because of the difficulty of framing the right sort of questions, because my informants and I were looking at the same phenomena from very different viewpoints, and because many people whom I had expected to know much about the substitution of English for Hawaiian and the development of the "pidgin" had observed but little. Nevertheless, I am under very deep obligation to those who have orally or through correspondence assisted me, here contributing a bit of knowledge, there a point of view. In the bibliography[2] and footnotes I have acknowledged those communications which I have used.

Valuable suggestions and encouragement have been given me by several friends, especially by Drs. Romanzo Adams, Andrew W. Lind, Edgar T. Thompson, T. T. Waterman, and Mr. Denzel Carr. Professor Ralph S. Kuykendall kindly checked Chapter 3 for historical facts, but he is not responsible for any of the views expressed therein. Finally,

> "But the wife drives, nor can man tell
> What hands so urge, what powers compel."

John E. Reinecke

HONOKAA, HAWAII   DECEMBER 1934

---

[2]See paragraph (3) in my Preface for changes made in the original bibliography.—*Ed.*

Language
and Dialect
in Hawaii

Chapter 1

INTRODUCTION:
THE PROBLEM OF
MAKESHIFT LANGUAGE
AND DIALECT IN HAWAII

The most casual observer is aware of the existence in Hawaii of a spoken English widely different from any accepted standard, either British or American. The difference from a standard may be greater or less, but apparently in the mind of the ordinary observer a continuum of deviation from his norm is evident. Locally this continuum has been known as "pidgin English," or simply as "pidgin."[1] This term has the support of popular usage, and in spite of its very misleading historical and linguistic associations, it may be expected to persist for many years in the face of protests from students.[2] The use of the term "pidgin" to cover all aspects of this continuum has been misleading in two senses; not only does it imply a greater similarity between the makeshift language of Hawaii and the language of the China ports than actually exists, but it has caused observers to lump together two somewhat different phenomena, a makeshift lan-

---

[1]Or much less frequently "broken English." I have not tried to find out the earliest date of the application of a term originally used for the trade language of the Chinese ports to the makeshift language of Hawaii. Probably its use dates from the 1850's, when the first Chinese were imported.

[2]T. T. Waterman, "Insular English," *Hawaii Educational Review*, February, 1930, pp. 145-146, 161-165.

3

guage of the creole dialect type and a regional dialect which has passed beyond the category of makeshift.[3] It shall be my task in this study to distinguish between these two forms of speech, the earlier makeshift language and the regional dialect that forms a later stage in the cycle of linguistic development.

This task, properly one belonging to the field of technical linguistics, has led me into a consideration of several of the chief elements of the sociology of language, as exemplified in Hawaii. The formation of a makeshift language and its evolution must be placed in their historical and social setting in Hawaii, and the factors in the social environment which were most important in giving rise to forms of speech aberrant from Standard English must be described. So also must the factors be indicated which have determined the functions which these forms of speech perform and the esteem (prestige value) in which they are held. In an environment such as that of Hawaii, the social basis of language can be seen with special clarity. The material at hand does not allow a full comparison between the environment and types of speech of Hawaii and of other countries where makeshift languages and colonial dialects have arisen; yet enough material is available to make it possible to attempt a classification of makeshift speech, based upon the functions of the various types and the social environment in which they have taken form. Since the interaction between English and other languages in Hawaii has had important effects upon the forms taken by the English language, I have also been led to give a cursory account of the competition of languages in these Islands, and of the position and functions of the various tongues now spoken here. Thus nearly the whole field of interaction between social and linguistic phenomena will be touched upon. I hope to present data on the linguistic situation of Hawaii which will be of help to later students of the sociology of language, and in addition to add somewhat to the theory of the function of makeshift speech and dialectal speech.

At the beginning of this study, two paragraphs of caution as

[3] This is evident in the first study of Hawaiian Island language problems printed in a technical journal: William C. Smith, "Pidgin English in Hawaii," *American Speech,* February, 1933, pp. 15-19.

to its limitations are in order. The practical person, whether educator or businessman, is interested in the nature of the roots of the "pidgin" continuum chiefly insofar as a knowledge of their nature will allow him to impose stricter standards of "good English" than now exist among the majority of the English-speaking population of Hawaii. Although a teacher, I have not tried to go into the technical side of language improvement. Some of the data which I present may be of aid to the schoolteacher, but I have no meliorative end in mind in presenting the material of this monograph.

The linguist, particularly the specialist in dialect, is interested in the details of pronunciation, stress and pitch, vocabulary, syntax, and accidence of a dialect, and a thorough treatment of the speech of Hawaii would have to include the linguistic problems as a necessary correlative to its social problems. Within the limits of this study, however, the purely linguistic treatment must be incidental to the elucidation of the difference between makeshift language and dialect and to a consideration of the factors that have affected the evolution of speech forms in Hawaii. The reader is referred to the studies by Reinecke and Tokimasa, Mowat, and Richmond;[4] and it is to be hoped that qualified students of language will continue the work which they have begun as amateurs.

[4]See the Bibliography.

Chapter 2

LOCAL DIALECT AND MAKESHIFT LANGUAGE IN THEIR WIDER SETTING

In studying the linguistic history of Hawaii, one soon finds that the phenomena observed here must be brought within a wide frame of reference and fitted with general terms in use in similar situations, so that their true nature will not be obscured by careless use of the local nomenclature. Unfortunately, to the reader's confusion, different writers in referring to the same general aspects of language have used different terms for them. Two tasks lie before us: to survey in brief fashion those aspects of language which must be known before the situation in Hawaii can be understood, and to choose a few terms suitable for bearing the weight of discussion. So important is the question of nomenclature in this problem that in this chapter the theoretical basis of this study will become apparent in large part.

Among the most prominent of the aspects in question are local dialect and makeshift language.

DIALECT

The term *dialect* is used in a remarkably inexact and all-inclusive manner.[1] For purposes of this study we may adopt the definition given by Vendryes, who says briefly: "Whenever in contiguous areas the current speech shows common peculiarities and a general resemblance apparent to the speaker, there is dialect."[2] That is, dialect is a local form of speech, confined areally. It may to a certain extent be also a mark of class because, if there is a standard language to which the local dialects stand in a sort of opposition (a situation found in many European countries), the "upper classes" of a dialect-speaking district are more likely than are the "lower classes" to speak the standard tongue. Yet the speaking of a local dialect is by no means a sure sign that the speaker is not a man of education and social position; and conversely one's class may be surmised from one's speech though one may use the standard language of the country.

Local dialects may be divided into two classes according to the historical and social circumstances of their formation. The typical dialects of European linguistic history have been formed primarily through the isolation of bodies of speakers of a "common prototype, known or inferred."[3] The dialects of France, which have been thoroughly studied and mapped, may be taken as an example. They were formed from the Low Latin

[1]The chief definitions may be outlined as follows:
1. Any variety of a language, including:
   a. Local dialects
   b. Special languages, including class dialects (*Enc. Brit.*, 11th ed., VIII, 155; Joseph Vendryes, *Language*, pp. 249-259)
2. Local or regional speech (Vendryes, *op. cit.*, pp. 249-259)
3. Local speech, as contrasted with a literary norm (Edward Sapir, *Language*, p. 164n; George Philip Krapp, *The English Language in America*, pp. 225-226)
4. Any unesteemed form of speech (a popular lay definition)
5. Local speech which contains a literature, as constrasted with patois (Vendryes, *op. cit.*, pp. 249-259)
6. A local form of speech related to another, especially if they be mutually intelligible (Edward Sapir, "Dialect," *En. Soc. Sci.*, V, 123)
7. A local form of speech related to another, and differing from it with respect to sound changes (statement of Denzel Carr, August, 1934).

[2]Vendryes, *op. cit.*, p. 260. Krapp (*op. cit.*, pp. 225-228) emphasizes the peculiarities and general resemblance apparent to those who do *not* speak the dialect.

[3]Sapir, "Dialect," *loc. cit.*

of the later Roman Empire, which was affected by the under-
lying Celtic habits of pronunciation and perhaps of syntax
among the Gallic population, and to a much less extent by the
Germanic languages of the invaders. Every district of medieval
France—one can almost say every manor—was largely self-
sufficient economically, besides being cut off from its neighbors
by poor communications and political particularism. Thus every
village of a small area may have a fairly stable dialect differing
slightly from that of every other village in the vicinity. So small
an area as the Department of Seine-et-Marne (2,273 square
miles) contains three quite distinct regional dialects.[4] Some of
these dialects (which together form the French language group)
became literary dialects, until one of them, that of the Île-de-
France, where the kings of France had their seat, has practically
crowded out all the others and has become the literary dialect
of the whole realm. The linguistic history of the other European
states has, roughly, paralleled that of France, while in the
United States the isolation of the mountaineers of the Appala-
chians and the Ozarks has given rise to a somewhat like formation of dialects of American English. "No known language,
unless it be artificially preserved for liturgical or other non-
popular uses, has ever been known to resist the tendency to
split up into dialects, any one of which may in the long run
assume the status of an independent language."[5]

The other class of local dialects is also formed through isolation, but under different circumstances than the typical dialect
of Europe. These dialects are due to the differentiation begun
and accelerated by the isolation of an overseas colony from the
parent stock and may be called *colonial dialects.* Usually a
second factor runs parallel to the isolation, namely, the contact
and consequent fusion of several local dialects of the mother
country. Thus a new dialect or group of dialects comes into
being, marked more or less by several of the dialects of the
homeland, yet differing in greater or lesser degree from them
all.

Because a common language has to be found for the speakers

[4]Vendryes, *op. cit.*, pp. 245-249, 260-261.
[5]Sapir, "Dialect," *loc. cit.*

of often widely divergent dialects, the colonial dialects some-times approach the standard speech of the mother country more closely than they do any one of the local dialects; thus Standard American and many of its local varieties are closer to Standard English (of southern England) than are broad York-shire or Lowland Scots or Somersetshire. Emigrants to the British colonies could not easily have been mutually intelligible if they had persisted in the use of the dialects of their several shires. They settled, therefore, upon the elements common to their respective dialects, and those who spoke both Standard English and dialect were encouraged to prefer the former in most of their conversation. Doubtless the same phenomenon is observable in the colonies of other countries. In countries already speaking a European language (the United States being the readiest example), as long as the immigrants retain their own languages, the same phenomenon can be observed.

To inhabitants of Hawaii this approach to the common language of the mother country should be especially interesting, for it is found to some extent among the speakers of both English and Japanese, and perhaps of other tongues as well. The English-speaking population was drawn from every part of the British Isles, the Dominions, and the United States, and no dialect has been preponderant enough to keep the English spoken by the Haoles[6] of the Islands from approaching Standard English. The isolation of the Japanese and the influence of their language schools have caused the natives of Yamaguchi, Kuma-moto, Niigata, Okinawa, and the other prefectures to speak more like the people of Tokyo (the linguistic as well as the political capital) than do their relatives who stayed at home.[7]

Furthermore, colonial dialects are often noteworthy for the vast areas over which they spread. Canadian French with few

[6]The local term "Haole" has been introduced to the reading public by such writers as Robert M. C. Littler in *Governance of Hawaii* and Lorna H. Jarrett in *Hawaii and Its People*. It is a Hawaiian word applied originally to foreigners in general but later restricted to people of European descent—with the exception of Portuguese, Spanish, Puerto Ricans, and sometimes minor groups such as the Russians, who are not popularly considered to belong to the same cultural and social level as the Americans, British, and North Europeans who compose the Haole ethnic group.

[7]Statements of several Japanese, particularly Yoshito Saigo, language school teacher in Honokaa.

local varieties covers a greater area than the Republic of France
with its many dialects; the Dutch language, spoken over a tiny
fraction of the surface of Europe, is divided into several widely
different dialects, while Afrikaans is practically the same
whether spoken in Cape Town or Johannesburg;[8] the multi-
plicity of dialects in Great Britain contrasts strongly with the
comparative uniformity of American and Canadian speech. In
the new countries the mobile colonists were able to spread over
great regions before relative fixity of residence and speech was
attained.

Few if any colonial dialects have been able to develop
unaffected by speech transfers and bilingualism. Icelandic and
the English of Australia have been among the freest from
foreign influence. Yet in the case of the former we may suspect
that the Celtic element of the population had some influence on
the speech of the Norwegians, and in Australia we find a
number of aboriginal words adopted into the English language.
The speech of the Spanish and Portuguese colonists in the
Americas has been influenced, in some cases very considerably,
by the Indian languages. In South Africa, Afrikaans contains
words from the native languages and from the Portuguese-Malay
pidgin and draws very extensively on the English, while conversely the English is colored with Dutch expressions. In
Canada, the United States, and Argentina the language of the
country has been changed by a tremendous influx of immigrants of many stocks. The influence of the aboriginal and
immigrant languages upon the English is to be seen in an
extreme form in Hawaii, and will form the substance of a large
part of the succeeding chapters.

Akin to the colonial dialects is the speech of immigrants who
form a socially dominated minority in their new land. This may
be called *immigrants' dialects.* There is one great difference
between the two; colonial dialects persist and take definite
form, sometimes becoming literary vehicles (as Afrikaans has
recently done), but the immigrants' dialects tend to disappear as
the immigrants are assimilated into the mass of the population.

[8]Adriaan J. Barnouw, *Language and Race Problems in South Africa*, pp. 24-25.

Religious bodies which practically form ethnic communities (as, for example, the Mennonites and the Yiddish-speaking Jews) and large, compact groups of rural settlers like the "Pennsylvania Dutch" and the Scandinavians of the northern Midwest may maintain their language for a considerable while—the Pennsylvania Dutch have done so for over two centuries.[9] These, however, are exceptional cases. Three generations usually sees the disappearance of the mother tongue among immigrants to the United States and Canada. While the foreign speech does maintain itself, however, it suffers progressive corruption at the hands of the native language, chiefly, at first, through wholesale adoption of loan words, later through adoption of the native intonation and stress, and through breakdown of the syntactical system. At last it becomes unrecognizable as part of the language to which it belonged and survives only in the influence it has locally upon the native tongue. While immigrants' dialects are still spoken extensively, they lack prestige. To speak or write them exposes one to the contempt of the population of the home country, as many a Hawaiian-bred Japanese can testify. They are links binding the immigrant to his old, familiar culture while he is engaged in adjusting himself to the new culture of his adopted country, but they cannot carry the old culture in its fullness, nor can they (except under the most exceptional circumstances) be the vehicle of any new cultural contribution.[10]

Immigrants' dialects should be of particular interest to the people of Hawaii, for these modes of speech are probably to be found in use among every linguistic-ethnic group of the Islands. They certainly exist among the Chinese and Japanese, and that of the Japanese may be studied in the columns of their news-

[9]Ernst Brauns, *Praktische Belehrungen und Rathschläge für Reisende und Auswanderer nach Amerika* (1929), pp. 351-352, 368, quoted in Lawrence Guy Brown, *Immigration*, pp. 73-74. See Edmund de S. Brunner, *Immigrant Farmers and Their Children*, for rural resistance to linguistic assimilation. Settlement in enclaves, where assimilation is extremely slow, as in much of Central Europe, is of the nature of colonization rather than of true immigration. See the beginning of Chapter IV for a discussion of it.

[10]Johanna Hamilton, "Zur Sprachbeeinflussung in anderssprachiger Umgebung," *Sociologus*, December, 1933, pp. 427-439; "Naturalization of Tongues," *The Interpreter*, April, 1928, pp. 7-15; H. L. Mencken, *The American Language*, examples in the appendix to the third edition.

papers as well as in their daily speech. Such phenomena as the adoption of both the Island (or "Portuguese") and the Standard English intonation in Japanese speech, and the loss of the Cantonese tones among the Chinese, may be observed by anyone having the barest acquaintance with these languages.[11] Among the Hawaiians, too, a similar influence of the English speech may be remarked. Unfortunately, only the influence of the English language upon the Hawaiian tongue has been studied.[12]

The concept of colonial dialect and the closely related concept of immigrants' dialect have been discussed at some length because of the part these dialects have in the speech of Hawaii. One may almost say that Hawaii is a land of colonial dialects. Even had the influence of the non-English-speaking stocks been less than it has, the isolation from the mainland of America would inevitably have brought certain linguistic changes in the English language. Some, indeed, are apparent. These are chiefly in the field of vocabulary; some words have been nearly dropped in an environment where they are not needed, while others have acquired specialized meanings. In addition, various American and British regional dialects have pooled their influ-

[11]Denzel Carr has pointed out that the reasons for the loss of the tones may be of interest. Inquiry among the writer's Chinese-American friends brought out three reasons, which are summed up by Violet U. Tsugawa in a letter dated November 9, 1934.

"I think there are several reasons why the young Chinese do not use the full Chinese tones in their speaking.

"1. (Generally true.) They *do not know* what the full tones should be. There are too many dialects. Even the people who speak the same dialect have numerous tone variations [from village to village].

"2. (True when speaking among ourselves.) In order to appear not too peculiar and different from their friends who use other dialects, many young friends of mine tone down and modify their speaking so as to make themselves sound and seem more like their companions.

"3. (True when we are speaking among 'foreigners.') I myself think the Chinese language is very musical, but there are some of us who are ashamed of its many tones and when speaking the language, modify it to suit ourselves. Some of us do not like to have our 'foreign friends' hear us using the full tones of our language. We do not wish to have them laugh at us."

[12]By Henry P. Judd in an unpublished study, "The Changes in the Hawaiian Language in the Last Hundred Years," and by Frederic B. Withington in an unpublished study, neither of which the writer has seen. There is a wide field here for investigation by language students of the University of Hawaii whose background is bilingual.

ence to make certain elements from each acceptable to all English-speakers.[13] The same holds true for the foreign languages; not only have the English and Hawaiian languages strongly influenced them, but the isolation from the homelands has reduced, narrowed, and specialized their vocabularies.

MAKESHIFT LANGUAGES

Throughout the world, wherever and whenever peoples of different speech have come in contact, two courses have been theoretically open to them: one of the languages in question might be learned carefully and with relative perfection by the speakers of the other languages; or one of the languages might be learned imperfectly and often in a corrupted form with elements, whether of vocabulary, of morphology, or of syntax, from the rest.

The first course was followed by the Japanese at the two cultural crises of their history, when in the sixth and seventh centuries A.D., select classes learned to read and speak Chinese in order that they might have access to the cultural riches of China, and again when, in the nineteenth century, the educated classes learned Western languages so that they might compete on equal terms with the Occident. The same phenomenon was seen in the Hellenistic Age, when the Oriental peoples—that is, certain classes among them, administrators, gentry, priests, *littérateurs,* and traders—learned the Greek *koiné*[14] or common language. By "learned" we are not to understand that all Orientals who set themselves to write and speak Greek came to use that language without an admixture of native speech elements; while the inability of the Japanese to use the Western languages naturally is proverbial. The point is that there was an effort on the part of well-equipped classes really to learn the foreign speech, to get at its cultural treasures as well as to use it as a mere instrument of communication with the foreigner. There were imperfections in the use of the foreign

[13]Reinecke and Tokimasa, "The English Dialect of Hawaii," *American Speech,* February, 1934, p. 53, col. 2 to p. 54, col. 1.

[14]"A form of language resulting from a compromise between various dialects and used as a common means of communication over an area covering all the contributing dialects." (Willem L. Graff, *Language and Languages,* p. xxxvii.) But the Greek *koiné* came chiefly from the Attic dialect.

language, but these were due to individual limitations, not to social limitations.[15]

The learning of a foreign language often is not confined to a small class. Bilingualism in the sense of effective and tolerably correct use of two languages is widespread. Some minor linguistic groups, such as those in parts of Europe and the partially Sinicized peoples of the Chinese Republic, are almost entirely bilingual. But such bilingualism requires long and generally peaceful contact between the two linguistic groups. It usually implies the superiority of one of the languages, whether because of its cultural richness, its widespread use in commerce, or the great number or the political superiority of its speakers.

But in many situations the relatively thorough learning of any language to serve as a common means of communication among different groups becomes difficult if not impossible. Thereupon arise what Jespersen in a penetrating study has called *makeshift languages* or *minimum languages.* That is, they are "means of expression which do not serve all the purposes of ordinary languages, but may be used as substitutes where fuller and better ones are not available."[16] Bearing a wide variety of local names—Lingua Franca, Sabir, Pidgin English, Chinook Jargon, Beach-la-mar (Bêche-de-mer English), Kitchen-Kaffir, Sudan Arabic, Bangala, Ki-Swahili (in its marginal forms), Mauritian Creole French, Creole French of the West Indies (notably of Haiti), Papiamento, *lingua gêral Brasilica,* Gullah, Bush Negro English of Surinam, *parau tinito,* etc., etc.,—they are found in most parts of the world and arise in various situations. But one thing they have in common, their extreme simplicity—or perhaps simplification is the better word, since they have been drawn from full languages.

---

[15]"In all these cases the theory of Windisch applies, that a people, when learning a foreign language, do not mix the foreign language with its own elements but its own language with the foreign elements, while its object is to speak the new language as correctly as possible and to understand it as well as it can." (G. W. J. Drewes, "The Influence of Western Civilisation on the Language of the East Indian Archipelago," in Schrieke, *The Effect of Western Influence on Native Civilisations in the Malay Archipelago,* p. 131.)

[16]Otto Jespersen, *Language,* p. 232 and pp. 216-236.

In all these languages . . . the grammatical structure has been simplified very much beyond what we find in any of the languages involved in their making, and simplified to such an extent that it may be expressed in very few words, and those nearly the same in all these languages, the chief rule being common to them all, that substantives, adjectives and verbs remain always unchanged. The vocabularies are as the poles asunder . . . but the morphology of all these languages is practically identical, because in all of them it has reached the vanishing point. . . . In all these seemingly so different cases the same mental factor is at work, namely, imperfect mastery of a language, which in its initial stage, in the child with its first language and in the grown-up with a second language learnt by imperfect methods, leads to a superficial knowledge of the most indispensable words, with total disregard of grammar.[17]

This phenomenon of the use of a minimum language is seen in the practice of almost any individual who has to express his needs in a language with which he has but a slight acquaintance. Thus while I was in China I spoke (and gesticulated) an individual pidgin Chinese. But it is only when a vocabulary and a morphology (though the one be the most limited and the other the most attenuated) common to a considerable body of speakers are developed that we may refer to a makeshift language. The makeshift languages of groups, not the makeshift speech of individuals, are historically and sociologically significant.

While there is not yet available any evidence to show that the linguistic and the psychological-learning conditions are different for any of these makeshift languages, socially considered they are divisible into groups. I distinguish three.

Pidgins. First, there is the class exemplified by such languages as Lingua Franca, Sabir, the Pidgin English of the China coast, the Chinook Jargon of the Pacific Northwest, the broken Portuguese and later the broken English of the Guinea coast, the earliest stages of the "pidgin English" of Hawaii, and probably some forms of the mixed Portuguese and Malay formerly used in the East Indies. The makeshift languages of this class arose in response to the need for an idiom in which trade could be

[17]Jespersen, *op. cit.*, pp. 233-234.

carried on between peoples,[18] neither of whom was in a position to learn the other's language at all fully. This class I propose to call *pidgins,* because this term recalls the word "business" of which "pidgin" is an adaptation, and these languages are preeminently languages of commercial intercourse.

Trade speeches or *trade languages* might serve as equivalent terms were there not a number of trade languages, such as Ki-Swahili and Malay, which are widely used as lingua francas yet are not necessarily corrupted or simplified to any great degree. It is to be remembered, however, that a lingua franca, by the very fact of its being such, is peculiarly liable to adaptation and simplification. The very word "pidgin," however, suggests the makeshift nature of the tongues it denominates. *Trade jargon* might serve were not "jargon" in the most nearly exact of its somewhat vague meanings reserved to denote the special—and to the outsider rather unintelligible—vocabulary of an occupational or like group.[19]

Something approaching equality characterizes trade relations. The Chinese may be able to restrict the European trader to a mudflat *shameen,* or a Western vessel may be able to blow a Chinook or Guinea village out of existence; yet if trade is to be carried on, there must be a modicum of trust, mutual dignity, and freedom of action. It would be interesting to know if the vocabulary of pidgins (as contrasted with creole languages) reflects to any considerable extent the circumstances under which they arise and the activities for which they function; but no study has yet been made inquiring into such a connection between milieu and expression.

Creole languages. The second class, following Vendryes and other writers,[20] I call *creole languages,* or *creole dialects,*

---

[18]Usually Westerners on the one hand and non-Westerners on the other, because the European peoples have been the greatest traders of recent times.

[19]N.E.D. definitions of *jargon;* Eric Partridge, *Slang To-day and Yesterday,* Chap. I.

[20]I owe the use of the term (in its form "creole dialect") for this class—minimum languages based on a European language, which have originated under conditions of forced, and usually imported, labor on plantations—to Vendryes. The *Enc. Brit.,* 11th ed., VII, 409, has: "The many patois founded on French and Spanish, and used chiefly by creole Negroes, are spoken of as creole languages, a term extended by some

depending on whether one is looking at them as independent media of communication or as offshoots of common languages. The plantation speech of Hawaii will usually be referred to as the "creole dialect" of Hawaii. Sometimes speakers of a makeshift language are mutually intelligible to speakers of the standard language from which it is chiefly derived, and sometimes not.

Creole languages arose under different circumstances than the pidgins. They are associated with the subjection to European masters[21] of a laboring class, usually and typically an imported servile class. This took place, typically, on tropical or semitropical plantations. The laborers were usually drawn from several linguistic groups, as were the Negro slaves of the West Indies, Surinam, Brazil, and the Southern states of America, the Malagasy and Negroes of Réunion and Mauritius, and the Melanesians of the Queensland plantations. In such a case there was need of a lingua franca among the groups of laborers as well as between them and their masters. Masters rarely deign to learn the speech of a servile population.[22] Even should they be

---

writers to include similar dialects spoken in countries where the word creole is rarely used." See also Rodolfo Lenz, *El Papiamento*, p. 31.

Some writers extend it to cover what I have denominated "pidgins"; the reference by Drewes to the work of H. Schuchardt seems to indicate that the author of *Kreolische Studien* included any makeshift or mixed language based on the Romance tongues, no matter what the circumstances of its formation. (Drewes, *op. cit.*, pp. 138-139.) I think that my restricted definition is more useful than the looser usage.

Ernst Schultze would call all makeshift languages, including the trade languages, "slave and servant languages"; but this is a term which is applicable only to the creole dialects and would only displace an already established, more concise term—though there is no denying that "slave and servant languages" is aptly descriptive of some creole languages. (Ernst Schultze, "Sklaven- und Dienersprachen [sogenannte Handelssprachen] : Ein Beitrag zur Sprach- und Wanderungs-Soziologie," *Sociologus*, IX, No. 4, 377-418.)

The term "creole dialect" is in a way misleading, for it may also be applied to the colonial dialects of the French, Spanish, and Portuguese creoles, such as the *idioma nacional* of Argentina. But as in practice there is little danger of confusion, and as the term "creole language" is already widely applied to a form of makeshift speech, we may safely apply the term only to minimum languages of the sort described in the text.

[21]The modern plantation system is the work of Europeans standing over non-Europeans. But it is conceivable that non-European creole dialects have arisen in similar circumstances of master-and-slave contacts.

[22]Jespersen, *op. cit.*, p. 202, subdivision 2a. For exceptions, see Maurice S. Evans, *Black and White in South East Africa*, pp. 51-52, and Thomas Jesse Jones (ed.), *Education in East Africa*, p. 116.

willing to learn the speech of their workmen, in many cases the number of languages spoken by the latter will make it virtually impossible for them to do so. A "language of command"[23] is needed on the plantation as decidedly as it is in the army, and that language will normally be the language of the ruling class. Yet its language "will appear shorn of its morphological peculiarities and reduced to a pulverized condition." It will be a minimum language, in part a mixed language. This is because "the Creole speech . . . is the speech of inferior beings and of a subordinate class whose superiors have never troubled nor desired to make them speak any language correctly."[24] Indeed, the European is apt to assume that a colored man of low class is incapable of speaking a European tongue correctly.[25]

The insufficiency of this type of speech for the communication of the complex groups of ideas which comprise the institutional side of culture is obvious. Margaret Mead has described with humor the difficulties of an Australian officer trying to understand the complexities of so concrete a thing as the exchange of a pig as part of a marriage price, as expressed in Beach-la-mar.[26] Just as the foreigner in China was able to carry on trade in Pidgin English, but could not grasp the complexities of Chinese culture until Chinese and Occidentals in sufficient numbers had learned each other's spoken and written language, so the plantation laborer, while able to absorb some of the more general and concrete parts of his master's culture, was cut off— by linguistic handicap as well as by servile status—from grasping the more abstract and complicated aspects. as even a humble white laborer would have grasped them. Intercourse was at the beginning merely a matter of giving and receiving orders. Later the master found it necessary to impart a modicum of European culture, but this was done in the creole speech, and the servant, we need not say, was not taught much above the minimum necessary for his station in life. He became a participant in his

---

[23]This concept is from Francis Delaisi, *Political Myths and Economic Realities*, pp. 174-177.

[24]Vendryes, *op. cit.*, p. 295.

[25]Jespersen, *op. cit.*, p. 225; William Churchill, *Beach-la-mar*, pp. 11-16.

[26]Margaret Mead, *Growing Up in New Guinea*, pp. 304-307.

master's culture, but a very limited participant. And even had there been the desire to teach more, only the servant's mastery of the master's language could have made possible access to the master's store of culture.

The servile or semi-servile population ends, like all immigrants, by losing its native languages qua languages, though traces of them will remain in its makeshift version of the master's language. Thus the creole speech differs from pidgin, which does not displace any one of its parent tongues but subsists beside them while its usefulness endures. The Englishman did not give up his use of English nor the Chinese his use of Chinese because he communicated in Pidgin English; the Indian tribes of the Pacific Northwest have maintained their native tongues, as complicated as ever, in spite of having used the Chinook Jargon in communication with the whites. When the term of a pidgin's usefulness is over, its speakers revert to their true languages. So Pidgin English is said to be disappearing from use on the China coast, and likewise, the Chinook Jargon of the American Northwest is passing. But as the mass of the speakers of a creole dialect have lost their native languages, only the master class has a pure language to revert to if the creole speech loses its usefulness. The masses may either make the creole practically their national speech, as the Haitian peasants have done, or they may, under conditions more favorable than those of the original plantation, learn a more polished form of the European tongue to which they have been apprenticed. The latter course is said by Jespersen to be followed, albeit slowly, in Mauritius[27] and, as will appear later in this study, is being followed more rapidly in Hawaii.[28]

To draw an exact line between pidgin and creole language is not always possible. The same speech is often used both by

---

[27] Jespersen, *op. cit.*, p. 228, relying on C. Baissac, *Étude sur le patois créole mauricien* and *Le folk-lore de l'Île Maurice.*

[28] An exception is probable, though the writer has no evidence at hand, in such situations as those of Latin America, where American Indian labor is drawn from reservoirs of tribal and village life, where Spanish is the medium of intercourse (in a minimum form, often) between master and *peón*, but where the Indian language of the locality remains the true vernacular of the servant class—especially if a large section of the population remains outside the plantation economy.

traders and by the masters of servile labor to communicate with the natives of a given region, and by those natives as a lingua franca among themselves. Such is the case with Beach-la-mar in Melanesia.

It has been suggested[29] that the vocabulary of makeshift languages which have grown up in trade and plantation situations respectively will differ, but this is a point to be determined only from careful examination of the recorded vocabularies of several languages of either type. In any case, it is unlikely that the morphology and syntax of pidgins and creole languages will differ much.

Foreign mixed speech. A third type of minimum language, *foreign mixed speech,* may be set beside the two already described, but with some doubt as to the validity of its inclusion.

Under modern conditions, outside the tropical plantation, immigrants tend to lose their native tongue rather rapidly. The first generation, especially the males, generally become bilingual, learning the language of their adopted country more or less adequately. Bilingualism may be preserved in their homes for an indefinite length of time, depending upon many circumstances. In the United States, bilingualism probably is exceptional beyond the third generation and not common beyond the second (i.e., the first reared in the new country). The immigrant will be distinguished in his use of his adopted language by what are generally termed "foreign accent" and "foreign idioms." His foreignisms of pronunciation and vocabulary may even color the language of his new country, particularly in those districts where he settles most thickly.[30]

There are "quasi-dialects," as Mencken styles them, of Yiddish, German, Italian, and Scandinavian speakers of American English, all based on the same principle of imperfect mastery of a language, as are the pidgins and creole dialects. One can recognize easily enough when a "Yid" or a "Wop" or a "Dutchman" is being caricatured on the stage. It is very hard, however, to put one's finger on the limits of one of these

[29]By Romanzo Adams and Edgar T. Thompson of the University of Hawaii.
[30]Henry L. Mencken, *The American Language,* 1st ed., pp. 158-159.

"quasi-dialects." They are so fluctuating, so much the creation of many complex circumstances, that they do not have a definite body of grammar and vocabulary as have, for example, the Chinook Jargon and Haitian Creole French. The composition of the body of people that speak them is such that they can not attain a uniformity in their makeshiftness, as pidgins and creole languages come to do. Neither do these "quasi-dialects" come to have the prestige that a few makeshift languages enjoy. Those who speak "quasi-dialects" do not wittingly write in them; they are reserved as "available only for farce or very broad comedy" written by those thoroughly familiar with the pure form of the language in question.[31] These foreign mixed speeches may be taken as paralleling the immigrants' dialects referred to earlier in this chapter.[32]

THE LANGUAGE MASTERY CONTINUUM

It is a matter of common-sense observation that individuals differ among themselves in their degree of mastery of a language, because of differences of age, social environment and education, and innate mental capacity. Even in an environment in which a trade pidgin or a plantation creole language is in use, fortunate individuals will be found who approximate more closely than do their fellows the standard speech of the foreign trader or of the master. And in an immigrant population such as we find in Hawaii, we observe such differences of language mastery even more plainly. There is, indeed, a continuum of mastery. At one end of the scale is the uneducated laborer who, in atrociously mispronounced and extremely simplified English,

[31] Krapp, *op. cit.*, Vol. I, p. 229. Krapp terms this type of speech "foreign mixed dialects" or "mixed foreign dialects." But as these are not true local dialects, I have avoided the use of the word "dialect."

[32] A phenomenon associated with foreign mixed speech and immigrants' dialects is the use of *macaronic speech*. By this term is meant that form of communication between persons acquainted with two languages, in which the speakers switch freely back and forth from one language to the other. Sometimes, for example, they speak a whole sentence or two in Japanese, then one or two more in English, and again a few in Japanese. Sometimes they change from clause to clause or from phrase to phrase within the same sentence. This type of speech is found among people of any degree of mastery of two tongues, but in Hawaii at any rate, it usually indicates a considerable mastery of both languages. Its psychology, so far as the writer knows, has never been investigated.

can barely make known his elementary wants; at the other end is the exceptional immigrant, or more likely the son or grandson of an immigrant, who expresses himself in fluent, idiomatic, and adequate English but who retains a scarcely perceptible smack of the "foreign accent" and idioms peculiar to his language group. The same phenomenon holds among the speakers of a local dialect in reference to their mastery of the standard language. While one's place on this continuum is a matter of great social importance, no sufficient term has to the present writer's knowledge been suggested for this phenomenon. Fully aware of the awkwardness and lack of precision of my nomenclature, I propose, until a better term is offered, *language mastery continuum.*

Chapter 3

THE HISTORICAL BACKGROUND OF MAKESHIFT LANGUAGE AND REGIONAL DIALECT IN HAWAII

Three factors stand out as of predominant importance in determining the character of the plantation "pidgin" or creole dialect of Hawaii, and through it of the colonial dialect which is succeeding it. They are the long-continued influence of the English and Hawaiian languages upon each other; the life and linguistic necessities of the sugar cane plantations, which drew a large-scale immigration of groups speaking neither English nor Hawaiian; and the development of the school system of Hawaii. Although these factors cannot be dissociated entirely, each will be discussed in its turn.

THE INTERRELATION OF THE ENGLISH AND HAWAIIAN LANGUAGES

Because of its central position in the North Pacific, inviting vessels bound between the American and the Asian or Australasian coasts to make it a stopping point, and because of its richness of agricultural resources, Hawaii has been inevitably exposed to foreign influences, linguistic and otherwise, almost from the time of its discovery. These influences were concentrated so heavily that Hawaii had by the middle of the nineteenth century already reached approximately the same stage that several other major Polynesian groups occupy today. The archipelagoes of Tonga and Samoa were discovered and missionized at approximately the same time as Hawaii. Nevertheless, in Tonga, isolated and of little economic account as it is, English has been generally taught for less than a generation and is now spoken by only one-fourth of the people,[1] while in Samoa, richer but similarly isolated, language dualism has reached about the same stage that it occupied in Hawaii in the 1860's and early 1870's.[2] And in Tahiti, the first of the Polynesian groups to feel the impact of Western culture, the Chinese coolies have learned not a makeshift French but a makeshift Tahitian,[3] just as the Chinese coolies in Hawaii learned a makeshift Hawaiian prior to about 1880.

Certain important language adjustments were made in Hawaii between the native population and the Western traders and colonists, beginning very early, almost a century before extensive immigration into the Islands, and continuing after the immigrants became established, down to the present. These language adjustments have been of importance in determining in turn the adjustments made by the immigrants. To understand the mutual influence of Hawaiian and English and how a makeshift language began to arise from their interplay, it is necessary to review some aspects of Hawaiian history.

From 1786 on, the archipelago became a convenient and frequented place of call for the vessels trading in furs between the American coast and China. These vessels were of several nationalities, with the American and British always greatly predominating. White men, mostly English-speaking, left their ships to reside in Hawaii from about 1790 on. These white men, isolated among the Hawaiians, naturally had to learn the language of the natives and were often available as interpreters. A few Hawaiians, too, were similarly isolated among whites when they shipped as sailors—as they did as soon as the trading

[1]"Tonga," *Enc. Brit.,* 11th ed.; letter dated March 6, 1934, from the Premier of Tonga.

[2]Felix M. Keesing, *Modern Samoa,* esp. pp. 444-447.

[3]Letter of March 23, 1934, from J. F. Stimson.

ships began to reach Hawaiian harbors. Thus native interpreters, such as the man who served Captain George Vancouver in 1792, were also available within less than two decades of the discovery of the Islands.[4] The traders appear usually to have picked up a little Hawaiian, mispronounced most barbarously if one is to judge by the spelling that they used, and often miscomprehended. So inadequate was their Hawaiian that they were glad to make use of the services of the few white settlers and the returned native sailors. Before approximately 1810 linguistic communication between foreign seamen and native Hawaiians was intermittent and comparatively restricted.

The intercourse between foreigners, chiefly English-speaking, and natives was enlarged by the sandalwood trade, which began to be important about 1810 and declined in the decade 1820 to 1830. This drew ships to Hawaii to trade on more intimate terms with the natives than when they merely stopped to take on supplies; and the resident merchant made his appearance. In May, 1825, Andrew Bloxam of the *Blonde* noted that in Honolulu, "now getting quite a civilized place," more than three hundred Americans, "with whom the principal trade consists," were resident.[5]

While the sandalwood trade was at its height, shortly after 1820, the whalers began making Hawaii their chief place of call for supplies. "The whaling era in Hawaii lasted for about sixty years (1820-1880), but it was at its height during the twenty years from 1840 to 1860. . . . The average number of arrivals between 1840 and 1860 was about four hundred [vessels] each year."[6] "After a while stores were opened. . . . A shipyard was established for doing necessary repair work. Hence a large number of foreign traders, carpenters, and mechanics were added to the population."[7] The trade and contacts with the Hawaiians were largely localized in Honolulu and Lahaina (the latter being until recently a stronghold of Hawaiian population and, like Lanai, having a negligible non-Hawaiian school population as late as 1901), but extended also to all parts of the

[4]Ralph S. Kuykendall, *A History of Hawaii*, pp. 72, 75.

[5]*Diary of Andrew Bloxam*, pp. 29-30.

[6]Kuykendall, *op. cit.*, pp. 189, 191.

[7]*Ibid.*, p. 139.

Islands which have good anchorages. Much of the sailors' business must have been carried on through Haole middlemen, yet the thousands of seamen touching annually at Hawaii also came in personal contact with other thousands of natives. Furthermore, a large number of natives shipped as seamen on the whalers.[8] For every Hawaiian who shipped in the days of the fur and sandalwood trade, more than ten must have shipped on the whaling vessels. The minister of the interior in 1846 estimated that nearly three thousand Hawaiians in the prime of life were serving on foreign vessels, scattered about the Pacific and indeed throughout the Seven Seas.[9] Many never returned to Hawaii, but those who did surely returned with a considerable knowledge of Yankee English.

The whaling trade and the incipient agricultural and grazing industries brought in a white, or Haole, population which early reached a size sufficient to be of linguistic importance in Honolulu and perhaps in other centers. As early as 1853 the Haoles comprised nearly 2 percent of the total population of Hawaii, a larger proportion than the whites comprised in 1930 in Samoa.[10]

At this point we must turn back in point of time to trace the influence of the missionary establishments in Hawaii. The four decades of contact between the Hawaiians and whites (1778 to 1820) prior to the arrival of the first missionaries had left little impression upon the native tongue,[11] and very few indeed of the natives had even a moderately adequate command of the foreign language.[12] The coming of the missionaries marks the

---

[8]For Hawaiian words carried to the Arctic by these whalers, see V. Stefánsson, "The Eskimo Trade Jargon of Herschel Island," *American Anthropologist,* XI, No. 2 (April-June, 1909), 217-232; and John Murdoch, "Ethnological Results of the Point Barrow Expedition," in *Ninth Annual Report of the Bureau of Ethnology to the Secretary of the Smithsonian Institution, 1887-1888,* pp. 3-441.—*Ed.*

[9]Kuykendall, *op. cit.,* pp. 196-197. The total population in 1846 was probably not over 80,000. But compare Golda Pauline Moore, "Hawaii During the Whaling Era 1820-1880": "Even in 1844 it was estimated that five to six hundred Hawaiian [*sic*] were on whaling vessels." (P. 53, citing E. P. Hohman, *The American Whaleman,* p. 53.)

[10]Romanzo Adams, *The Peoples of Hawaii,* rev. ed., p. 8; Keesing, *op. cit.,* p. 32.

[11]It was probably confined to a few loan words. *Pepa,* "paper," playing cards, was certainly one; another was probably *amara,* "armorer," blacksmith.

[12]This is evident from the specific references to the few natives whose English was passably good.

beginning of intensive mutual influence of the two languages, an influence of considerable local importance to the English language and of overwhelming importance to the vernacular.

The Protestant missionaries came imbued with New England ideals of the value of universal education in raising the economic, intellectual, and religious level of any people. They almost immediately realized that the only feasible way of introducing the principles of Christianity, the Scriptures, and the rudiments of Western education to the masses of natives was through the widespread use of the native language, reduced to writing. The chiefs, to whom the English language was immediately useful, were flattered by having it taught them from the beginning of the mission's ministry—at which time, indeed, the missionaries could not have given instruction in Hawaiian. Soon afterwards half-bloods and other select *maka'ainana* (commoners) were also taught English; so an opening wedge for literate bilingualism and the ultimate loss of the vernacular was introduced. But the chief efforts of the missionaries were applied to learning the phonological and grammatical structure of Hawaiian, in order that they might reduce it to writing and through the agency of the printing press diffuse their teachings throughout the archipelago. They were remarkably successful, partly because of the opportune arrival in 1822 of the Reverend William Ellis, who had served for six years in Tahiti, where a related language had been reduced to writing, and who volunteered his services in aiding the members of the American mission to master the Hawaiian tongue. Only twenty months after entering the Islands (in January, 1822, before the arrival of Ellis), the missionaries had partially fixed the Hawaiian orthography and were able to print a spelling book in the vernacular. One month after the printing press began to function, the chief Kuakini was able to write a letter in his own language. He was followed by thousands. "Epistolary correspondence, thus commenced in that language, suddenly opened to the chiefs and people a new source of pleasure and advantage, of which hundreds soon availed themselves."[13]

13Hiram Bingham, *A Residence of Twenty-One Years in the Sandwich Islands,* p. 157.

Hawaiian had become overnight a written language. "As early as 1826 there were four hundred native teachers, and ten years after the coming of the missionaries it was estimated that one-third of the entire population was enrolled in the schools."[14] These students were almost all adults. As the enthusiasm for the *palapala* (book learning) died down almost as suddenly as it had flared up, the missionaries turned to the slower but more fruitful task of instructing the children in the Hawaiian language. This was fairly successful. Formal literacy became almost universal, and the native language was used to a considerable extent as a carrier of Western ideas.[15]

The reduction of the Hawaiian tongue to writing and the creation of a written literature had several important results. First, the alphabet was standardized.[16] Within the same Hawaiian phoneme there existed what to the English ear was a wide variety of sounds. "The following appeared sometimes to be interchangeable: *b* and *p*, *k* and *t*, *l* and *r*, *v* and *w*, and even the sound of *d*, it was thought by some, was used in some cases where others used *k*, *l*, *r*, or *t*."[17] The elimination of *b*, *t*, *r*, and *d* from purely native words as they were spelled encouraged the Hawaiians, after the passage of some time, to drop the sounds which they represent to the English-speaker, and to approximate their own phonemes to the English phonemes.[18] Second, the vocabulary of the native language was greatly

[14]Kuykendall, *op. cit.*, p. 131.

[15]Kuykendall, *op. cit.*, p. 132, gives 1833 as the date of the decline of the adult schools and 1828 as the beginning of the attention to juvenile education. The founding of Lahainaluna seminary in 1831 was a great step toward securing fairly competent native instructors.

[16]In 1825. Howard M. Ballou and George R. Carter, "The History of the Hawaiian Mission Press," p. 22, quoting Elisha Loomis, the first printer.

For a detailed history of the development of Hawaiian orthography, see C. M. Wise and W. D. Hervey, "The Evolution of Hawaiian Orthography," *The Quarterly Journal of Speech*, XXXVIII, No. 3 (October, 1952), 311-325. See also: S. H. Elbert, "The Hawaiian Dictionaries, Past and Future," in *Sixty-Second Annual Report of the Hawaiian Historical Society for the Year 1953*, pp. 7-9; and D. B. Walch, "The Historical Development of the Hawaiian Alphabet," *The Journal of the Polynesian Society*, LXXVI, No. 3 (September, 1967), 353-366.—Ed.

[17]Bingham, *op. cit.*, p. 155. See also the letter by Wm. Richards (1828) quoted in T. M. Spaulding, "The Adoption of the Hawaiian Alphabet," pp. 31-32.

[18]One competent observer reports that the sound *t* will be pronounced by some natives of all the islands, but if they are asked what they have said, they will pronounce *k*. (Helen H. Roberts, *Ancient Hawaiian Music*, pp. 72-73.)

enriched. Some words were Hawaiianized directly from the English, the Greek, or the Hebrew. More commonly, as one of the chief translators of the Bible wrote:

... We were able to form new words to an indefinite extent, in perfect accordance with the genius of the language, and intelligible to the native reader. The constant use of this power enabled us to meet and overcome nearly every difficulty arising from the paucity of Hawaiian words, besides enriching the language with hundreds of new terms, which are now in common use throughout the archipelago.

Another method of obtaining words, was to take those in vulgar use and appropriate them to a religious sense for a definite purpose.[19]

Third, in spite of the endeavor of the translators to maintain the purity of the native language, it was impossible that some English idioms should not creep into their work. The effect of the English idioms was more plainly seen when the Hawaiians essayed writing for the newspapers. As they had no tradition of style for this particular type of composition, they were influenced by English idiom and journalistic style.[20] Whether because of the influence of the English language or because the native writers became more occupied with matter than with form, a slight carelessness became evident. Kamakau, for example (1868 to 1870), was careless of his particles.[21] Fourth, the attention of the nation to the *palapala* and to the foreign culture which accompanied it could not but have a destructive influence upon the preservation of, and further composition in, the elevated, extraordinarily allusive, and obscure poetic and religious special language. True, while a court existed poetic Hawaiian endured, but no longer were monarch and courtiers able to devote so much time to its cultivation and encouragement as before the strenuous and complex life of semi-Westernized Hawaii began. The cultural changes also destroyed such secret dialects as the *kake*.[22]

[19]Artemas Bishop, "Address. A Brief History of the Translation of the Holy Scriptures into the Hawaiian Language," *The Friend*, August, 1844, p. 74. Compare the development of the Samoan language now taking place: Keesing, *op. cit.*, pp. 444-445.

[20]Interview with John H. Wise, August, 1933.

[21]Interview with John F. G. Stokes, August, 1933.

[22]The *kake*, at least in one form, was a jargon used by criminals.

For a period the net results of the reduction of Hawaiian to writing under the influence of English were hopeful for the native language. There was the prospect of creating a native literature of some promise. The foundation of that literature, as so often among languages reduced to writing by missionaries, was the Bible. Formal translation was begun in 1824; the Gospel of Luke was printed in December, 1827; the entire Scriptures were printed by May 10, 1839; and a revised translation was printed in 1843. There was of course a flood of catechisms, religious leaflets, and translations of textbooks, themselves often of a religious nature; and there were legal documents and government papers. But there were also a few works of more substantial worth—e.g., historical accounts, legends and romances, and translations of religious works and hymnals.[23] A Hawaiian press also came into existence. The first newspaper, for the students at Lahainaluna, *Ka Lama Hawaii,* began publication on February 14, 1834.[24] Thereafter until the present time there have been Hawaiian periodicals, chiefly of educational or religious inspiration but, since the 1800's, often political in their aims. The *Kuokoa* (1861 to 1927) in particular was for a long while a journal of opinion as well as of information and afforded an outlet for the literary and didactic ambitions of Hawaiians.

But at the same time that the Hawaiian language was clothing itself with a literature in the Western style, profound changes in the social and economic life of the natives and in the structure of the population were rapidly weakening the vitality of the native tongue. First of all, the aboriginal population was very rapidly declining in numbers, largely because of the foreigners' diseases, and this decline deepened the feeling of hopeless discouragement in the face of Western culture. The people were dying, the language was dying with the people—such was the feeling of many. The foreign population was increasing both relatively to the Hawaiian stock and absolutely. A Part-Hawaiian group was also coming into existence; by 1866 it

[23]For examples of these works written in Hawaiian, see: Howard Malcolm Ballou, "Bibliography of Books in the Native Hawaiian Language."

[24]"Hawaii Journalism Ends Its First Century Today; Maui Paper Blazed Trail," *Honolulu Star-Bulletin,* February 14, 1934, pp. 1, 8-9.

comprised approximately 2.8 percent of the whole Hawaiian stock. It is obvious that many of the mixed bloods would be thrown within the English-speaking circles of Honolulu and other ports, and that they would not have the same traditions, and therefore not the same incentives to perpetuate those traditions in carefully chosen Hawaiian, that an unmixed native population would have. As the mixed-blood group increased it drove the wedge of bilingualism, of language dualism,[25] deeper and deeper.[26]

The social changes and their attendant political changes during the reigns of the Kamehamehas, and especially during the period 1839 to 1854 under Kauikeolani, were rapid as well as profound. In 1800 there was a Polynesian *ali'i* (sacred chief) governing, according to a Polynesian polity, a people divided into rigid classes, rather evenly distributed on the arable land, regulating their life according to the needs of their agriculture- and-fishing economy and the traditional demands of their chiefs and *konohiki* (chiefs' stewards), and proud of their own culture and traditions because they knew little of Western culture and had no traditions besides their own. Such was an ideal field for the perpetuation of the native tongue. But in 1854 a "constitu- tional and Kanaka" king with Anglo-Saxon advisers ruled a people among whom class lines were fast breaking; who were becoming accustomed to such Anglo-American institutions as representative government, official intercourse with foreign governments, written and impersonal laws, government schools, money, and landholding in fee simple; whose dependence upon the chiefs was being pulverized into individualism; who were detaching themselves from their small holdings to crowd into the ports and onto the plantations and ranches owned by Haoles; whose social structure and traditions were shattered irreparably, to be imperfectly replaced by the church.[27] In Samoa at the present time, Keesing finds the phenomenon of

[25]Language dualism is the sociological aspect of bilingualism—the reservation of one language for certain fields in which it functions best and of another language for other fields. See Keesing, *op. cit.*

[26]It would be valuable to know the language of communication between husband and wife, and between parents and children, in the early mixed marriages, but the present writer has no data on it.

[27]E. S. Craighill Handy, *Cultural Revolution in Hawaii.*

language dualism bound up with cultural changes of somewhat the same sort but less profound and acute, and with the incipient urban life of Apia and Pago Pago; he finds, together with the introduction of English on a rather large scale, a partial disintegration and loss of niceties in the native language. With the social and economic changes in Hawaii so profound, the way was opened for a very rapid change in the linguistic situation in the second half and especially in the last quarter of the nineteenth century, when the institutions of the plantation and the English school finally, as it were, fell with a crash upon the weakened structure of aboriginal Hawaiian society.

Economic and administrative necessities combined to give English currency and prestige at the expense of the native language. Merchants established in Hawaii might depend upon the native tongue for their retail trade, but the trade with foreign ships and the bookkeeping of Honolulu firms required the use of the English language. The Hawaiian with a knowledge of English could often obtain a position with a Haole firm. Official intercourse with the representatives of foreign governments of course required the rulers of Hawaii to use a European language. The administration of the machinery of the government was necessarily for the most part in the hands of English-speaking Haole advisers of the king. The native Hawaiian language was not well adapted to the exact uses of the law-makers and the courts, and even if it had been, several of the advisers were not masters of that tongue. At the same time the legislative enactments and other important papers had to be placed before the chiefs and people in their own language. Therefore bilingualism became the rule in the printing of government documents, reports, laws, and papers generally. For a few years the translation was from Hawaiian to English, or no translation was made; but before the end of the Kamehameha dynasty, English became the original language of government papers, from which the Hawaiian was translated and which was referred to for the meaning.[28] While the folk language was still

[28]William C. Smith ("Pidgin English in Hawaii," *American Speech*, February, 1933, p. 17) gives a very brief account of how English became the language of communication in governmental affairs.

definitely Hawaiian and a majority of the people were unable to speak English, English became the administrative language, bringing prestige and advancement to the Hawaiians who could use it.

Ralph S. Kuykendall has indicated 1874, the date of the accession of Kalakaua to the throne, as the beginning of a new era in the political, economic, and social history of Hawaii. Perhaps, however, September 9, 1876, the day that the Reciprocity Treaty between Hawaii and the United States went into effect, is a better date to take as one of the four great turning points of Hawaiian history.[29] We may pause at this point, before going on to consider the results of the political, economic, and educational revolutions consequent to Reciprocity, to inquire into the linguistic conditions of the Hawaii of 1820 to 1876.

The upper classes and certain individuals closely attached to the homes of missionaries and other foreigners (whether as students, servants, or wives) early learned some English. As will be seen in the section dealing with the schools, education in English, from the 1850's on, was accessible to a limited number of well-to-do students. That much formal education in English failed to "stick" may be taken for granted, however. What of the mass of the natives, who were unable to afford a formal education in English? Direct testimony as to the number who could speak good English at any time previous to the Hawaiian Census of 1896 is very limited, being confined chiefly to the "Blount Report" of 1893. For the period prior to 1876 the present writer has found no direct evidence and therefore must arrive at his conclusions from negative evidence and from analogy with similarly situated groups. Apparently the genuinely English-speaking natives were very few and were mostly confined to Honolulu, Hilo, and Lahaina. Both Charles Nordhoff and Isabella Bird Bishop, tourists who published accounts of Hawaii in 1874 and 1875, respectively, recorded that it was hard to find natives outside Honolulu and Hilo who could understand more than a bare smattering of English.

[29]Kuykendall, *op. cit.,* p. 240. The other three are January 18, 1778 (discovery by Captain Cook); March 30, 1820 (arrival of the first American missionaries in the brig *Thaddeus*); August 12, 1898 (annexation to U. S.).

Nordhoff advised that "your guide . . . be instructed in your wishes before you set out."[30]

How, then, did the Haole employers and merchants, and the great crowd of seamen from the whalers, communicate with the natives? Except for missionary and Part-Hawaiian families, few foreigners learned Hawaiian fluently and well. A considerable number, however, learned it well enough to get along in simple conversation. James Girvin makes the hero of his *Master Planter* on a Maui plantation learn Hawaiian so that he may deal readily with his workmen and neighbors, apparently in the early 1870's. But it may be taken as axiomatic that the average member of a dominant nationality will not take the pains to learn the language of a less advanced group if he can make the members of that group learn his own. Certainly the transient sailors could not be expected to learn more than a few words of Hawaiian. The natives, at least those in often-frequented ports, found it advantageous to learn a little English for purposes of trade. (But in the more remote places, no English at all was learned; in Waimanu Valley, Island of Hawaii, Mrs. Bishop in 1873 found only one man who knew a little broken English.) This English was of a makeshift character and was mixed with Hawaiian words, probably mispronounced by most whites. It was sometimes called *hapa haole* (half white). It was the most common means of communication between Haole residents and Hawaiians and practically the sole means between sailors and Hawaiians.[31] Probably it arose about 1830 or 1840, with the development of the whaling trade and the beginning of the plantations.

Doesn't this *hapa haole* fulfill the definition of a pidgin? We do not find it classed as such. William Churchill wrote that "we should note that there never was a permanent jargon based

[30]Charles Nordhoff, *Northern California, Oregon, and the Sandwich Islands*, p. 33; Isabella L. Bishop, *The Hawaiian Archipelago*, passim.

[31]For the data in this paragraph, I am indebted almost wholly to Ella H. Paris of Kealakekua. Miss Paris, the daughter of a missionary, was born in Kona in the early 'fifties and has lived there most of her life. She knows Hawaiian very well and distinctly recalls the later days of the whaling trade. What she has told me is corroborated by hints gained from letters and interviews and from reading accounts of Hawaii during its middle period. Nevertheless, it requires further corroborative evidence to be accepted as true beyond a doubt. Conditions may have differed in the various districts of Hawaii.

upon English and Polynesian."[32]   J. Frank Stimson, Research
Associate in Polynesian Linguistics for the Bernice P. Bishop
Museum, wrote: "I believe Wm. Churchill to have been quite
correct in stating that there never has been a true pidgin jargon
current in any part of Polynesia."[33]   This statement is con-
curred in by E. S. Craighill Handy of the same museum, an
authority on Hawaiian ethnology.[34]   All *kamaaina* (old time)
Islanders whom I have asked have said that a "pidgin English"
did not arise until after the Chinese and Portuguese immigration. At least in the popular mind, *hapa haole* was not an
impressive linguistic phenomenon, and it attracted so little
attention that no one has recorded it as an example of a mixed
language.

Perhaps the solution to the problem may be found in the
shifting, unfixed nature of the *hapa haole* speech. Apparently it
never attained any sort of fixity in either grammatical structure
or vocabulary. Each Hawaiian spoke the best English he could.
And there was no uniformity from plantation to plantation,
locality to locality, in the use of Hawaiian, English, or a mixture
of the two. No doubt some of the elements of the *hapa haole*
were those common to any makeshift language based on
English, and others were based on a direct translation of
Hawaiian idioms. The strong Hawaiian influence found in the
later makeshift language makes this assumption reasonable. But,
while the *hapa haole* was the forerunner of plantation "pidgin
English" and no doubt the chief reservoir from which the latter
drew, all available evidence fails to show that it possessed a
definite character of its own.

Though it was apparently used to some extent on the early
plantations, its chief field of utility was in intercourse between
the Hawaiians and the whites who had business relations with
them. Sociologically, therefore, it may be classified as a trade
pidgin.

Here it may be added parenthetically that even in formal

[32]*Beach-la-mar*, p. 6.

[33]Letter of March 23, 1934. This is because "all Polynesian dialects are more or
less mutually intelligible." However, "In Tahiti a 'pidgin' Tahitian has become
established due to the inability of the several thousand Chinese immigrants to learn
Tahitian. This is a unique local development, so far as I am aware. . . ."

[34]Letter of March 21, 1934.

colloquial English, resident Haoles soon after the advent of the missionaries were using numerous Hawaiian words, for many of which there are no English equivalents. The influence of Hawaiian upon Standard English is limited to loan words, of which the present writer has estimated about one thousand to be in use (often a very limited use) in Hawaii. Perhaps 250 to 350 are in fairly common use colloquially, but not nearly so many are used in formal speech and writing. A few have passed into general currency and beyond Hawaii, such as *ukulele, poi, hula, aa,* and *pahoehoe.*[35]

Let us now return to the thread of Hawaiian history. The effects of the economic and educational revolutions are of such importance that they must be treated separately in the following sections. Suffice it to point out here that the rapid development of the sugar cane plantations increased both the number and the importance of the Anglo-Saxon Haoles and afforded funds to hasten the teaching of their language, now grown still more important and rich in prestige. The Hawaiian Islands were swung more and more closely within the orbit of the United States. Business and social contacts with the mainland became more frequent, especially after the establishment in 1867 of steamer service from San Francisco to Honolulu. The investment of great sums of money in the plantations made the Haole population more sensitive than it had hitherto been to the administration of Hawaii and to relations with the United States. While the general lot of the native population seems to have improved with the development of the plantation economy, the upper classes became increasingly submerged economically and socially.[36]

The "nativism" of the Kalakaua court was a protest against this submersion, an ineffectual eddy against the inevitable

[35]John E. Reinecke, unpublished collection of Hawaiian loan words. [This collection was subsequently compiled in the form of a mimeographed word list: John E. Reinecke, "A List of Loanwords from the Hawaiian Language in Use in the English Speech of the Hawaiian Islands." A revised version of this list is now available in published form: John E. Reinecke and Stanley M. Tsuzaki, "Hawaiian Loanwords in Hawaiian English of the 1930's," *Oceanic Linguistics,* VI, No. 2 (Winter, 1967), 80-115.—*Ed.*] J. M. Lydgate, "The Hawaiian Contribution to English," *The Hawaiian Almanac and Annual,* 1914, pp. 131-135.

[36]The first clause of this sentence I owe to Romanzo Adams.

current; it may, however, for a short while have bolstered the prestige of the Hawaiian language.[37] Finding that the native rulers were not amenable enough to their ideas of efficient government, the middle class Haoles overthrew the Kalakaua dynasty in 1893. Thus the foreign group which had for some years exercised practical control set up their rule openly, to the detriment of native prestige. No longer was there an effective rallying point for Hawaiian sentiment. The Americanization of the Islands had been conceded as inevitable under the native monarchy, but now it was accelerated and emphasized; and the transfer of sovereignty on August 12, 1898, made little difference in the sentiment of the people.

The break-up of the royal court with its literary hangers-on was probably the critical blow to the prestige of elevated Hawaiian speech. Dispersed throughout the Islands, with no chiefly patron to look to, the composers of chants in the ancient manner and the masters of the meaning of the elevated poetic style no longer had a strong incentive to pass on their knowledge and attainments to their children. Literary Hawaiian began rapidly to disappear. John H. Wise told the author in 1933 that "probably I could count on the fingers of my two hands" the Hawaiians who could at that date understand the inner meaning of the old poems. The purity of the Hawaiian language had suffered from the contact with English during the whaling period, but now, reduced in prestige and utility as it was, the language was bound to suffer much more. At the beginning of Kalakaua's reign there was a true dualism of language which, had there been a continuation of peasant agriculture, might have endured indefinitely. At the annexation to America, the dualism still existed among the Hawaiians,[38] but it was obvious to all observers that, with the passage of the then

[37]Government reports under Kalakaua and Liliuokalani regularly appeared in both languages, but this may have been due merely to political graft. At any rate, English alone was usually found sufficient after 1894.

[38]According to the census of 1896, only 3,973 Hawaiian males (about 32.6 percent of the total) and 2,972 Hawaiian females (about 29.6 percent) could read and write English. Of the Part-Hawaiians, however, 2,169 males (about 74.4 percent of the total) and 1,911 females (about 78.0 percent) could read and write English.

These figures must be understood in the light of a statement by William Brewster

adult generation, the native tongue would begin its decline to a patois of little practical importance outside the home.[39]

In spite of all unfavorable circumstances—the cultural breakdown of the Hawaiian people, their detachment from the soil, the educational changes, the dominance of the Haole population, the now complete dependence upon the United States, the deluge of immigrants, the decline of the pure native population and the growth in its stead of mixed-blood population—the native language has persisted. It is safe to presume that almost all the 22,636 Hawaiians of "pure" stock returned by the 1930 census speak the Hawaiian language. (How well they speak it is another matter.) Indeed, 1,467, or 8.3 percent of those ten years old and over, are unable to speak English. One can only guess what fraction of the 28,224 Part-Hawaiians (many of them having but little native blood) can speak the native tongue; one-third is probably a generous estimate. The native language still occupies a favored position officially as compared with other non-English tongues. Its history and the number of voters who are at home in no other language give it some prestige still.[40] The reasons for the persistence of Hawaiian are dealt with in Chapter 5.

Oleson, principal of Kamehameha School ("Blount Report," 1893, p. 507): "But a great many of them are able to read in an English book who can not talk English, except indifferently." At the same date William DeWitt Alexander stated (p. 269) that the English language was spoken: "By the rising generation; not the adults." Peter Cushman Jones stated that the Hawaiian language was still used extensively for business in Honolulu (p. 221); although, according to Chief Justice A. F. Judd (p. 1650): "Lately they [Hawaiians] are losing the ability to speak Hawaiian well, by reason of their minds being directed in school to English." In 1884, according to Capt. C. E. Dutton, U.S.A.: "few of the natives are able to converse or read except in their own language," and the whites had to learn Hawaiian (p. 91).

[39]Vernacular publications usually furnish a good index to the strength of a tongue. Unfortunately Ballou's bibliography runs only to 1908. In the field of periodicals, however, we have testimony of the decline of the native language. One small paper after another struggled to hold subscribers during the first two decades of the twentieth century; most lasted only one to four years. The *Nupepa Kuokoa*, although supported by the *Honolulu Advertiser,* gave up the ghost in 1927; only Jonah Kumalae's *Ke Alakai o Hawaii* (Honolulu, founded about 1919) and Stephen Desha's *Ka Hoku o Hawaii* (Hilo, founded about 1907) have survived to the present date (1934). Publication in Hawaiian is now practically limited to trivial religious writings.

[40]The use of the Hawaiian language is prescribed or optional in some twenty-six situations by the present laws.

THE PLANTATION SYSTEM
AND THE IMPORTATION OF LABOR

The political events and the social development of Hawaii during the second half of the nineteenth century, as has already been pointed out, rested chiefly upon the development of the Islands into a plantation area. Upon the change from a small farming economy to a plantation economy depended also, in large part, the transformation of the school system. The plantation system and the part played by the sugar planters in introducing diverse linguistic groups into Hawaii should therefore be briefly reviewed.

The establishment in 1835 at Koloa, Kauai, of a sugar cane plantation is commonly taken as marking the beginning of the plantation system in Hawaii. A plantation as it appears in Hawaii, a century after this first establishment, may be defined as a large estate cultivated under a capitalistic economy, devoted chiefly to the cultivation of one staple crop—sugar cane or pineapples—and tilled by hired labor under the direction of a hierarchy of foremen (*lunas*) culminating in a manager. The laborers are generally housed on the plantation, concentrated in plantation towns, villages, or camps of varying sizes. The sugar cane plantations are almost invariably centered about a sugar mill (in the Spanish colonies aptly called a *centrál*) at which crude sugar and molasses are manufactured. The pineapple plantations, which were not developed until after 1903, of course lack the concentration about the mill, and their laborers are in some instances more scattered than those on the sugar plantations. Maunaloa on Molokai and Lanai City are, however, good examples of the concentration of pineapple labor. Social lines are very closely drawn on the plantations and are dependent upon both occupation and race. (Throughout this work, the terms "race," "nationality," and "ethnic group" have been used interchangeably.) There is a strong tendency for the various ethnic groups, known in Hawaii as "races" or "nationalities," to be segregated spatially as well as socially; thus we hear references to the "Haole Camp," the "Puerto Rican Camp," the "Chinese Camp," etc., in a mill village. Each group that is numerous enough has its own social life, and this tendency is especially marked today among the Haoles, the Japanese, and most of all among the Filipinos.

Between 1835 and 1876 the sugar cane plantations grew but slowly because of the competition of sugar from the Philippine Islands and the tariff barrier to their chief market, California.[41] The bulk of the labor force was drawn, until about 1878, from the native Hawaiians. They were so averse to working continuously for a long period that a system of contract labor was enforced. The laborer was held in a semi-servile position until the expiration of his five-year—later his three-year—contract, and plantation labor received a corresponding stigma.

To supplement the unreliable native labor, Chinese were imported or came of their own initiative. The first group was imported in 1852. The following year the census recorded 364 in Hawaii; in 1860 there were about 700; in 1866 there were 1,200; in 1872 there were 2,038, only 157 of them females.

This was the beginning of a type of immigration much different from that of the few hundred entrepreneurs, commercial agents, skilled laborers, and seamen, chiefly Americans and Europeans, who had drifted into Hawaii and were concentrated in Honolulu. Now, with the development of the plantation, was seen the contract laborer immigrant. He was usually ignorant not only of the native language but of English as well; he was in a dependent position because of his lack of money, his legal bonds, and his ignorance of conditions; he was tied for some years to a plantation in a rural district which undeveloped transportation often made remote from the capital—a plantation was frequently a little world in itself. He was often—among several groups, typically—a young bachelor. For several years, even under favorable conditions, he was exposed to very limited social and linguistic contacts with his bosses and the native population. In time the emancipation of some members of each immigrant group from plantation occupation brought them into contact with the established groups as shopkeepers, independent farmers, skilled or semi-skilled laborers, and domestics, and sometimes as husbands of native wives or, later, as wives

[41]Kuykendall, *op. cit.*, pp. 199-202, 205-207.

drawn from immigrant groups established long enough to have learned English.

Conditions prevalent in the early period of wholesale immigration, it should be borne in mind, came to change considerably. In 1900, after annexation to the United States, contract labor was legally abolished, and the worker was legally free to leave the plantation at any time when he felt that he could support himself outside it. As a matter of fact the free laborer both before and after annexation often remained confined to the plantation milieu because of his ignorance of the English language and of economic opportunities. Living conditions on the plantations have been steadily improved, but the stigma attached to plantation labor has not been eradicated. Educational opportunities in rural districts have been added to. The isolation of the plantation has largely disappeared before the extension of regular steamship service, good roads, and telephone lines, and recently before the radio and the talkies. Ethnic separatism has in part broken down before the schools, the churches, and the pressure of proximity with other nationalities. Every year the body of inhabitants assimilated to Hawaiian-American culture has grown larger. With the increasing complexity of Island life, opportunities for making a living in the cities and towns increased, and with them increased the movement of partially adapted immigrants to swell the population of Honolulu, Hilo, and some smaller places. Although the milieu in which a Filipino immigrant found himself in 1925 was essentially the same as that which a Chinese or a Portuguese entered in 1880, the nonessential changes had been so great that the Filipino had a much better chance to learn the English language and American customs than had his predecessors of two generations before.

Immediately after the operation of the Reciprocity Treaty in 1876, the sugar cane industry grew by leaps and bounds, with the export of sugar increasing ten-fold between 1875 and 1890. This extraordinary development required great numbers of laborers, who were imported wholesale by the sugar planters or by the Hawaiian government. The reader is referred to Table 1 for the transformation in the character of the population wrought by this immigration.

TABLE 1

POPULATION OF HAWAII AT VARIOUS CENSUS DATES[a]

Date	Total	Hawaiians	Caucasian-Hawaiians	Part-Hawaiians	Asiatic-Hawaiians	Portuguese	Puerto Ricans	Spanish	"Other Caucasians"	Chinese	Japanese	Koreans	Filipinos	All Other
1853	73,138	71,019							1,262	364				493
1860	69,800	66,984							1,600	700				516
1866	62,959	57,125		1,640					2,200	1,200				794
1872	56,897	49,044		2,487					2,520	2,038				384
1878	57,985	44,088		3,420					3,262	6,045				684
1884	80,578	40,014		4,218		9,967			6,612	18,254	116			1,397
1890	89,990	34,436		6,186		12,719			6,220	16,752	12,610			1,067
1896	109,020	31,019		8,485		15,191			7,247	21,616	24,407			1,055
1900	154,001	29,799	7,185		2,672	18,272			8,547	25,767	61,111			648
1910	191,909	26,041	8,772		3,734	22,301	4,890	1,990	14,867	21,674	79,675	4,533	2,361	1,071
1920	255,912	23,723	11,072		6,955	27,002	5,602	2,430	19,708	23,507	109,274	4,950	21,031	658
1930	368,336	22,636	15,632		12,592	27,588	6,671	1,219	44,895	27,179	139,631	6,461	63,052	780
1934[b]	378,948	21,796	18,169		16,250	29,236	7,280	1,267	45,888	26,989	148,024	6,638	56,700	711

[a] After Table 1, Adams, *The Peoples of Hawaii*, rev. ed.
[b] From the estimate in *Annual Report of the Governor of Hawaii . . . June 30, 1934.*

For various reasons—among them official preference for a particular stock, the reputation of several nationalities for industry and docility, the availability of different nationalities at different times, and fear that one group of labor should grow too large and powerful—the plantation workers were imported from several sources. Today, in the face of cultural and biological amalgamation, several large groups hold their own: Filipinos, Japanese, Chinese, Koreans, Puerto Ricans, and Portuguese, besides the native Hawaiians, the two mixed Hawaiian groups, and the "Other Caucasians" or Haoles, among whom the British still constitute a distinct subgroup. Other immigrant peoples have been present at one time or another in sufficient numbers to stand out as distinct minor ethnic groups: Spanish (still returned separately by the census), Germans, Norwegians, Russians, Galician Poles, and South Sea Islanders (chiefly Gilbert Islanders).

Since its first decade in Hawaii, each of the immigrant groups has undergone several changes: in age and sex composition, in ethnic solidarity, in locality of settlement, and in occupations followed and hence in economic and social status and in opportunity for secondary and higher education. In the final analysis almost everything in the economic and social history of Hawaii has had a bearing on the various ethnic groups' attitudes toward language, and consequently on the development of language in the Islands. This study can, however, deal only with those characteristics of the several groups and of the interrelationships between groups that have been most immediately influential in the linguistic field. At this point the reader need only bear in mind the large number of languages introduced into Hawaii by the plantation laborers and the economic and social position of those laborers, which made the formation of a makeshift language necessary.

THE SUBSTITUTION OF ENGLISH FOR HAWAIIAN
AS THE LANGUAGE OF INSTRUCTION

When the majority of the adult population had become literate in the vernacular and the emphasis of the educators had shifted (about 1828 to 1840) to the education of the children, the question was raised as to which language should be taught. At least as early as in the 1850's some persons, presumably whites, expressed the opinion that English should be immediately and everywhere introduced into the schools.[42] On the mainland of America, too, the "oft-repeated and not unimportant question" had been raised: "Why did you not teach the nation English, and open to them, at once, the rich stores of learning, science and religion, to be found in that language?"[43] The obvious answer was that instruction in a foreign language would be vastly more difficult than in the vernacular, and that it would require foreign teachers in large numbers, whom the little Kingdom could not afford to pay. No one seems to have questioned that some English should be taught in some of the schools. The practical question was in what proportions the foreign and the native language should divide the schools. The general opinion probably was that instruction should for the most part be given in the Hawaiian language, and that this was necessary for the maintenance of a separate Hawaiian nation.[44] This opinion, however, was not fully shared by the Ministry of Education.

Richard Armstrong, who did much to shape the course of education in Hawaii during his thirteen years at the head of the educational system (December 6, 1847, to September 23,

[42]*Report of the President of the Board of Education to the Hawaiian Legislature, 1858.* The Reports vary in title. They will be quoted simply in this form: *Report* of 1858. Usually made on January 1 or on December 31, they cover the preceding biennium.

[43]Bingham, *op. cit.,* p. 104.

[44]The present writer has not read the original sources, other than the *Reports,* covering this point. R. S. Kuykendall, in a communication of October 25, 1934, gives as his opinion that the missionary policy was in general the preservation of the Hawaiian language and that Armstrong rather broke away from this policy. "It was a maxim with the Mission that in order to preserve the nation, they must preserve its speech." (Mrs. Judd, *Honolulu,* 1928 ed., quoted by Kuykendall.) Rufus Anderson, Corresponding Secretary of the American Board of Commissioners for Foreign Missions, in a letter to the Sandwich Island Mission, dated April 10, 1846, wrote: "I trust you will not fall in with the notion, which I am told is favored by some one at least in the government, of introducing the English language, to take the place of the Hawaiian. I cannot suppose there is a design to bring the Saxon race in to supplant the native, but nothing would be more sure to accomplish this result, and that speedily." (Quoted by Kuykendall.)

Concerning this language problem, as well as other educational developments in the period under consideration, now also see Ralph S. Kuykendall, *The Hawaiian Kingdom, 1778-1854,* esp. pp. 360-367; *The Hawaiian Kingdom, 1854-1874,* pp. 110-114.—*Ed.*

1860), advocated the extension of education in English as rapidly as the finances of the Kingdom would permit, and he seems to have had the support of the legislature and of administrators generally.[45] The attitude represented by Armstrong and his supporters was thoroughly unselfish in that it aimed at the material advancement of the Hawaiian people, and was thoroughly charged with a sense of the superiority of the English language over the Hawaiian and of the desirability of introducing the former at the expense of the latter.[46]

[45]Kamehameha III and Kamehameha IV strongly supported English education for the Hawaiians. In his opening address to the Legislature of 1855, young Kamehameha IV said: "It is of the highest importance, in my opinion, that education in the English language should become more general, for it is my firm conviction that unless my subjects become educated in this tongue, their hope of intellectual progress, and of meeting the foreigners on terms of equality, is a vain one." (Quoted from Lydecker, *Speeches of Sovereigns and President*, p. 58, by George Allen Odgers, "Educational Legislation in Hawaii, 1845-1892" [M.A. thesis, University of Hawaii], p. 125.)

[46]"He [Armstrong] would have Hawaiians learn English that they might take better places in the inevitable commercial and industrial development of the country, and earn more money." (Henry Schuler Townsend, Inspector-General of Schools, in a sketch of the educational history of Hawaii appearing in the *Report* of 1900, p. 46.)

Armstrong's official views are set forth in his *Report* of 1858, pp. 11-12: "But it may be a question whether a larger proportion of the school revenue ought not to be appropriated to teaching the people the English language. The Board is of opinion that it should . . .

"The aim of the government should be as it has been, to impart at least an elementary education, however imperfect, to every Hawaiian youth, and until this can be done in a better language, let it continue to be done in their own vernacular tongue, any direct attempt to supersede which at once, would be as impolitic as it would be impracticable. Were the means at our command, it would be an unspeakable blessing to have every native child placed in a good English school, and kept there until it had acpuired [*sic*] a thorough knowledge of what is now, in fact, to a great extent, the business language of the Islands, and which would open to its mind new and exhaustless treasures of moral and intellectual wealth. But such is not the fact. The means are not at our disposal. . . . The entire school revenue would not more than support through the year, fifty well conducted English schools taught by suitable foreign masters; and these could not do justice to more than two thousand children allowing forty to a school. From five to ten years in school, is required to give a native child even a tolerable knowledge of English; and what in the mean time would become of the more than seven thousand children that must be left without any government provision whatever, for their education?

"The idea, therefore, of abandoning all instruction in the native language in the schools at once, and confining our educational efforts to the introduction of the English language among the natives, however well it may answer for newspaper talk, will not be entertained by any sober minded man. . . . The language of a nation is a part of its very being and never was and never will be changed except by a very gradual process. That of Hawaiians is no exception to the general rule."

Under the Kamehamehas, the more farsighted whites probably expected the English to drive out the Hawaiian language, but in the remote future. For the immediate future, they sought to lay the foundation for a bilingual nation, but even this process they expected to be gradual. The natives do not appear to have apprehended to any great extent the undermining of their tongue.[47] Nevertheless, there may have been more opposition to the extension of English education than appears in the official sources. Only in the *Report* of 1864, prepared by a subordinate and issued in the name of M. Kekuanaoa,[48] does there appear an attack on the Anglicization of the schools and the diversion of a disproportionate amount of the revenues to the English language schools. The clerk's reasoning was forceful and often cogent, anticipating many of the arguments now advanced by ethnologists for the preservation of instruction in the native tongues; nevertheless, it appears to have carried little weight with those in power.[49]

[47]See the preceding note; also Bingham, *op. cit.*

[48]Townsend in *Report* of 1899, pp. 48-49.

[49]From the *Report* of 1864, pp. 6-12: "The result of experience warrants the assertion, that the attempt to give Hawaiian children, whose language out of school, in the playground, and at their homes, is exclusively Hawaiian, an education in *day schools,* through the medium of English textbooks only, has not met with success enough, when compared with the advantages to be derived from a common school education in their own language, to warrant the change in favor of the English, even were the expense not so enormously disproportionate.

"That Hawaiian children should be doubly tasked, first, to learn a language that has no analogy whatever, either in its construction or its pronunciation, with their own, and then to acquire through it an education, is much more complimentary to the natural powers of the Hawaiian race, than to the common sense of a Government, who would seek under such a system to educate the people."

The preservation of the Hawaiian language, the writer further pointed out, was necessary to the preservation of the individuality of the Hawaiian nation. The vernacular, he maintained, is "full and comprehensive" enough for teaching any subject.

The neglect of the common schools conducted in the native tongue, for the benefit of a small class receiving English instruction, the writer attacked very strongly. School books and books on general subjects in Hawaiian were not available to the people; while a weekly journal of general practical and cultural content was to be desired. As for English journals and books, they were beyond the pocketbook of the average Hawaiian.

The family schools indirectly if not directly taught the native girl "to consider her mother's tongue as one unfitted for her to speak," and in short turned the pupils into "no longer Hawaiian, but American or English bred young women."

Competent schoolteachers were needed, and these could not be secured from a class educated in a foreign language and brought to think of themselves as a "superior caste, having nothing, not even a language, in common with the rest."

Schools for instruction of children in the English language were opened for certain classes early in Hawaii's educational history: Oahu Charity School, known for a while as Kula Hapahaole, for half white and some white children, in 1833; Punahou School, for the secondary education of white children, in 1842; Royal School, at first for children of *alii* (chiefly) rank, in 1839. Private boarding schools in the charge of missionary and other foreign families gave instruction in English, often very effectively, to a limited number as early as the 1840's, while for many years there was an ephemeral class of English day schools. By 1860 the institution of the English private school for natives was well established. The state soon took a hand in English instruction by granting financial aid to, and exercising more or less supervision over, the private schools. These came to be known as *select* schools, as distinct from the *common* schools where only Hawaiian was taught. (A few select schools gave instruction also in Hawaiian.) "In 1854 a law was passed providing for English schools for Hawaiians whenever the parents would pay half the salary of the teacher. From that time on English education for Hawaiians has continued to grow in favor...."[50] The spread of instruction in English, though not the efficiency and effectiveness of that instruction, can be traced in the successive reports of the heads of the school systems (see Table 8).

The chief obstacle in the way of the rapid supersession of Hawaiian by English in the schools was evidently not opposition or even apathy on the part of the parents, but lack of money. So long as there was no industry rich enough to furnish large revenues, English schools with their foreign masters and superior equipment could be extended but slowly. Even so, a disproportionate amount of the revenues devoted to education was early expended on the English schools. Thus in 1857, although only 691 native students, together with 65 half castes and 155 whites (altogether only 9.7 percent of the total enrollment), were in schools in which English was taught, more than 21 percent of the school funds was expended on their education. The government expenditure per pupil that year in the

[50]Townsend, *op. cit.*, p. 46. The law referred to is found in H. L. 1854, pp. 18-22.

common schools was less than $3.26, but in the select schools it was more than $9.96.[51] Little wonder that friends of the common schools complained!

As the successive reports show, instruction in English continued to grow, at the expense of the common schools conducted in Hawaiian, at a moderate but rather steady pace, until 1876. Had the great impetus given the sugar cane plantations been delayed, say until the end of the century, all indications point to a maintenance, perhaps to a slight acceleration, of this change in the schools. But when Reciprocity did supply impetus to the growth of the plantations, the situation was radically changed. Revenues from taxation were now sufficient to allow a rapid extension of more expensive schools. The composition of the student body within two decades came to be, in most districts, greatly changed; Hawaiians, whether school children or adults, at first mingled with and then became almost lost among a congeries of immigrants. As the economic bonds between Hawaii and the United States quickly grew in importance and communication with the West Coast became regular and rapid, the manifest destiny of the Islands, their not-far-distant Americanization, became clearly evident to the Haoles who in fact directed Hawaiian affairs. English more than ever was seen to be the language of commerce and business relations, the language of command, the language of Anglo-Saxon culture, in which Hawaii was rapidly becoming a participant. The native tongue was increasingly dismissed, by those concerned with education, as unprofitable.[52]

Because the educational authorities of the 1870's and 1880's frankly felt Hawaiian to be dying as a medium of instruction, they were, it appears from the *Reports,* not deeply concerned with the unsatisfactory nature of the common schools taught in the native language. The low standard of these schools was in turn a direct incentive for Hawaiian parents to send their children to the select schools, even at the expense of a tuition fee. The following analysis of instruction in the common schools is typical: "The teaching in these schools, so far as may

[51]*Report* of 1858, pp. 3, 23-24.
[52]Townsend, *op. cit.,* pp. 55-56.

be judged from an examination of some of them, is very poor. This result may be attributed to several causes. In the first place, Hawaiians who have any ability and aptitude for teaching generally drift into other more lurcrative [*sic*] occupations; and secondly, those who do teach prefer to teach in English, thus leaving the more incompetent for the Board of Education to select from." [53]

Some elements of the native population, and perhaps of the Haoles as well, in this period appear to have expressed their fear (which events soon showed to be well-grounded) that the rapid and complete Anglicization of the schools would destroy literacy in Hawaiian, if not its use as a spoken language, among the young natives. This is seen in the defense of their policy submitted by the heads of the school system in their reports of the 1880's. The report prepared while Walter Murray Gibson was President of the Bureau of Public Instruction reads in part:

> In giving preference, however, to schools taught in the English language, no desire is entertained to suppress the Hawaiian schools, or language. Indeed, such is not possible, were it desirable. The child learns his vernacular by the easiest and sweetest of methods—from a mother and father.
>
> With one or two hours per week, a Hawaiian boy or girl will soon learn to read and write the native language. It is perfectly feasible in all the larger schools, in which, at present, only English is taught, to have a competent Hawaiian instructor take two or three hours per week for the purpose of giving instruction in the Hawaiian language, only to Hawaiian children. [54]

Ten years thereafter, when only fifty-nine pupils in three isolated schools received (officially) [55] instruction in Hawaiian,

[53]*Report* of 1886, p. 12. On page 11 of the *Report* of 1884 is a frank statement of the attitude: Why worry over the quality of teachers in Hawaiian? We shan't need them much longer, anyway. See also the following *Reports*: 1858, p. 4; 1874, p. 8; 1878, pp. 3-4, 11; 1880, pp. 8-12, esp. p. 9; 1884, p. 2; 1886, pp. 4, 8-9, 12-13, 26-27; 1888, pp. 2, 3; 1890, pp. 9, 22-24; 1892, pp. 8-9; 1896, pp. 6-7; 1899, pp. 46-49, 55-58 (Townsend's historical summary).

[54]*Report* of 1886, p. 5. See also *Reports* of 1880, pp. 9-10, and 1884, p. 2. A similar argument was advanced in the 1920's regarding the teaching of the Oriental languages in the public schools.

[55]In out of the way places, Hawaiian continued to be a language of instruction for some years after it had officially ceased to be so. John F. G. Stokes of the Bishop Museum heard it so used in the Waipio Valley school as late as 1906.

the supplanting of the Hawaiian language, not only in the schools but in the mouths of the native population, was passed over in one sentence: "The gradual extinction of a Polynesian dialect may be regretted for sentimental reasons, but it is certainly for the interest of the Hawaiians themselves."[56]

Whatever arguments might be advanced in favor of maintaining instruction in the native language lost weight before the argument of the presence of a heterogeneous youth, the children of immigrant laborers, who according to American ideals were entitled to primary education at least, and who would form a large minority, if not a majority, of the future population of the nation. The Portuguese school population in the biennium 1884 to 1886 leaped from 1.9 percent of the total enrollment to 9.8 percent. The Chinese enrollment grew slowly, but its future influence was apparent by 1886. The Japanese group in the schools was appreciably large by the turn of the century. Obviously the Hawaiian language, almost lacking in literature and spoken by a dwindling race, was of no use to these later inhabitants of the Islands; obviously, too, these elements must be made citizens in feeling if not in law. The *Report* of 1886 said: "In the future, therefore, if these heterogeneous elements are to be fused into one nationality in thought and action, it must be by means of the public free schools of the nation, the medium of instruction being the English language chiefly."[57]   Twelve years later, almost at the same moment that Hawaii relinquished its sovereignty, the same view was officially enunciated: "It is the chief purpose of our schools to make our heterogeneous population a homogeneous people and to develop in that people a common good citizenship."[58]   Since the Hawaiian nationality, as represented by the dominant element, had been American in spirit for several years before annexation, the transition to American sovereignty brought no change of spirit in the schools, except that the feeling that English was the only possible language for the future citizenry was confirmed. The sentence last quoted above remains the maxim of the schools.

[56]*Report* of 1896, pp. 6-7.

[57]*Report* of 1886, p. 6.

[58]*Report* of 1898, p. 41. See also *Reports* of 1886, pp. 4-6; 1894, p. 2; 1896, pp. 23-24, 103, 107; 1898, pp. 6-7, 41-42; 1900, pp. 4-5, 156.

An immediate result of the Portuguese immigration was the extension of the scope of the English or select schools, which had been reserved for the children of those able to pay for the privilege of attendance. This led to all public schools' being placed on the same level in 1888.

Up to this time the English schools were considered as giving more than a common school education, and had always been conducted partially at the direct expense of the patrons. But in recent years complications had arisen which aroused public sentiment against this. The Portuguese immigrants came with the express provision in their contracts that they should have free schools for their children. Now no man could seriously contend that education in the Hawaiian language was a suitable provision for these Europeans. At first the Board of Education attempted to make their education in the English schools a charge against the employers, but later yielded the point and gave them free tuition. Others, especially the sons of the soil, wishing to send their children to these same schools, complained that aliens should be more favored than they. The matter was agitated in the Legislature, and in 1888 a law was enacted abolishing all tuition fees in the English schools generally. This was the death sentence of the vernacular schools. From this date they disappeared with great rapidity, giving place to English schools.[59]

THE COMPOSITION OF THE LANGUAGE GROUPS OF HAWAII

Chinese

Provenance. The Chinese, entirely from Kwangtung, are divided into three main dialectal groups. (a) Hakkas—most of whom come from the districts of Doong Goon, Pao On, Wai Yang, Chung Shan, Bock Lo, Ing Wah, Lung Chuen, Kwei Sin, Mui, Hing Ping, Hock Shan, Nam Hoy, Sam Sui, Ching Yen, Poon Yee, and Fah—speak a dialect somewhat akin to the northern Chinese dialects. The sub-dialects appear to differ little from one another. Hakkas from predominantly non-Hakka-speaking districts also speak their district's dialect. The Hakka-speakers constitute about 7,000 of the 27,000 Chinese in Hawaii. (b) See Yup, from the Four Districts of Toy Shan, Sun Wui, Hoy Ping, and Yen Ping, constitute about 3,000 of the Chinese population. (c) Inhabitants of Chung Shan (formerly Heung Shan) District, a peninsula formed by a cluster of islands at the mouth

[59]Townsend, *op. cit.,* pp. 57-58.

of the West River, with the city of Macao at its tip, speak a sub-dialect of Cantonese with several local subdivisions. The four most important of these are Shekki in the central part—the standard dialect of Chung Shan, because Shekki is the *hsien* town; See Dai Doo or Nam Long spoken on the northeastern coast; Loong Doo spoken in the west; and Sam Heung spoken in a group of contiguous villages of Gook Doo. The last is said to bear some resemblance to the Amoy dialect. The dialect of Wong Leong Doo in the extreme southwest of the district is similar to that of Sun Wui District of the See Yup. The Chung Shan people, exclusive of the Hakka-speakers, make up nearly 65 percent of the total Chinese population. The Loong Doo Benevolent Society alone numbers 4,000 members, and the Leong Doo society, 2,000 members. There are in addition (d) a few Sam Yup people from near Canton city, from the Three Districts of Nam Hoy, Poon Yee, and Doong Goon. The three latter dialect groups, See Yup, Chung Shan, and Sam Yup, are commonly called Puntis in distinction from the Hakkas. Their dialects are on the whole mutually intelligible but differ considerably. Differences in the pronunciation of words and the placing of tones are found from village to village, but the syntax is nearly the same everywhere.[60]

Date of settlement. A very few came in fur-trading days. Over 2,000 came between 1852 and 1876, so that in 1876 they constituted 2,038, or nearly 3.2 percent of the population. During the chief immigration, from 1877 to 1897, with a break from 1887 to 1890, over 37,000 entered. Some women, children, and men who entered illegally, professional men, and merchants came after annexation in 1898.[61]

Age and sex composition. The males have always heavily out-

---

[60]Most of the data in this paragraph, including the figures, were obtained from Chock Lun, journalist, in an interview of August, 1933, and letters of October, 1934, and from his series of articles appearing in *The United Chinese News,* January 20 and 27, February 3 and 10, 1934. Other information was given by Tin Yuke Char, Kum Pui Lai, James Chun, and Margaret Lam.

All of the Chinese characters representing names of dialects, districts, villages, etc., which appear in the original typescript, were deleted.—*Ed.*

[61]Lorna H. Jarrett, *Hawaii and Its People,* p. 35; Adams, *op. cit.,* Table 5; Ta Chen, *Chinese Migrations, with Special Reference to Labor Conditions,* pp. 111-127.

numbered the females. According to the estimates of Romanzo
Adams, based on the Hawaiian censuses, the distribution was as
follows (including Hawaiian-born with foreign-born):[62]

Census	No. Males	No. Females	% Males	% Females
1853	344 (?)	20 (?)	94.5 (?)	5.5 (?)
1860	620 (?)	80 (?)	88.6 (?)	11.4 (?)
1866	1,090	110	90.8	9.2
1872	1,881	157	92.3	7.7
1878	5,751	294	95.1	4.9
1884	17,243	1,011	94.5	5.5
1890	15,343	1,409	91.6	8.4
1896	19,167	2,449	88.7	11.3

In 1884, out of 4,812 male and 513 female (foreign-born)
Chinese in the city of Honolulu, only 184 of the former and
134 of the latter were under ten years of age, while 184 of the
males were already over fifty.[63] The 1890 census classified the
(foreign-born) Chinese by age and sex, for the entire kingdom,
as follow:[64]

Sex	1-6	6-15	15-30	30-45	45-60	60+
Males	33	124	5,591	6,671	1,770	333
Females	36	68	360	248	44	23

The American census returns for age and sex groups are given in
Table 2.

Locality of settlement. Upon arrival, the Chinese were
scattered through the rural districts, although some plantations
had a much higher proportion of Chinese than had others. Later
they were concentrated in Honolulu, Hilo, and lesser towns.
The more successful Chinese who could afford wives got into
urban and suburban occupations, leaving the unsuccessful men
to die off as bachelors in the country districts. Of plantation
districts, Kohala alone for some time had a considerable

[62]Population from Adams, *op. cit.,* Table 1; percentages by the present writer.
The estimates for 1853 and 1860 are of doubtful validity, according to Adams.

[63]Hawaiian Census of 1884, p. 4. The Hawaiian censuses 1872-1890 show only
the foreign-born of immigrant ethnic groups.

[64]Hawaiian Census of 1890, Table 5.

TABLE 2

AGE AND SEX DISTRIBUTION OF CHINESE IN HAWAII, 1900-1930

Age Group	1900 M	1900 F	1910 M	1910 F	1920 M	1920 F	1930 M	1930 F
Total	22,296	3,471	17,148	4,526	16,197	7,310	16,561	10,618
Under 5 yrs.	1,648	1,371	859	759	1,450	1,429	1,753	1,619
5- 9 yrs.	438	302	999	898	1,281	1,239	1,808	1,759
10-14 yrs.	1,240	352	856	765	1,052	924	1,547	1,563
15-19 yrs.	2,337	366	650	450	1,002	898	1,354	1,218
20-24 yrs.			405	294	828	745	1,078	938
25-29 yrs.	7,330	640	790	329	667	503	1,076	877
30-34 yrs.			1,828	269	426	346	1,139	741
35-39 yrs.	5,379	300	2,714	282	764	375	1,229	879
40-44 yrs.			2,299	184	1,547	272		
45-49 yrs.	2,431	93	2,040	117	2,122	231	1,739	559
50-54 yrs.			1,399	86	1,681	143		
55-59 yrs.	1,289	35	870	42	1,178	89	2,293	333
60-64 yrs.			872	22	1,184	61		
65-69 yrs.	204[a]	12[a]	368	15	586	30	1,142	99
70-74 yrs.			152	8	286	15		
75-79 yrs.			30	3	100	6	395[b]	31[b]
80-84 yrs.			7	2	23	3		
85 and up			5	1	10			
Unknown			5		10	1	8	2

Data from U. S. Census of 1900, Vol. III, p. 1174; U. S. Census of 1910, Vol. III, pp. 1162-1163; U. S. Census of 1920, Vol. III, pp. 1178-1179; U. S. Census of 1930, *Population—Hawaii*, Table 4.

[a]65 years and over.   [b]75 years and over.

community of Chinese families. At present small concentrations are still found in the rice and general farming sections of Hanalei on Kauai, Keokea on Maui, and Koolaupoko and Waiahole precincts on Oahu. In Honolulu the Chinese are heavily concentrated in "Chinatown" of lower Nuuanu Valley and also in Bingham Tract, Makiki, and parts of Kaimuki ("areas of second settlement"). In precincts 25 of the Fourth Representative District and 23, 24, and 25 of the Fifth, they amounted to more than one-fourth of the population in 1930.[65]

Portuguese

Provenance. A few hundred Portuguese came in pre-Reciprocity days, some being "black Portuguese" from the Cape Verde Islands. Practically all the immigration for plantation labor was from the Madeira Islands (about 40 percent) and the Azores (about 60 percent). Apparently the latter came chiefly from the island of São Miguel, for Portuguese speak of themselves as St. Michael and Madeira folk, respectively. The two groups speak mutually intelligible dialects.[66]

Date of settlement. The chief immigration, about 10,000 in number, was between 1878 and 1887. The second immigration, from 1906 to 1913, brought about 5,000, many of whom soon went on to California.[67]

Age and sex composition. The Hawaiian censuses give the following figures:[68]

Census	No. Males	No. Females	% Males	% Females
1872	382	42	90.1	9.9
1878	403	83	82.9	17.1
1884	5,549	4,418	57.5	42.5
1890	6,870	5,849	54.0	46.0
1896	8,202	6,989	54.0	46.0

[65]Adams, *op. cit.,* pp. 14-15; U. S. Census of 1930; school *Reports* of 1888-1901 (which give the number of children of school age in each of the districts of the islands); The Hawaiian Immigration Society, *Report of the Secretary* (Honolulu, July, 1874), table of statistics of distribution of labor, p. 19.

For present distribution, see the maps.

[66]Jarrett, *op. cit.,* p. 40.

[67]*Ibid.,* pp. 40, 42; Adams, *op. cit.,* p. 13.

[68]Hawaiian Census of 1884, p. 4.

Classification by age and sex (of foreign-born) in 1890 was:[69]

Sex	1-6	6-15	15-30	30-45	45-60	60+
Males	157	944	1,501	1,437	577	154
Females	198	924	1,361	989	309	51

In the 1900 United States Census the Portuguese were enumerated with the other Caucasians, but the age and sex distribution in the 1910, 1920, and 1930 censuses is given in Table 3.

Locality of settlement. At first, the Portuguese settled throughout the Islands. Nearly one-half are still located in rural districts, while the rest are in the two cities of Honolulu and Hilo. There was early concentration in the districts of Hamakua, Hawaii; Makawao, Maui; and to a lesser degree in Hilo. At present the Portuguese are still concentrated in these districts, and in Kalaheo and Eleele, Kauai. They are also concentrated in several parts of the cities of Hilo and Honolulu. "Punchbowl" immediately suggests "Portuguese." Other sections, such as Kalihi-uka in Honolulu and Villa Franca in Hilo, are strongly Portuguese. Between 5 and 10 percent of the population are of this nationality in Olaa and Waiakea near Hilo, in Honomakau precinct of Kohala, in parts of North Kona, in several districts of central Maui, along the Kauai coast from Koloa to Kawaihau, and in Koolaupoko and Haaula on windward Oahu, as well as in most precincts of Honolulu. The widespread distribution of the Portuguese over a long period, and their rural concentration, contrast with the early urban concentration of the Chinese.[70]

Japanese

Provenance. The present writer, not having available any good studies of Japanese dialects, depends upon a rough dialectal division found in Mori's *The Pronunciation of Japanese.* The following percentages are approximate for the Japanese in

[69]Hawaiian Census of 1890, Table 5.

[70]Early concentration of all nationalities found in the *Reports;* present concentration in U. S. Census of 1930.

TABLE 3

AGE AND SEX DISTRIBUTION OF PORTUGUESE IN HAWAII, 1900-1930

Age Groups	1900 M	1900 F	1910 M	1910 F	1920 M	1920 F	1930 M	1930 F
Total	9,785[a]	8,487[a]	11,571	10,730	13,737	13,265	13,870	13,718
Under 5 yrs.			1,953	1,989	2,406	2,337	1,681	1,624
5- 9 yrs.			1,618	1,611	2,185	2,086	1,897	1,795
10-14 yrs.			1,407	1,343	1,757	1,797	1,888	1,906
15-19 yrs.			1,404	1,332	1,503	1,483	1,707	1,720
20-24 yrs.			1,113	1,055	1,121	1,178	1,269	1,395
25-29 yrs.			856	854	929	1,030	1,057	1,091
30-34 yrs.			690	556	826	796	861	893
35-39 yrs.			586	485	683	691	1,560	1,533
40-44 yrs.			367	317	543	472		
45-49 yrs.			376	324	526	359	979	929
50-54 yrs.			304	297	262	263		
55-59 yrs.			259	204	239	198	515	444
60-64 yrs.			333	165	261	209		
65-69 yrs.			155	90	238	159	313	225
70-74 yrs.			84	56	120	103		
75-79 yrs.			45	34	79	56	139[b]	160[b]
80-84 yrs.			6	10	34	26		
85 yrs. and up			12	8	20	15		
Unknown			3		5	7	4	3

Data from U. S. Census of 1910, Vol. III, pp. 1162-1163; U. S. Census of 1920, Vol. III, pp. 1178-1179; U. S. Census of 1930, *Population—Hawaii,* Table 4.

[a]Estimate by Romanzo Adams, *The Peoples of Hawaii,* Table 1.   [b]75 years of age and over.

Hawaii in 1924 (120,074) according to the distribution by prefectural origin given in the *Hawaii Nenkan*.[71]

Dialect Regions and % of Total

Eastern Honshū 7	
Northeastern (chiefly Miyashiro Ken)	1
Kantō 6	
Fukushima Ken 4	
Central Honshū <5	
Hokuriku (chiefly Niigata Ken) >5	
Tōkai-Tōsan >1	
Western Honshū and Shikoku 50	
Kyōto-Ōsaka (chiefly Wakayama Ken)	1
Tosa >1	
Idzumo-Hōki >1	
Inland Sea 47	
Hiroshima Ken <25	
Yamaguchi Ken <21	
Kyūshū 21	
Western Kyūshū 21	
Kumamoto Ken 14	
Fukuoka Ken 6	
Eastern Kyūshū >1	
Southern Kyūshū >1	
Luchu (Okinawa Ken) 14	
Amami-Ōshima ?	
Okinawa ?	

The dialects of Okinawa Ken are so different from other Japanese dialects that they can be considered a separate language. The other dialects of Japanese are mutually intelligible.

Date of settlement. The flow of Japanese into Hawaii (and also out of Hawaii to the West Coast) was strong from 1885 to 1907, with the exception of 1904 to 1905. Most of the immigrants during this period were men, though a considerable number were women and children. From 1907 to 1924 there was a large immigration of children and especially of women, who have not gone on to the mainland.[72]

[71]Masatoshi Gensen Mori, *The Pronunciation of Japanese*, p. 1 and map; *Hawaii Nenkan*, 1931-32, pp. 30-31.

[72]Adams, *op. cit.*, p. 13; Jarrett, *op. cit.*, pp. 44-45; National Bureau of Economic Research, *International Migrations*, Vol. I, pp. 940, 1022-1023.

Age and sex composition. The census of 1890 shows strikingly the adult composition of the early Japanese immigration.[73]

Sex	1-6	6-15	15-30	30-45	45-60	60+
Males	6	28	5,345	4,583	105	12
Females	9	20	1,754	490	8	—

For the United States censuses of 1900 to 1930, see Table 4.

Locality of settlement. From the beginning, the Japanese have been the most widely and evenly distributed of the immigrant groups. Only thirteen precincts in 1930 returned less than 10 percent of their population as Japanese. In the period 1888 to 1901 the Japanese with families were somewhat concentrated in Hilo, Kona, and Kauai. Localities having more than one-half of the total population Japanese in 1930 were: the Puna plantations, Waiakea-kai in Hilo, the coast north of Hilo as far as Honohina, middle Kona; Anahola precinct, Kauai; and several sections of Honolulu, where the Japanese form "camps," or ghettos. The Japanese number less than 5 percent of the population in a few districts still inhabited chiefly by natives and in Maunaloa on Molokai, where the laborers are mostly Filipinos. Elsewhere they make up a consistently large part of the population, important especially in the younger age levels. Their urbanization has gone on apace, but they are still predominantly inhabitants of plantation and small farming districts.[74]

Koreans

Provenance. Immigration was from most parts of Korea, especially the south. The provincial dialects differ little from one another.

Date of settlement. Nearly all, except a few women who came later, arrived during the Russo-Japanese War, 1904 to 1905.[75]

[73]Hawaiian Census of 1890, Table 5. Foreign-born only.
[74]*Reports,* 1888-1901; U.S. Census of 1930.
[75]Adams, *op. cit.,* p. 13; *International Migrations, loc. cit.*

TABLE 4
AGE AND SEX DISTRIBUTION OF JAPANESE IN HAWAII, 1900-1930

Age Groups	1900		1910		1920		1930	
	M	F	M	F	M	F	M	F
Total	47,508	13,603	54,784	24,891	62,644	46,630	75,008	64,623
Under 5 yrs.	3,011	2,771	4,945	4,855	9,552	9,237	11,149	10,636
5- 9 yrs.	219	153	3,532	3,393	6,842	6,682	11,795	11,474
10-14 yrs.	1,901	599	1,655	1,443	4,499	4,125	9,483	9,111
15-19 yrs.	9,791	2,872	1,743	941	4,416	3,439	6,722	6,445
20-24 yrs.	22,304	5,712	7,707	2,457	3,320	4,270	4,335	3,984
25-29 yrs.			7,457	3,299	2,391	4,785	4,193	4,109
30-34 yrs.	8,889	1,393	8,965	3,536	6,730	3,941	3,168	4,235
35-39 yrs.			7,749	2,600	5,825	3,413	7,778	7,256
40-44 yrs.	1,263	93	5,659	1,448	6,689	3,079		
45-49 yrs.			3,093	632	5,253	1,917	9,137	4,792
50-54 yrs.	120	8	1,508	204	3,773	1,072		
55-59 yrs.			424	56	1,802	454	5,732	2,163
60-64 yrs.			274	21	1,170	157		
65-69 yrs.	10[a]	2[a]	53	3	294	41	1,401	382
70-74 yrs.			7	—	51	5		
75-79 yrs.			3	—	16	4	100[b]	27[b]
80-84 yrs.			1	1	1	2		
85 and up			2	—	4	1	15	9
Unknown			7	2	16	6		

Data from U. S. Census of 1900, Vol. III, p. 1174; U. S. Census of 1910, Vol. III, pp. 1162-1163; U. S. Census of 1920, Vol. III, pp. 1178-1179; U. S. Census of 1930, *Population—Hawaii*, Table 4.

[a] 65 years and over.   [b] 75 years and over.

Age and sex composition. See Table 5. The Koreans, like the Chinese, have been a group of bachelors.

TABLE 5
AGE AND SEX DISTRIBUTION OF KOREANS IN HAWAII, 1910-1930

Age Groups	1910		1920		1930	
	M	F	M	F	M	F
Total	3,931	602	3,498	1,452	3,999	2,462
Under 5 yrs.	140	123	398	375	464	456
5- 9 yrs.	91	99	209	183	530	509
10-14 yrs.	65	45	123	123	401	407
15-19 yrs.	81	32	78	84	222	176
20-24 yrs.	255	42	52	237	120	121
25-29 yrs.	889	60	68	99	76	152
30-34 yrs.	994	56	301	77	55	235
35-39 yrs.	636	43	691	82	327	161
40-44 yrs.	394	37	633	55		
45-49 yrs.	210	23	433	44	1,115	136
50-54 yrs.	78	20	268	40		
55-59 yrs.	40	6	111	22	560	73
60-64 yrs.	44	6	83	16		
65-69 yrs.	9	6	29	9	111	31
70-74 yrs.	2	3	7	4		
75-79 yrs.	—	1	3	2	17[a]	5[a]
80-84 yrs.	—	—	1	—		
85 and over	1	—	—	—		
Unknown	2		10		1	

Data from U. S. Census of 1910, Vol. III, pp. 1162-1163; U. S. Census of 1920, Vol. III, pp. 1178-1179; U. S. Census of 1930, pp. 8-10.

[a]75 years and over.

Locality of settlement. The Koreans were at first scattered among the plantations. They have moved rather rapidly to the cities, so that the proportion included in the urban population in 1930 was 43.2 percent. Areas of relative concentration include Wahiawa, Schofield Barracks, and Waialua in rural Oahu; lower Nuuanu Valley and Precinct 24 on Punchbowl in Honolulu; Hilo and Honohina precincts in Hawaii.[76]

[76]United States Census of 1930.

Puerto Ricans[77]

Provenance. Puerto Rico, so far as the present writer knows, has no dialectal areas. The inhabitants speak a dialect of Spanish.
Date of settlement. Chiefly 1900 to 1901.
Age and sex composition. See Table 6. Note the unusual proportion of minors.

TABLE 6

AGE AND SEX DISTRIBUTION OF PUERTO RICANS IN HAWAII,
1910-1930

Age Groups	1910		1920		1930	
	M	F	M	F	M	F
Total	2,878	2,012	3,133	2,469	3,635	3,036
Under 5 yrs.	528	500	467	434	503	545
5- 9 yrs.	264	277	447	434	491	495
10-14 yrs.	170	132	412	403	441	373
15-19 yrs.	274	228	254	273	424	400
20-24 yrs.	387	234	178	134	353	319
25-29 yrs.	373	164	147	157	195	210
30-34 yrs.	253	147	198	129	155	102
35-39 yrs.	208	123	277	155	349	259
40-44 yrs.	121	80	194	103		
45-49 yrs.	110	61	260	94	374	189
50-54 yrs.	60	27	93	58		
55-59 yrs.	36	19	66	30	216	86
60-64 yrs.	60	10	77	28		
65-69 yrs.	21	3	38	21	106	30
70-74 yrs.	4	1	13	6		
75-79 yrs.	2	–	5	5	26[a]	27[a]
80-84 yrs.	3	2	1	2		
85 and over	1	2	2	2		
Unknown	3	2	4	1	2	1

Data from U. S. Census of 1910, Vol. III, pp. 1162-1163; U. S. Census of 1920, Vol. III, pp. 1178-1179; U. S. Census of 1930, pp. 8-10.

[a]75 years and over.

Locality of settlement. The Puerto Ricans tend to settle in the same localities as the Portuguese. Their areas of concentration are Hamakua, especially Paauilo and Kukuihaele, and on

[77]Known in Hawaii as *Porto Ricans.* Data from U. S. Censuses of 1910, 1920, and 1930.
For linguistic data on Puerto Rico, now see Tomás Navarro Tomás, *El español en Puerto Rico,* esp. pp. 163-176.—Ed.

School Street east of the Bishop Museum in Honolulu. Only in the 18th precinct of the Fifth Representative District did they number more than 10 percent of the total population in 1930; they are highly dispersed.

Spanish

Provenance. Chiefly from Málaga province.

Date of settlement. Mostly 1907 to 1913. Most moved on to California.

Age and sex composition. There was at first a slight preponderance of males, but this has now nearly corrected itself. The age distribution is about normal.

Locality of settlement. The Spanish are extremely scattered. A few more than half the total are in the two cities of Honolulu and Hilo.

This group has now almost lost its identity among the Portuguese.[78]

Filipinos

Provenance and *date of settlement.* From 1907 through 1915 18,379 Filipino laborers entered Hawaii, but the present writer has found no figures concerning their provenance. It is said that the first comers were chiefly Tagalogs, who were soon followed and displaced by Bisayas, who in turn have given way to the Ilocanos, mixed with a few Pangasinans (who were probably Ilocano speakers). Bruno Lasker furnishes figures on the provinces of origin of the immigrants from 1916 through 1928, and there has been little immigration since 1930. During that period the immigration of Tagalogs dropped almost to zero, the Bisayas dropped moderately, and there was a marked increase of Ilocanos. As many laborers, especially those coming in earlier years, have left Hawaii, it is probable that the Ilocano element is larger than the number of immigrants from the Ilocano-speaking provinces would indicate. On the other hand, the settled families are likelier to come from the earlier immigration.

[78]For the Spanish, data are drawn from U. S. Censuses of 1910, 1920, and 1930; Adams, *op. cit.,* p. 13; Jarrett, *op. cit.,* p. 55.

The immigrants of the period 1916 to 1928 were distributed as follows:[79]

	Approx. No.		Approx. %	
	Totals	Subtotals	Totals	Subtotals
Ilocano-speaking				
From Ilocano-speaking provinces (including 275 speakers of allied Batan)		39,777		53.6
From provinces containing Cagayan, Tagalog, and Sambal elements		861		0.1
From Pangasinan and Tarlac Provinces; probably from one-half to two-thirds Ilocano and the rest Pangasinan-speaking		9,015		12.2
Probable Ilocano-speaking element	c. 45,146		c. 61.0	
Pangasinan-speaking (probable)	c. 4,508		c. 6.1	
Bisaya-speaking				
Aklan sub-dialect		384		0.5
Hiligainon sub-dialect		705		0.9
Samar sub-dialect		86		0.1
Mixed Samar and Cebuan, probably Cebuan element		1,470		1.9
Cebuan sub-dialect		20,915		28.2
Bisaya and other dialects		33		0.0
Probable Bisaya element	23,593		31.9	
Tagalog-speaking (including natives of mixed Tagalog and Bikol Provinces)	597		0.8	
Bikol-speaking	109		0.1	
Pampanga-speaking	140		0.2	
Total Filipino immigration, 1916-1928	c. 74,092		c. 100.0	

Age and sex composition. The Filipinos are overwhelmingly a group of young bachelors, while the married men have often left their wives in the Philippines. See Table 7.

[79]Bruno Lasker, *Filipino Immigration to Continental United States and to Hawaii,* Appendices B and C.

TABLE 7

AGE AND SEX DISTRIBUTION OF FILIPINOS IN HAWAII, 1920-1930

Age Groups	1920		1930	
	M	F	M	F
Total	16,851	4,180	52,566	10,486
Under 5 yrs.	956	989	2,854	2,858
5- 9 yrs.	614	552	1,825	1,794
10-14 yrs.	320	241	956	930
15-19 yrs.	660	258	3,308	566
20-24 yrs.	5,441	721	13,696	792
25-29 yrs.	4,347	643	12,057	1,388
30-34 yrs.	2,033	313	7,911	852
35-39 yrs.	1,108	245	7,606	966
40-44 yrs.	518	105		
45-49 yrs.	485	66	1,845	258
50-54 yrs.	151	24		
55-59 yrs.	83	9	402	56
60-64 yrs.	68	6		
65-69 yrs.	38	3	85	16
70-74 yrs.	12	2		
75-79 yrs.	4	–	13[a]	9[a]
80-84 yrs.	1	2		
85 and over	–	–		
Unknown	12	1	8	1

Data from U. S. Census of 1910, Vol. III, pp. 1162-1163; U. S. Census of 1920, Vol. III, pp. 1178-1179; U. S. Census of 1930, pp. 8-10.

[a]75 years and over.

Locality of settlement. The Filipinos, being the latest comers, are still concentrated on the plantations, with only 11 percent found in the cities. Indeed, some city precincts contain no Filipinos at all. Neither have the Filipinos found employment in the predominantly native districts. But on the plantations they are distributed fairly evenly, forming a majority of the workmen but a minority of the total population.[80]

South Sea Islanders

"In all, 2,448 South Sea Islanders were brought during 1869-1885." About 1,800 of these were Gilbert Islanders, and almost all were from Micronesia. Most returned to their native

[80]U. S. Census of 1930.

islands as soon as they were able, and those who remained were soon lost among the native Hawaiian population.[81]   South Sea Islander children were separately enumerated in the schools from the *Report* of 1882 (when they numbered 182) to the *Report* of 1900 (when they numbered 28). This group appears to have had no linguistic influence on Hawaii. It is likely that those who remained learned to speak the Hawaiian language fluently.

Russians

This group still maintains its individuality to some extent and is often distinguished from the Haoles. From 1906 to 1912 about 3,000 Russians (Molokan sectarians and Siberiaks) came to Hawaii, but most have moved to the mainland, leaving only about 700 at present, one-third of them foreign-born. They appear to have had no specific linguistic influence.[82]

Germans

"Between 1882 and 1885, 1,052 Germans came to the islands as laborers."[83]   This was in addition to the mercantile population established in Honolulu and elsewhere. These laborers, most of whom were from Hannover, were concentrated on the Isenbergs' plantation at Lihue, where they formed a compact little community. This community still maintains its identity and, thanks to an excellent language school kept up from 1882 to 1917, until lately maintained its language. In 1930 there were 739 Germans and Austrians of foreign birth in the Islands, but they are not now differentiated from the other Haoles.[84]

Scandinavians

The only large compact group of Scandinavian immigrants for plantation labor was 615 Norwegians who were imported in 1881. Most of these soon moved away. Some Swedes and Danes

[81]Jarrett, *op. cit.,* pp. 51-52. [The recent immigration of Samoans is the first non-plantation immigration in the usual American pattern.—*Ed.*]

[82]*Ibid.,* pp. 53-54; U. S. Census of 1930; *Hawaiian Annual,* 1907, p. 146.

[83]Jarrett, *op. cit.,* p. 52.

[84]Bernhard Hörmann, "The Germans in Hawaii" (M.A. thesis, University of Hawaii); U.S. Census of 1930.

also came to Hawaii. But all the Scandinavians soon became indistinguishable from the rest of the Haole population. In 1930, there were 382 foreign-born Scandinavians in Hawaii.[85]

Other Europeans

In 1898, 365 Galician Poles were imported as plantation laborers, who soon scattered.[86] There has always been a scattering of foreigners of non-English-speaking stocks in Honolulu: Dutch and Flemish (including several parochial school teachers), Italians, French, Slavs, and others. Their linguistic problems are those of immigrants in any part of the United States; their linguistic influence, if any, is extremely slight; and they very soon are indistinguishable from the other Haoles.

Haoles

The Haoles comprise most of the "Other Caucasians" of the census, but they are not identical with that category. The Haoles as a group occupy a preferred position in Hawaii. It is considered beneath their dignity to do unskilled labor on a plantation. Many come of old established families; those who immigrated to Hawaii often came as skilled laborers, office workers and other white collar employees, salesmen, government employees, professional men, entrepreneurs—few to work on the plantations, most to the cities. About 20,000 belong to the military and naval establishments and are concentrated in forts and at Pearl Harbor, where they come into little contact with the civilian population. There is, however, some linguistic contact between the servicemen and the Islanders, especially those residing in Honolulu and Wahiawa. The officers and their families come into more extensive contact with non-Haoles than do most enlisted men, because they hire Oriental servants and their children meet all nationalities in the schools. Thus the linguistic influence of the military and naval population is felt, though not so much as the influence of the civilian Haoles.

---

[85] Jarrett, *op. cit.*, p. 52; Hawaiian Sugar Planters' Association, *Story of Sugar in Hawaii*, p. 27; *Hawaiian Annual*, 1882, p. 65.

[86] *Story of Sugar in Hawaii*, p. 27.

The Haoles have always been very thinly spread in the country districts; not one rural precinct contains Haoles to the proportion of one-tenth of its population. Practically none are found in many districts, especially outside the plantations. In the cities and in the larger plantation towns, they congregate in certain localities; thus in Honolulu some districts are more than 50 percent Haole while in other precincts their percentage is zero.

Outside the service population, the sex and age distribution of the Haoles approaches normality. A number of Haole men are married to non-Haole women, especially to Part-Hawaiians and Portuguese, and this affects the language situation in the homes.[87]

British. The British, who in 1930 numbered 3,056 (foreign-born only) out of 44,895 Other Caucasians, and who therefore constitute about one-eighth of the civilian Haole population, have undoubtedly had some influence, distinguishable from that of the Americans, upon the English spoken in Hawaii. Scotch, English, and Canadians, in that order, are the most numerous of the British group. Scotch plantation employees are well known, especially in East Hawaii.[88]

Hawaiians

The Hawaiians have concentrated in the cities and in the rural districts unsuitable for plantation agriculture. Nearly one-half (47.8 percent) now live in Honolulu and Hilo. A few, however, are found in almost every precinct of the Islands. While scattered, the Hawaiians still maintain enough centers of concentration for their language to be preserved. The strongest rural concentration is on the coasts of Puna and Kona, in Kona outside the Japanese coffee farming area, on the Parker Ranch, and in the Waipio Valley on Hawaii; on Niihau and in Hanalei District on Kauai; on Molokai, excepting Maunaloa pineapple plantation; in Hana District and about Kahakuloa on Maui; in Koolau and on the Waianae homesteads of rural Oahu. The

[87] U. S. Census of 1930.
[88] U. S. Census of 1930, *Population—Hawaii*, Table 15.

urban concentration is generally in the poorer districts. Lahaina, until the beginning of the twentieth century a stronghold of Hawaiian population, has lost most of that population since the agricultural development of the district. The same is true of most of Lanai. A record of the advance of plantation lands would account for the changes in the rural distribution of the natives.[89]

Part-Hawaiians

The Part-Hawaiians are divided into Caucasian-Hawaiian and Asiatic-Hawaiian groups, the former of which is largely part-Haole and the latter largely part-Chinese in blood. Their rapid numerical increase may be traced in Table 1. Both are chiefly city-dwelling (59.4 percent of the Caucasian-Hawaiians and 54.4 percent of the Asiatic-Hawaiians), like their fathers. In the rural districts their distribution largely follows that of the pure Hawaiians. The distinction between so-called pure Hawaiians and Part-Hawaiians is probably more a matter of culture than of blood, so that we may expect the Part-Hawaiians to be more Americanized in manners, to have lost more of the Hawaiian language, and to have learned the English language better than the pure Hawaiians.

The sex distribution of both Hawaiians and Part-Hawaiians, as is natural of native groups, is normal, but the Part-Hawaiian group is heavily weighted with young people—as may be expected of a recent and still growing hybrid group.[90]

To know the home languages of Part-Hawaiians would throw valuable light on linguistic processes in Hawaii. This information could in large measure be obtained from school records and merely awaits the student.

STATISTICAL MATERIAL RELATING TO THE
SCHOOLS OF HAWAII

Proportion of students receiving instruction in the English language. In interpreting Table 8 it must be borne in mind that until about 1870 the *Reports* prepared by the educational

[89]U. S. Census of 1930; *Reports* of 1882-1900.
[90]U. S. Census of 1930; *Reports*, 1888-1900; Adams, *op. cit.*, pp. 8-9, 15, 27.

TABLE 8

STUDENTS RECEIVING INSTRUCTION IN THE HAWAIIAN AND ENGLISH LANGUAGES

Year	Total Schools	Total Students	Schools Conducted in Hawaiian	Students Enrolled in Hawaiian Schools	% of Total Enrollment	Schools in (or Offering) English	Students in English Schools	% of Total Enrollment
1832[a]	—	23,123						
1839[b]	—	c. 16,000						
1842[c]	—	c. 13,080						
1846[d]	—	c. 18,393	—	c. 18,193	c. 98.9	6	c. 200	c. 1.1
1847[e]	—	18,644	—			—		
1848[f]	631	c. 19,844	624	c. 19,644	c. 99.0	7	c. 200	c. 1.0
1849[g]	553	c. 16,147	545	15,841	c. 98.1	8	306	c. 1.9
1850[b]	c. 555	15,729	543	15,308	97.3	c. 12	421	2.7
1851[i]	551	15,967	540	15,660	98.1	11	307	1.9
1852[j]	455	14,541	445	14,188	97.6	10	353	2.4
1853[k]	435	c. 12,755	425	c. 12,255	c. 96.1	10	500	c. 3.9
1854[l]	c. 433	c. 11,101	c. 415	c. 10,341	c. 93.1	c. 18	760	c. 6.9
1855[m]	c. 386	c. 11,226	363	10,076	c. 89.7	c. 23	c. 1,150	c. 10.3
1856[n]	c. 352	c. 9,599	332	8,671	c. 90.3	c. 20	928	c. 9.7
1857[n]	c. 327	9,371	312	8,460	90.3	c. 15	911	9.7
1858[o]	c. 321	—	293	8,628	—	c. 28	—	—
1859[o]	c. 312	c. 9,782	284	c. 8,628	c. 88.2	c. 28	c. 1,154	c. 11.8
1860[p]	c. 292	c. 9,682	c. 269	8,532	c. 88.1	c. 23	c. 1,150	c. 11.9
1861[p]	c. 289	9,530	c. 266	8,317	87.3	c. 23	1,213	12.7

Year								
1862[q]	—		c. 236	c. 7,606	—	—	—	—
1863[q]	292	c. 9,367	255	7,857	c. 83.9	37	c. 1,510	c. 16.1
1864	No report avail.							
1865	No report avail.							
1866[r]	262	c. 8,590	230	7,590	c. 88.4	32	c. 1,000	c. 11.6
1867	No report							
1868[s]	266	8,404	221	6,323	75.2	45	2,081	24.8
1869	No report							
1870[t]	—	7,927	224	5,938	74.9	—	1,989	25.1
1871	No report							
1872[u]	245	8,287	202	6,274	75.7	43	2,013	24.3
1873	No report							
1874	242	7,755	196	5,522	71.2	46	2,233	28.8
1875	No report							
1876	224	6,981	180	4,799	68.7	44	2,182	31.3
1877	No report							
1878	222	6,991	170	4,344	62.1	52	2,647	37.9
1879	No report							
1880	210	7,164	150	4,078	57.0	60	3,086	43.0
1881	No report							
1882	201	8,046	134	3,528	43.8	67	4,518	56.2
1883	No report							
1884	200	8,723	114	2,841	32.6	86	5,882	67.4
1885	No report							
1886	172	9,016	77	2,018	22.4	95	6,998	77.6
1887	No report							
1888	179	8,770	63	1,370	15.7	116	7,400[v]	84.3
1889	No report							
1890	178	10,006	36	768	7.7	142	9,238	92.3
1891	No report							
1892	168	10,712	28	552	5.2	140	10,160	94.8
1893	No report							

TABLE 8 — continued

STUDENTS RECEIVING INSTRUCTION IN THE HAWAIIAN AND ENGLISH LANGUAGES

Year	Total Schools	Total Students	Schools Conducted in Hawaiian	Students Enrolled in Hawaiian Schools	% of Total Enrollment	Schools in (or Offering) English	Students in English Schools	% of Total Enrollment
1894	176	11,307	18	320	2.8	158	10,987	97.2
1895[w]	187	12,616	3	59	0.5	184	12,557	99.5
1896[x]	–	14,023	–	–	–	–	–	–
1897[y]	192	14,522	1	26	0.2	191	14,496	99.8
1898	No report							
1899	189	15,490	1	31	0.2	188	15,459	99.8
1900[z]	195	15,537	1	41	0.2	194	15,496	99.8
1901	No report							
1902	203	18,382	0	0	0.0	203	18,382	100.0

[a]Report of 1846, p. 56; number of readers, probably including adults.
[b]Ibid.; estimated attendance.
[c]Ibid.; estimated attendance (regular) of Protestant schools.
[d]Report of August 1, 1846; figures approximate.
[e]Report of April 29, 1847; number of students under government supervision.

f *Report* of April 28, 1848; 19,644 students in National Schools and "not far short of" 200 studying English.

g *Report* of April, 1850; number studying English is approximate.

b *Report* of May 12, 1851; number studying English probably overstated by about 200.

i *Report* of April 14, 1852.

j *Report* of April 6, 1853.

k *Report* of April 8, 1854; figures approximate.

l *Report* of April 7, 1855; all figures approximate and unsatisfactory.

m *Report* of April, 1856; "Students in English Schools" include all those studying any English or French, but the figure seems too high.

n *Report* of 1858; figures on English schools uncertain.

o *Report* of 1860; figures for 1858 incomplete; those for 1859 contain an error of 100 in the total; number of English school students approximate.

p *Report* of 1862; figures for 1860 approximate.

q *Report* of 1864; figures unsatisfactory; out of about 1,510 students studying English in 1863, only about 639 were doing so effectively.

r Number at date of *Report*, 1866; 962 students accounted for in English schools, the others estimated.

s *Report* of January 1, 1868.

t *Report* of January 1, 1870.

u *Reports* dated only by years until 1895; figures probably are of January 1 for every even year.

v English schools include a few bilingual Chinese and one bilingual German school.

w *Report* of 1896, which really covers 1895.

x From *Report* of 1897.

y *Report* of December 31, 1897.

z Figures for 1899 and 1900 from *Report* of December 31, 1900.

authorities were not well organized statistically, and that the number of students returned as receiving instruction in the English and Hawaiian languages is sometimes uncertain. Most of the figures given before that date must be taken as approximate, though they are as careful approximations as the present writer can make. For the earlier reports, it is also to be remembered that many of the pupils listed as receiving instruction in English were taught English as a foreign language but did most of their school work in Hawaiian. Conversely, some students returned as

TABLE 9

NATIONAL DERIVATION OF STUDENTS IN THE SCHOOLS OF HAWAII, 1880-1932

Year	Total No.	Hawaiian No.	%	Part-Hawaiian No.	%	American & British No.	%	Other Foreign No.	%	Portu- No.
1880	7,164	5,657	79.2	955	13.3	337	4.7	75[a]	0.8	55
1882	8,043	6,064	75.4	1,057	13.1	346	4.3	282[b]	3.5	157
1884	8,723	5,885	67.5	1,186	13.6	419	4.8	249[c]	2.9	858
1886	9,016	5,881	65.2	1,042	11.6	491	5.4	287[d]	3.2	1,185
1888	8,770	5,320	60.7	1,247	14.3	416	4.7	251[e]	2.8	1,335
1890	10,006	5,599	56.0	1,573	15.7	398	4.0	322[f]	3.2	1,813
1892	10,712	5,353	50.0	1,866	17.4	502	4.7	325[g]	3.0	2,253
1894	11,307	5,177	45.8	2,103	18.6	469	4.1	365[h]	3.2	2,551
1895	12,616	5,207	41.3	2,198	17.4	586	4.6	438[i]	3.5	3,186
1896	14,023	5,480	39.1	2,443	17.4	673	4.8	499[j]	3.6	3,600
1897	14,522	5,330	36.7	2,479	17.1	764	5.3	496[k]	3.4	3,815
1898	14,885	5,406	36.0	2,568	17.1	760	5.7	426[l]	2.8	3,818
1899	15,490	5,043	32.5	2,721	17.5	814	5.2	575[m]	3.7	3,882
1900	15,538	4,977	32.0	2,631	16.9	931	6.0	549[n]	3.5	3,809
1901	17,519	4,903	28.0	2,869	16.4	1,052	6.0	597[o]	3.4	4,124
1902	18,382	5,076	27.6	2,934	16.0	1,011	5.4	593[o]	3.2	4,335
1903	18,415	4,893	26.6	3,018	16.4	1,016	5.6	632[o]	3.4	4,243
1904	20,017	4,983	24.9	3,267	16.3	1,157	5.8	537[o]	2.7	4,448
1905	21,644	4,943	23.0	3,430	16.0	1,293	6.0	934[p]	4.2	4,683
1906	21,900	4,906	22.4	3,500	16.0	1,196	5.5	554[p]	2.5	4,437
1907	23,087	4,658	20.2	3,546	15.4	1,157	5.0	1,028[p]	4.5	4,537
1908	24,856	4,767	19.2	3,691	14.9	1,188	4.8	926[p]	3.7	4,777
1909	25,410	4,536	17.9	3,841	15.1	1,242	4.9	842[p]	3.3	4,722

"Other Foreign" is in short a catch-all term which, especially in later years, need not mean of foreign birth.

[a]Other Foreigners, French, Germans. [b]103 Other Foreigners, Germans, Norwegians; 182 South Sea Islanders. [c]As above, 200 and 49 respectively. [d]230 Germans and Norwegians; 57 South Sea Islanders and Japanese. [e]216 Germans and Norwegians; 35 South Sea Islanders and Other Foreigners. [f]256 Germans, Norwegians, French; 66 South Sea Islanders and Other

receiving instruction in Hawaiian also learned some English in school. Furthermore, all pupils are returned for the purposes of this table, although the number who could read and write was much less. In 1850, for example, of 15,308 students, only 7,851 were able to read and 4,210 were able to write.[91] No distinction has been made between public and private schools. It is obvious that most of the schools conducted in the Hawaiian language, especially in the latter part of the century, were public schools.

[91]*Report* of 1851, table.

ese	Spanish		Puerto Rican		Chinese		Japanese		Korean		Filipino	
%	No.	%	No.	%	No.	%	No.	%	No.	%	No.	%
0.8					85	1.2						
1.9					137	1.7						
9.8					126	1.4						
13.1					130	1.4						
15.2					147	1.7	54	0.6				
18.1					262	2.6	39	0.4				
21.0					353	3.3	60	0.6				
22.6					529	4.7	113	1.0				
25.3					740	5.9	261	2.1				
25.7					931	6.6	397	2.8				
26.3					1,078	7.4	560	3.9				
25.5					1,170	7.8	737	4.9				
25.1					1,314	8.4	1,141	7.4				
24.5					1,289	8.3	1,352	8.7				
23.5			596	3.4	1,385	7.9	1,993	11.4				
23.6			593	3.2	1,499	8.2	2,341	12.7				
23.1			538	2.9	1,554	8.4	2,521	13.7				
22.2			437	2.2	1,875	9.4	3,313	16.5				
21.8			405	1.9	2,087	9.3	3,869	18.0				
20.3			392	1.8	2,197	10.0	4,557	20.8	161	0.7		
19.7			368	1.6	2,548	11.0	5,035	21.8	210	0.9		
19.2			447	1.8	2,797	11.3	6,095	24.5	168	0.7		
18.6			381	1.5	2,840	11.2	6,758	26.5	248	1.0		

Foreigners. [g]As above, 273 and 52 respectively. [h]As above, 296 and 69. [i]As above, 357 and 81. [j]476 Germans, French, Other Foreigners; 23 South Sea Islanders. [k]As above, 486 and 10. [l]396 Germans and Other Foreigners; 30 South Sea Islanders. [m]545 Germans, Norwegians, Other Foreigners; 30 South Sea Islanders. [n]521 Germans, Scandinavians, Other Foreigners; 28 South Sea Islanders. [o]Germans, Scandinavians, Other Foreigners. [p]Germans and Scandinavians given first, Other Foreigners second. Figures for the years are: 397 and 537 for 1905; 355 and 199

TABLE 9—continued

NATIONAL DERIVATION OF STUDENTS IN THE SCHOOLS OF HAWAII, 1880-1932)

Year	Total No.	Hawaiian No.	%	Part-Hawaiian No.	%	American & British No.	%	Other Foreign No.	%	Portug No.
1910	25,770	4,354	16.9	3,718	14.4	1,208	4.7	846[p]	3.3	4,890
1911	28,435	4,301	15.1	4,060	14.3	1,325	4.7	1,121[p]	3.9	5,153
1912	32,300	4,370	13.5	4,182	12.9	1,405	4.5	832[q]	2.6	5,580
1913	33,139	4,179	12.6	4,108	12.4	1,608	4.9	626[q]	1.9	5,521
1914	35,988	3,963	11.0	4,482	12.4	1,585	4.4	624[q]	1.7	5,780
1915	38,229	4,011	10.5	4,652	12.2	1,705	4.5	583[q]	1.5	5,973
1916	39,004	3,914	10.0	4,918	12.6	1,939	5.0	664[q]	1.7	6,012
1917	41,679	4,024	9.7	5,173	12.4	2,094	5.0	538[q]	1.3	6,302
1918	43,136	3,960	9.2	5,347	12.4	2,132	4.9	471[q]	1.2	6,408
1920	48,923	4,030	8.2	6,119	12.5	2,453[r]	5.0	485[s]	1.0	6,678
1922	57,502	4,339	7.5	6,798	11.8	2,989[r]	5.2	554[t]	1.0	7,189
1924	65,469	4,213	6.4	7,633	11.7	3,553[r]	5.6	792[t]	1.2	7,403
1926	72,776	4,100	5.6	8,453	11.6	4,010[r]	5.5	951[t]	1.3	7,655
1928	81,391	3,986	4.9	9,716	11.9	5,372[v]	6.6	884[u]	1.1	7,958
1930	88,577	3,873	4.4	10,518	11.9	5,331[v]	6.0	1,124[u]	1.3	7,981
1932	93,063	3,551	3.8	11,366	12.2	5,786[v]	6.0	1,415[u]	1.5	7,794

for 1906; 376 and 652 for 1907; 332 and 594 for 1908; 263 (Germans only) and 579 for 190
261 (Germans) and 585 for 1910. [q]Germans, Russians, and Other Foreigners. [r]Americans an
British combined as Anglo-Saxons. [s]Scandinavians and Others. [t]Others. [u]All Others. [v]"Oth
Caucasians" substituted for Anglo-Saxons.

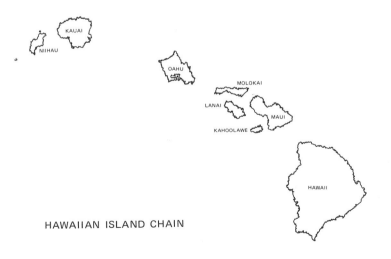

HAWAIIAN ISLAND CHAIN

%	Spanish		Puerto Rican		Chinese		Japanese		Korean		Filipino	
	No.	%	No.	%	No.	%	No.	%	No.	%	No.	%
19.0			350	1.4	2,872	11.0	7,262	28.2	270	1.0		
18.1			352	1.2	3,184	11.2	8,600	30.3	339	1.2		
17.3	592	1.8	653	2.0	3,839	11.9	10,288	31.9	390	1.2	169	0.5
16.5	1,037	3.1	774	2.3	3,625	10.9	10,976	33.1	399	1.2	286	0.9
16.1	1,069	3.0	855	2.4	3,886	10.8	12,917	35.9	460	1.3	367	1.0
15.6	1,008	2.7	963	2.5	4,008	10.5	14,324	37.5	512	1.3	490	1.3
15.4	940	2.4	1,037	2.7	4,070	10.4	14,440	37.0	518	1.3	552	1.4
15.1	679	1.6	1,116	2.7	4,455	10.7	16,071	38.6	543	1.3	684	1.6
14.9	524	1.2	1,063	2.5	4,518	10.4	17,213	39.9	622	1.4	878	2.0
13.7	441	1.0	1,143	2.3	5,068	10.4	20,651	42.2	729	1.5	1,126	2.3
12.5	459	0.8	1,330	2.3	5,759	10.0	25,424	44.2	949	1.7	1,712	3.0
11.0	401	0.6	1,185	1.8	6,495	9.9	30,487	46.6	1,180	1.8	2,127	3.3
10.5	356	0.5	1,158	1.6	7,156	9.8	34,626	47.6	1,477	2.0	2,834	3.9
9.8	324	0.4	1,165	1.4	7,661	9.4	39,290	48.3	1,728	2.1	3,307	4.1
9.0	305	0.3	1,276	1.4	8,092	9.1	43,910	49.8	2,047	2.3	4,120	4.6
8.4	324	0.3	1,457	1.6	8,070	8.7	46,352	49.8	2,210	2.4	4,738	5.1

HAWAII

Honomakau 2 ● Hawi
● Makapala
Mahukona ● 1
KOHALA
3
Kaauhuhu
Waimanu
17 Waipio
16 Kukuihaele
16 Honokaa
Paauhau
Kawaihae 5 ●
4 ●
Kamuela
Ahualoa
14 Kalopa
13 Paauilo
Kukaiau
12 Ookala
12 Laupahoehoe
Papaaloa
11 Honohina
WAIMEA
Hakalau
10 Honomu
N. HILO
Peepeekeo
6 Puuanahulu ●
HAMAKUA
9 Papaikou
(20 Villa Franca
(18 Keaukaha
8 Hilo (19 Kapiolani School
7 Kalao
S. HILO
7 Waiakea-kai
N. KONA
6 Waiakea-waena
8 Kailua
5 Olaa
9 Keauhou
Kainaliu ●
4 Pahoa ●
10 Kahauloa
3 Kapoho ●
Napoopoo ●
Glenwood ●
2 Opihikao ●
Honaunau ●
S. KONA
Volcano ●
PUNA
1 Kalapana
Hookena ● 11
KAU
Ala-e 12
Milolii 13
16 Pahala ●
15 Punaluu
14 Waiohinu ●

0 5 10 15
Miles
Precincts numbered
Districts in capitals

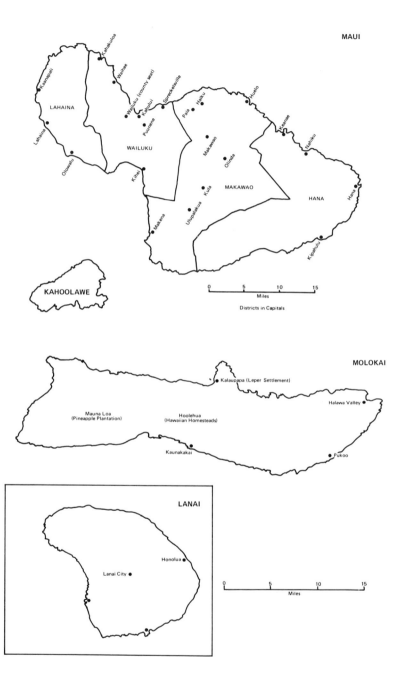

MAUI

LAHAINA

Kaanapali
Kahakuloa
Waihee
Wailuku (county seat)
Kahului
Spreckelsville
Puunene
Paia
Haiku
Huelo
Keanae
Nahiku

Lahaina

WAILUKU

Olowalu

Kihei

Makawao

Olinda

Makena

Kula

Ulupalakua

MAKAWAO

HANA

Hana

Kipahulu

0   5   10   15
Miles
Districts in Capitals

KAHOOLAWE

MOLOKAI

Kalaupapa (Leper Settlement)

Halawa Valley

Mauna Loa
(Pineapple Plantation)

Hoolehua
(Hawaiian Homesteads)

Kaunakakai

Pukoo

LANAI

Honolua

Lanai City

0   5   10   15
Miles

78

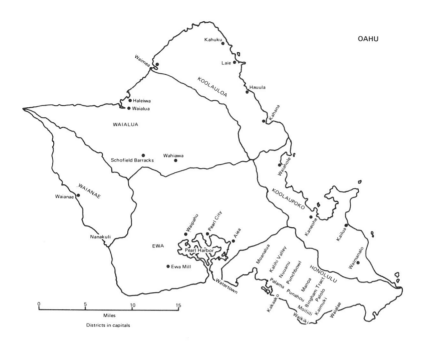

OAHU

Kahuku

Waimea

Laie

KOOLAULOA

Hauula

Haleiwa

Kahana

Waialua

WAIALUA

Schofield Barracks

Wahiawa

Waiahole

WAIANAE

KOOLAUPOKO

Waianae

Kaneohe

Kailua

Nanakuli

Whipahu

Pearl City

Aiea

Waimanalo

EWA

Pearl Harbor

Watertown

Moanalua

Kalihi Valley

Nuuanu

Punchbowl

HONOLULU

Palama

Punahou

Manoa

Bingham Tract

Palolo

Ewa Mill

Kakaako

Moiliili

Kaimuki

Waialae

Waikiki

0   5   10   15
Miles
Districts in capitals

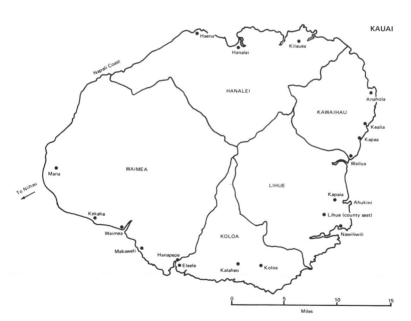

KAUAI

Haena

Kilauea

Hanalei

HANALEI

Napali Coast

Anahola

KAWAIHAU

Kealia

Kapaa

Wailua

Mana

WAIMEA

LIHUE

To Niihau

Kapaia

Ahukini

Kekaha

Lihue (county seat)

Waimea

KOLOA

Nawiliwili

Makaweli

Hanapepe

Eleele

Kalaheo

Koloa

0   5   10   15
Miles

79

TABLE 10

NATIONALITY OF TEACHERS IN THE HAWAIIAN SCHOOLS, 1888-1933

Year	Total	Hawaiian No.	%	Part-Hawaiian No.	%	American No.	%	British No.	%	Other No.
1888	210[a]	79	37.6	42	20.0	54	25.7	32	15.4	3
1890	368[b]	90	24.4	47	12.8	143	38.9	53	14.4	25
1892	390	93	23.7	47	12.0	154	39.3	57	14.5	27
1894	405	80	19.7	61	15.1	155	38.3	57	14.1	24
1895	426	68	16.0	60	14.1	177	41.6	66	15.5	26
1896	482	68	14.2	59	12.2	226	47.0	76	15.8	27
1897	507	57	11.2	62	12.2	253	49.8	69	13.6	30
1898	516	61	11.8	64	12.4	254	49.3	67	13.0	30
1899	544	62	11.4	68	12.5	282	51.8	66	12.1	30
1900	559	64	11.4	58	10.4	299	53.5	59	10.5	39
1902	629	79	12.5	72	11.4	321	51.0	60	9.5	46
1904	663	70	10.5	110	16.6	328	49.5	53	8.0	39
1906	704	89	12.6	124	17.7	326	46.4	61	8.7	45
1908	755	83	11.0	164	21.7	348	46.1	51	6.8	37
1910	777	85	10.9	172	22.2	355	45.7	40	5.2	41
1912	973	89	9.2	191	19.6	457	47.0	52	5.3	43
1914	1,044	85	8.1	202	19.3	481	46.1	57	5.5	49
1916	1,171	99	8.5	233	19.9	561	47.8	49	4.2	48
1918	1,433	102	7.1	295	20.6	695	48.5	53	3.7	36
1924	1,566[b]	86	5.5	137[i]	8.8	464	29.6	71	4.5	46
1926[j]	—	(See Part-Hawaiian)	—		26.0[k]	—	45.0[l]	—	—	—
1929[m]	2,892									
1933[n]	2,587	114o	c. 4.5	—	—	—	—	—	—	—

[a]Government schools only.

[b]Government and private schools until 1918; thereafter government schools only.

[c]The first year in which Chinese appeared as teachers in the public schools was 1904; Japanese in 1910.

[d]Including 1 Spanish.

[e]Including 3 Spanish.

[f]Including 6 Spanish.

[g]Including 2 Spanish.

[h]From *Honolulu Star-Bulletin*, [?] , 1924, p. 6.

[i]The large "mixed, excluding Part-Hawaiian" group undoubtedly does contain a good many Part-Hawaiians.

Foreign	Portuguese and Spanish		Chinese		Japanese		Korean		Other	
%	No.	%	No.	%	No.	%	No.	%	No.	%
1.4										
6.8	2	0.5	8	2.2^c						
6.9	8	2.2	4	1.0						
5.9	10	2.5	17	4.2	1	0.2^c				
6.1	13	3.1	14	3.3	2	0.5				
5.6	13	2.7	11	2.3	2	0.4				
5.9	20	4.0	13	2.6	3	0.6				
5.8	22	4.3	15	2.9	3	0.6				
5.5	22	4.0	10	1.8	4	0.7				
7.0	25	4.5	12	2.1	3	0.5				
7.3	28	4.5	14	2.2	9	1.4				
5.9	33	5.0	23	3.5	7	1.0				
6.4	32	4.5	18	2.6	9	1.3				
4.9	44	5.8	20	2.7	5	0.7	3	0.4		
5.3	51	6.6	23	3.0	6	0.8	4	0.5		
4.4	68	7.0	43	4.4	27	2.8	3	0.3		
4.7	87^d	8.3	47	4.5	36	3.4	–	–		
4.1	100^e	8.5	55	4.7	23	2.0	2	0.2	1	0.1
2.5	115^f	8.0	96	6.7	41	2.8	–	–	–	–
2.9	131^g	8.4	174	11.1	80	5.1	–	–	377^i	24.1
–	–	7.0	–	11.0	–	7.0	–	–	–	7.0
			415	14.4						
–	196^p	c. 8.0	400^q	16.0	400^r	16.0	13	0.5	–	–

^{j}Percentages approximate, from Littler, *Governance of Hawaii*, p. 76. It is to be noted that the total is 103 percent.

^{k}Hawaiians and Part-Hawaiians.

^{l}Haoles.

^{m}Kalfred D. Lum, *The Chinese of Hawaii*, p. 18.

^{n}The present writer's estimate from the *School Directory* of 1933-1934, based on the approximate number of names belonging to each nationality.

^{o}Hawaiian surnames and given names—a very imperfect way of estimating.

^{p}Portuguese and Spanish surnames.

^{q}Chinese surnames.

^{r}Japanese surnames.

Nationality of students. The *Reports* of 1880 to the present date give the number of students by national or racial descent, from which their home language can usually be deduced. The totals given in Table 9 are for students in both public and private, select and common, schools. In the private schools were a majority of the Americans and British and other Haoles, and a large proportion of the Part-Hawaiians. Other nationalities have been represented in smaller proportion in the private schools. Thus the influence of the students best acquainted with the English language has been concentrated in a few schools.

The totals give a picture of national linguistic influence in the schools as a whole, not by localities. The Chinese children, for example, have from the start been concentrated in Honolulu.

Nationality of teachers. One frequently hears the statement that the poor quality of the English spoken by the students of Hawaii is the fault of the teachers, that a stream can rise no higher than its source. The Oriental teachers are frequently blamed by members of other nationalities, by Haoles in particular, while the Orientals tend to blame the elderly Portuguese and Hawaiians. Rather plainly, this assignment of the blame depends upon the economic rivalries of the various ethnic groups. In the formative period of the local dialect, the blame seems to rest on the Haoles and Hawaiians, if someone must be blamed. Unfortunately the government did not begin publishing a record of the nationalities of teachers in both private and public schools until 1890, and after 1918, because economic rivalry had become so much of a sore spot, these statistics were discontinued.[92] In Table 10, the teachers have not been divided according to whether they taught in private or public schools. Almost all the pure Hawaiian teachers were in the public schools. Most of the Chinese before 1906, of the Japanese until 1915 or 1916, and of the Koreans until about the same date, were in the private schools, as were most of the "Other Europeans." A disproportionate number of the Americans and British have also been in the private schools.

[92]Statement of Superintendent of Public Instruction Will C. Crawford, August, 1933.

Chapter 4

THE CREOLE DIALECT
OF HAWAII: ITS ORIGIN
AND ITS FUNCTION

Three general types of immigration, from the linguistic point of view, may be distinguished.

The first partakes of the nature of colonization and may be termed settlement in enclaves. Central Europe is the classic field of this type of immigration. A typical instance is the settlement of Germans in Transylvania from about 1150 to 1786, since which date they have remained isolated from the main body of Germans, without receiving further accretions through immigration. Other examples are the Germans of the Volga (settled in 1764) and the Albanians of Calabria (settled about 1460 to 1480). A body of immigrants, often directly planted by a sovereign for political and economic purposes, has found it possible to maintain its ethnic individuality and language though it is cut off for the most part from its parent group. This has been basically because of the political and religious particularism and the economic self-sufficiency of small communities prevailing in most parts of Europe prior to the

83

nineteenth century. Given a firm rooting in such conditions, many of these immigrant communities have been able to build up a resistance to assimilation which has lasted into the twentieth century. Ethnic groups of this sort typically become bilingual or even trilingual but jealously retain their own language. While accommodating themselves to the surrounding population, they strenuously resist assimilation, whether in language or in culture and sense of individuality. Indeed, they conceive of their language as a very potent force in the maintenance of their culture.

In new countries without traditions of ethnic particularism and with many incentives to assimilation, especially if the countries are highly industrialized, such enclaves have little opportunity to form, and indeed are combated (as the Doukhobors in Canada) if they do seem to be taking form. Instead, in such countries of European settlement as Canada, the United States, South Africa, Australia, Brazil, Chile, Argentina, and Uruguay, a second type of immigration is typically found, in which the immigrant loses his ethnic identity and his language—usually his language before his identity— within a relatively short time, sometimes even within the lifetime of the immigrant himself. The immigrant comes to a country having the ideal of assimilation of the various immigrant stocks into a fused new nationality, an ideal already based in the colonial immigration which has fused the various provincials of the mother country into a new colonial nationality. Very frequently his fellow immigrants are spread throughout a wide, undeveloped country. Economic opportunities are those of an industrial civilization, not those of self-sufficient medieval Europe. Frequently the immigrant's assimilation is welcomed by the established population; he is a valuable addition to its manpower. While he usually arrives in his adopted land at an economic disadvantage, sometimes even as an indentured laborer, he is politically a free man and normally becomes a free agent economically. In this he contrasts with the plantation laborer. Usually, too, he belongs to the same color group as the established nationality and shares its Christian European culture; his assimilation to it is therefore a matter of culture and economic status, not necessarily of intermarriage, though that, too, takes place speedily.

The third type of immigration furnishes the bulk of plantation labor. The plantation laborer is typically of a different race and culture and language from his master. He is typically held in a servile or semi-servile economic and political status and is, at any rate, completely dependent economically upon his master or employer. On the plantation there is a complete organization into an economic-social hierarchy. The imported laborer frequently is, by the exigencies of his position, pulverized ethnically. Contact with his homeland is completely or almost completely broken. Frequently speakers of many languages are thrown together and must have an interlanguage, and grow to have a common culture and a common ethnic identity. This was the situation in those parts of the Americas which depended upon African slave labor, in Mauritius during the period of slavery, and in the Cape Colony during the formation of the Cape Coloured population.

But later in the history of the plantation, as outright slavery fell into abeyance in the nineteenth century, a modified form of servile economic status has been more common: that of the importation of labor under contract, which it is a penal offense to break. This is the form seen in much of the immigration to Hawaii from 1852 to 1900, and in the importation of Indian labor to the Fiji Islands, Mauritius, Trinidad, and British Guiana, and of Annamites to French Oceania. When the laborer's term of contract is up, he may usually turn to extra-plantation occupations. Economically and legally he occupies a position halfway between the completely servile plantation worker and the free immigrant. (There are gradations, naturally, depending on the laws and economic and social circumstances of each country.) But as a general rule, socially he is not regarded as the European immigrant to the white man's new countries is regarded. The East Indian in Trinidad, for example, though he may enrich himself by trade, is not regarded as assimilable to either the Negro or the European population. The stigma of a semi-servile occupation, present or past, is upon his group, and there are between him and the European upper classes the barriers of cultural and racial differences. Though he may be a millionaire, he is a coolie. Not being admitted to assimilation, he is likely to retain a lively sense of his cultural inheritance, thus approaching the first or enclave type of immigration.[1]

Hawaii's place is on the extreme edge of the more liberal sub-type of the third type of immigration. Its immigrants have been drawn mostly to serve on the plantations. For half a century, contract labor laws confined most of them in their movements during at least the first three-year period of their residence. On the other hand, the immigrants to Hawaii were able within a very short time to go into other kinds of work, and a considerable proportion of the immigrants came proposing to enter non-plantation occupations from the start. Off the plantation, class lines were not as strictly drawn as on it. There has been a conscious attempt to assimilate the native and immigrant population to American cultural and political life. (This is excepting the latest comers, the Filipinos, who are still regarded as a largely transient group living symbiotically outside the true Hawaiian civic body.) Members of non-American groups have in turn exerted more or less effort to accommodate themselves or even to become assimilated. Intermarriage has been legally and socially sanctioned and is becoming more common, even between Haoles and non-Haoles. Social lines, based partly on American conceptions of racial differences and partly on plantation traditions, still hold, as do social lines based on ethnic separatism of the immigrant groups, but in certain spheres these lines are little emphasized. Thus Hawaii's immigration, while it stands definitely within the plantation economy, has so many points of resemblance with the free, assimilated immigration of new countries populated chiefly by Europeans that it is a borderline example.

Linguistically, too, the borderline position of Hawaii is manifest. In some features of its linguistic history Hawaii offers a parallel to the linguistic experience of immigrants to the continental United States; in other features it matches the experience

---

[1] Leroy-Beaulieu, *De la colonisation chez les peuples modernes,* 4th ed., pp. 203, 230.

of other plantation regions. The various ethnic communities, native and immigrant, have retained their respective languages and have not, by any manner of means, lost them in exchange for a makeshift dialect (some cases of individuals excepted).[2] A makeshift language, the "pidgin English" of Hawaii, has arisen but can scarcely be said to have taken durable form, so rapid has been its passage to a less makeshift and more refined sort of English. That a makeshift language should arise and take form enough to be recognizable as an entity, however, is a mark of the plantation community. Yet, that speakers of the "pidgin" should be recognizable as Japanese, Portuguese, Hawaiians, Filipinos, etc., by their peculiarities of speech is on the other hand proof that this makeshift language, this creole dialect of Hawaii, is not a unified, comparatively stable compound such as the creole languages of (for example) Haiti and Mauritius. Instead, it approaches being a congeries of immigrants' mixed dialects, all of which have common features. The unity which the creole dialect lacks is, however, being established in its off-shoot, the dialect of the Hawaii-bred generations. Among them it is growing increasingly difficult to distinguish a member of one nationality from a member of another, so thoroughly are the common elements of the dialect overcoming the national "accents."

This somewhat amorphous phenomenon, the makeshift language of Hawaii which because of its close connection with plantation needs I have called "creole dialect," requires historical and sociological definition. The first is far from easy, for the available material is scanty and confused. Nevertheless, I shall try to set forth, first the factors in the formation of the creole dialect of Hawaii, and second the functions of the creole dialect.

In Chapter 3 the evidence for the presence of a makeshift language built on English and Hawaiian, the *hapa haole*, has been discussed. No doubt had the population of Hawaii been confined principally to speakers of these two languages, the linguistic history of the Islands would have been limited to a struggle of the two for position, with an intermediate makeshift

[2]See Chapter 5 for a full discussion of this point.

speech like the *hapa haole* occupying the midst of the contested ground until all the Hawaiian natives had become truly bilingual. With the development of commerce, the strengthening of Haole political control, the increase of the Anglo-Saxon population, and the steady though not rapid transformation of the Hawaiian language schools into English schools taught by American, British, and half-white teachers, the Hawaiians, except those in the farthest outlying districts, would have found it advantageous to learn English. Yet it would have been impossible for all but a small minority to learn it fully in the somewhat artificial milieu of the classroom and the limited contacts which most natives would have with whites. A great many imperfections based on faulty apprehension of English idiomatic grammar and on literal translations from the vernacular, together with a poverty of vocabulary and of expression, would perforce have characterized the speech of the average Hawaiian.[3] As the resident Haoles had already adopted many Hawaiian terms, English speech would have been sprinkled generously with them. In the long run, however, the native language would have lost prestige and would have lost its purity and its literary quality.

All that has been described in the preceding paragraph as suppositional was in fact true in the actual struggle between the Hawaiian and the English language, but not in a simple, isolated form. It was complicated, instead, by the presence of half a dozen other competing languages. Therefore, instead of a steady absorption of the whole population into the English-speaking body of inhabitants, we find the *hapa haole* expanding into a creole dialect which shows mingled influences from several linguistic stocks, and a great mass of immigrants learning this makeshift language instead of either Hawaiian or Standard English. Thus at the same time that the usefulness and scope of the English language was being rapidly extended, its proper mastery was being retarded.

The first immigrant group likely to have affected the formation of the creole dialect was the Chinese. The first Chinese plantation laborers, who arrived during the period 1852

---

[3]Compare the present linguistic development in Samoa, described by Felix M. Keesing, *Modern Samoa*, pp. 444-447.

to 1876 while the plantations were being built up, were comparatively few in number and confined to a few plantations. They were thrown into contact with the natives rather than with the Haoles. Many Chinese left plantation work and entered occupations such as peddling, shopkeeping, and farming, where they were thrown into still closer contact with the Hawaiians. As they were almost all young males, a considerable number married native women. It was more usual for the husband to learn and use his wife's language, which gave him business and social advantages, than for the wife to learn her husband's. To broken forms of Hawaiian used by certain Haoles were added other broken forms used by Chinese. There does not appear to have been, however, any fixed Chinese-Hawaiian makeshift speech, probably because the Chinese were so few in number.[4]

At the same time, some of the Chinese laborers learned a broken English. The basis of this naturally was the *hapa haole*, because the English-speaking bosses would already have learned to adapt their speech to the comprehension and idiomatic peculiarities of the Hawaiians. If one finds that a particular broken and simplified speech works in one situation, one will be apt to use it in another situation—just as I have heard a Hawaiian-Chinese use Island "pidgin," intonation and all, to Peking coolies. This theoretical analysis is supported by the structure of the present dialect, which contains many Hawaiian words and some Hawaiian idioms and traces of intonation, stress, and pronunciation, but very few Chinese words and few ascertainable traces of specifically Chinese influence in other lines.[5] The Chinese no doubt added a few of their idioms to the creole dialect, spoke it with Chinese intonation, and adapted the English and Hawaiian sounds to the Cantonese phonetic system. These influences, however, do not appear to have been lasting—though the information available on the subject, it is to

[4]That the early Chinese learned Hawaiian and some English is a matter of common knowledge; see also the statement by C. B. Wells in the "Blount Report," p. 1806. For Sinicized Hawaiian, the writer is indebted to Albert Judd.

[5]The Hawaiian contribution to the vocabulary can be determined with comparative ease, in spite of the large number of words that have gone out of use. The contributions based on Hawaiian idiomatic constructions may in part be traced by comparing the writings of Hawaiians whose mastery of English was imperfect with the writings of non-Hawaiian youths in our schools today. See the examples in the Appendix. The Hawaiian contributions to intonation, pronunciation, and stress are

be remembered, is very scanty.[6] The failure of the Chinese to contribute to the creole speech is really remarkable.[7] Judging from the preponderance of Hawaiian words among the technical terms used on the plantations, the Hawaiian language had already been established as the reservoir for plantation terminology before the Chinese arrived in considerable numbers, and the Chinese set themselves to learn this technical vocabulary.

The Chinese mark on the creole dialect is apparently slight, perhaps because Chinese is in structure so like almost any makeshift language that would arise on the basis of an Indo-European tongue. Chinese is a language which depends almost wholly on the position of the words, not on inflection; makeshift languages do the same. When one tries to talk broken English, the structure of the English tongue will cause any simplication to take much the same form as a literal translation from Chinese into English.

There is no indication that the true Pidgin English of the Chinese ports had any influence whatever on the creole dialect of Hawaii except to give it its misleading name and the word *kaukau* (i.e., *chowchow*).[8]

Even after the Chinese immigrated in large numbers, their influence upon the creole dialect continued, apparently, to be slight. The large numbers of single males, keeping pretty much to themselves, probably had little opportunity to imprint their linguistic peculiarities upon the rest of the population. With the

harder to determine. One informant (Ella H. Paris) believes that the prolonging of vowels to indicate emphasis is peculiarly Hawaiian; this, however, is more than doubtful. Pronunciation is probably often Hawaiianized; the substitution of [w] for [v] as in *wote* for *vote*, which Portuguese "Joe Manuel of the Raddio Patrol" uses, is Hawaiian in its origin. So, too, to give one definite instance, is the pronunciation of *opium* as [o'pjum], which corresponds to the Hawaiian *opiuma* (opium tree).

[6]Madorah Smith of the University of Hawaii, who is studying the speech of Hawaiian-born Chinese, is of the opinion that the Chinese have contributed more than they are generally credited with.

For an annotated list of publications on language by Madorah E. Smith (1887-1965), see Stanley M. Tsuzaki and John E. Reinecke, *English in Hawaii* (Oceanic Linguistics Special Publication No. 1; Honolulu, 1966).—*Ed.*

[7]I do not know of any direct contribution to the vocabulary of plantation English. *Kaukau* (food, to eat) and *pākē* (Chinaman, Chinese) are the only Chinese words that have passed into the Hawaiian. On the other hand a Chinese meat dumpling has received a Hawaiian name, *pepeiao* (ear).

[8]Denzel Carr suggests that *side*, very much used in Hawaii to denote locality (*upside, downside, overside, Hilo side, stateside,* etc.), may have gained its wide currency from Chinese or Japanese port English.

intensification of the plantation economy and with the Chinese working beside other immigrant nationalities rather than with natives, the trend of the Chinese was increasingly away from dependence upon the Hawaiian language and toward "pidgin English" as their chief means of communication with the community generally. It must be remembered that the Hawaiians, too, were becoming increasingly bilingual.

Almost all observers credit the Portuguese with great, and some with predominant, influence in the formation of the creole dialect. The present writer is of the opinion that the Portuguese influence is less than that of the Hawaiians, and that neither nationality is so responsible as the Haoles with their conscious attempt to simplify their speech. He is fully aware that an effort to evaluate the relative weight of the three languages is little better than guesswork for one ignorant of two of them. However, those who know something of Hawaiian and Portuguese trace the influence of the latter chiefly in the "Portuguese inflection" and certain peculiarities of stress accent associated with it, and in certain sound substitutions, little in the syntax, and scarcely at all in the vocabulary.[9] The Hawaiian influence, on the other hand, is evident in all fields. Apparently the Portuguese, finding a *hapa haole* makeshift tongue, perhaps slightly modified by Chinese influence, already at hand upon their arrival, merely took it over and used it on a large scale, doing little to its syntax, accidence, and vocabulary.

Whatever may have been the actual contribution of the Portuguese to the structure of the creole dialect, it is the unanimous testimony of those who have paid attention to the rise of

[9]"Portygee accent" depends partly on misplacing the stress accent of English words and partly on the use of the circumflex tone where English would have rising or falling tone and of the rising tone where the proper English tone is level or falling. Sound substitutions are most marked in the vowels, because English and Portuguese consonants are largely similar. The sound $\breve{a}$ [æ] takes the place of $\breve{e}$ [ɛ], $\overline{oo}$ [u] of $\overline{oo}$ [ʊ], $\breve{o}$ [ɑ] of $\breve{u}$ [ʌ]; sometimes [ʌ] instead of [ɑ] and an open o instead of the English closed o.

One verbal auxiliary of the creole dialect, *stay*, used for "is" and to show present or even past action, is plainly the Portuguese *está*.

For possible influences of Portuguese on the English spoken in Hawaii, now see Edgar C. Knowlton, Jr., "Portuguese in Hawaii," *Kentucky Foreign Language Quarterly*, VII, No. 4 (December, 1960), 212-218; and "Pidgin English and Portuguese," in F. S. Drake, ed., *Proceedings of the Symposium on Historical, Archaeological and Linguistic Studies on Southern China, S. E. Asia and the Hong Kong Region*, pp. 228-237.—Ed.

the dialect that the Portuguese were the group that precipitated its formation from the formless mass of *hapa haole* expressions. This was due to several reasons. The Portuguese came as families, and their children were placed in the English schools, where they at once began learning English instead of Hawaiian and carried their English speech into their homes. (Naturally it was English strongly tinged with the Hawaiianisms of their native schoolmates and often of Hawaiian or Part-Hawaiian schoolteachers.) The Portuguese, being white, rose to positions of trust more readily than did Orientals and soon occupied a disproportionately large number of positions as skilled laborers, lesser foremen, and even clerks, where they could issue orders— in broken English—to workmen of other nationalities.[10] Many Portuguese entered skilled trades outside the plantations under circumstances which threw them into closer contact with Haoles and Part-Hawaiians than most Orientals enjoyed. Notwithstanding their generally inferior economic and social status when compared with the Haoles and lighter Part-Hawaiians, the Portuguese, because of their racial and cultural kinship with the dominant Haoles, have always enjoyed fuller participation in the general community life of Hawaii than have the Orientals. Their political and social assimilation was expected as a matter of course. They were thought of as a counterpoise to the too numerous Orientals. Furthermore, the Portuguese immigrant, being a family man, was more "on his own," less dependent upon his local and national group for support and advancement and for social life, than either the Chinese or Japanese. After the first few years the Portuguese were more scattered about the Islands than were the Chinese and were seldom present anywhere in such numbers as were the Japanese. In religious services they were often thrown into contact with Hawaiians and Haoles. Mostly illiterate, and separated geographically from their native country, they did not have the same incentives as the Orientals to look back to it, expect to return to it, and so regard Hawaii as a temporary stopping place. In short, they

[10]Letter from H. H. Brodie, veteran schoolteacher on Kauai, February 3, 1933; reports of the Commissioner of Labor on Hawaii. The report of 1901 lists 154 Portuguese as against 32 Chinese "overseers"; that of 1905 lists 273 Portuguese "overseers" as against only 24 Chinese.

were much less isolated culturally and in social relations than the Oriental groups were, and had more reason to learn English rapidly than had the latter. It must not be forgotten that English is easier for a Portuguese, speaking a kindred language, to master than it is for an Oriental or Polynesian. And once a smattering of English had been gained (according to a prominent *kamaaina*), a certain self-assured volubility enabled the Portuguese to talk more than did members of other nationalities, and so they have had more to do with the propagation of "pidgin English" than any other nationality had.[11]

We may pass over the minor groups brought in during the nineteenth century, who appear to have had no influence in particular upon the creole dialect, and go on to the Japanese, the third major group and the most numerous. The first large immigration of Japanese did not occur until 1888, when the Hawaiians, Chinese, and Portuguese between them had pretty well fixed the form of the "pidgin" spoken on the plantations. It is the unanimous testimony of observers that the Japanese had only to learn the creole dialect and that they added little to it. Yet one may be allowed to doubt this general impression, in view of the forty-seven Japanese words found in "Terms Used on Hawaiian Plantations," compiled in 1930 by U. K. Das for the Hawaiian Sugar Planters' Association (though it is true that few of these terms have carried over into the later colloquial dialect, as so many of the Hawaiian words have done). It is probable, however, that the Japanese influence has been more noticeable upon the later stages of the creole dialect and upon the colonial dialect which grew out of it. In the present colloquial dialect (not makeshift), certain Japanese idioms and peculiarities of pronunciation are apparent. Probably the Japanese influence has been felt chiefly through the presence of Japanese children in the schools. This presumption is strength-

[11]Did the Beach-la-mar of Melanesia have any influence upon the plantation speech of Hawaii? The two makeshift languages took form at about the same time, and some foremen in Hawaii may have been acquainted with Beach-la-mar. (Several plantation men were originally seamen.) Certain words and forms of expression are common to the two, but there is no direct evidence of connection. The similarities may be those likely to occur in any two systems of makeshift English. There is also the third possibility that both Beach-la-mar and early "Pidgin English" drew from a common reservoir of broken English in use by Pacific seamen. See Reinecke and Tokimasa, "The English Dialect of Hawaii," *American Speech,* IX, No. 1, 58.

ened by the statement of an informant[12] that he noticed the influence of the Japanese in the common speech only about 1905, a generation after the arrival of the first laborers and about ten years after the Japanese children began to form a considerable part of the student population.

The later minor immigrations of the Koreans, the Puerto Ricans, the Spanish, the Russians, and the second wave of Portuguese seem to have had no influence upon the creole dialect except to confirm it in its usefulness in so polyglot a population. Only with the arrival of the Filipinos (1907 to 1931) do we find a group large enough to have a potential influence upon the course of language in Hawaii. There appears to be some difference in the response of the Filipinos and of the other nationalities to the creole dialect. The other groups apparently adopted the makeshift dialect with comparatively little appreciation of its limited usefulness. The Filipinos, on the other hand, have come into an environment wherein both the makeshift dialect and a more refined, though still local and non-standard, form of speech are in use. On the plantation they have inherited the "pidgin" from their fellow-laborers and from their old-style Haole *lunas*. Off the plantation they come into contact with young Orientals and others speaking the colonial dialect and become aware of its superiority. The Filipinos are very generally, and rightly, given credit for striving more than the earlier groups to learn and use correct English. This may be due in part to the linguistic traditions of the Filipinos, many of whom are already bilingual or trilingual and before immigrating had an acquaintance with English. It is probably due also to the keener competition now obtaining, in which superior attainments are necessary to raise the Filipino to the same position that an Oriental or Portuguese relatively careless of his speech could formerly attain. And most of all it is due to the more general use of tolerably good English. Nevertheless "pidgin English," the creole dialect, is still perpetuated among the Filipinos and is receiving some accretions and changes from their tongues.[13]

[12]Albert F. Judd.

[13]Das, in "Terms Used on Hawaiian Plantations," lists twenty-three Filipino terms in use on the plantations.

A large number of people claim that there is no one make-shift dialect in Hawaii that can be singled out and called "pidgin English" and that there are instead several national dialects. Their contention is in large part correct. A Portuguese, a Japanese, a Chinese, a Filipino, a Hawaiian, all can be rather easily distinguished by their national accents—as we may unscientifically call the sum total of their habits of intonation, stress, timbre of voice, and pronunciation—and sometimes by their word order and vocabulary. These five major groups and sometimes minor groups as well are mimicked by would-be humorists. The speech peculiarities of some are almost a stock in trade of the amateur entertainer. These peculiarities are used also in serious communication. In speaking to a group of Japanese, for example, a member of another ethnic group will use such Japanese words as he knows (very likely in an adapted form) and perhaps fall into Japanese intonation. Thus "The Story of the Prodigal Son," as retold by Hattie Saffery Reinhardt,[14] contains several words that the narrator would not have used with any group other than elderly Japanese.

Nevertheless, there are common elements which bind together these forms of speech which individually might almost be called immigrants' mixed dialects. Most obvious of the common elements is the vocabulary; and in the vocabulary the numerous Hawaiian terms are in turn most obvious. Numerous idioms (often derived from the Hawaiian construction) are common to all national varieties of the creole dialect. Thus it comes about that a Haole foreman can address a mixed group of workmen in "pidgin" and be equally well understood by all of them, although they in return when addressing him will perhaps introduce peculiarly Japanese, Portuguese, or other elements into their "pidgin." The foreman himself, if speaking to members of only one ethnic group, might use some peculiarities of idiom appropriate to that group.

Parenthetically, it may be remarked that on certain plantations or in certain districts the influence of one or more nationalities may have been strongly impressed and the creole dialect may therefore be expected to vary slightly from locality

[14]*Honolulu Advertiser,* May 11, 1924; part reprinted in W. C. Smith, *American Speech,* VIII, No. 1, 16. This piece of dialect is rather well known locally. [Now also reprinted in Harry A. Franck, *Roaming in Hawaii,* pp.148-150.—*Ed.*]

to locality. No survey, however, has been made to establish either the common elements of the creole dialect or its local variations. Yet it is certain at least that the Portuguese influence has colored the speech of the Japanese in Hamakua, Hawaii, and that the Hawaiian influence has been unusually strong in parts of Kona.

FUNCTIONS OF THE CREOLE DIALECT

The phenomenon of language mastery continuum is illustrated by taking a cross section of immigrant population of a given age group as well as by taking a cross section of an immigrant community of all ages and lengths of residence in their adopted land. Among the immigrants of any nationality who have come to Hawaii at about the same time will be found some individuals who can speak no English whatever, or at most so few words that they can not form even a broken "pidgin English" sentence. There will also be found individuals who have mastered the English language in the fields of vocabulary and the essentials of syntax and whose mistakes are limited chiefly to a "foreign accent." Between these extremes, forming a series with insensible gradations, are the bulk of the immigrants, speaking a more or less broken and makeshift English. What proportion of the first generation of any immigrant group speaks the creole dialect cannot be determined, essentially because the creole dialect has no exact limits. It may be taken as practically certain that a large though indeterminate number of immigrants and native Hawaiians are incapable of carrying on any sort of conversation in makeshift English. Possibly 10 percent of the total population ten years of age and over is a reasonable guess at their number.

The number of persons ten years of age and over "unable to speak English" is no sure indication of the lower limits of the creole speech, for undoubtedly a considerable number of these speak a little broken English. The United States Census of 1930 returned 66,822 out of a total of 273,037 persons ten years of age and over, or 24.5 percent, as unable to speak English. The sex and ethnic distribution are given in Table 11, adapted from the United States Census of 1930. It will be seen that in the groups whose immigrant members are divided fairly evenly between the sexes, namely the Portuguese, Puerto Ricans, Spanish, and Japanese, the percentage of females unable to speak English is higher than the percentage of males. The same is true of the Hawaiians. But among the groups in which the male immigration is much larger than the female and most of the females consequently are Hawaiian-bred (Koreans, Chinese, Filipinos), the reverse is true. In 1920 and before, however, the percentage of females unable to speak English was greater for all groups than was the percentage of males.

TABLE 11

MALES AND FEMALES UNABLE TO SPEAK ENGLISH, 1930

Ethnic Group	Males Unable to Speak English		Females Unable to Speak English	
	No.	%	No.	%
Total	46,308	26.6	20,514	20.8
Hawaiians	625	7.1	842	9.5
Part-Hawaiians	44	0.5	67	0.9
Portuguese	408	4.0	652	6.3
Puerto Ricans	537	20.3	435	21.8
Spanish	42	8.7	64	14.5
Chinese	3,419	26.3	1,109	15.3
Japanese	14,095	27.1	14,055	33.1
Koreans	970	32.3	357	23.8
Filipinos	26,112	54.5	2,881	49.4
Others	56	—	52	—

Many students report that their parents can speak no English or practically none. At Maui High School in 1929 the students reported as follows about their parents' ability to speak English:[15]

	Speaking Good English	Speaking Poor English	Speaking No English
Fathers	143	165	82
Mothers	131	134	135

[15]Jane Stratford, "Cross-Section of a High School Student's Life" (M.A. thesis, University of Hawaii), p. 45.

The persons unable to speak English are of three general classes. First are the recently arrived immigrants who have had no time to learn any English. The Filipinos are the only nationality now having any members in this class, but all immigrant nationalities have passed through the stage of total ignorance of English. Second are males who have been able to live outside the necessity of communication in the creole dialect, a few Hawaiians in remote communities and a few old immigrants in separate camps. Third, and most numerous among the older established groups, are the women whose contacts outside the home and the circle of neighbors of the same nationality have been negligible.

It may readily be seen how an immigrant woman can remain ignorant of any English. If she lives in a ghetto-like plantation camp or section of a city, is at home most of the time attending to her housework, calls only on members of her own ethnic community and trades only with them, and insists that her children speak their parents' language at home, she can get along without learning any English except a few loan words. Also, it can be readily understood how a few elderly Hawaiians in remote country districts can rely upon their bilingual children for any necessary communication with English-speaking people. But how is it possible for an immigrant male to avoid learning the language of command of his employers?

Probably, in the long run, very few do avoid learning something of it. But for a while it is possible to escape learning any English whatever, and it is easily possible to avoid learning adequate English during one's whole lifetime, because of the presence of two figures important in all linguistic contacts between an employing native and an employed immigrant population using different languages. These are the interpreter and the bilingual under-foreman or "straw boss." The latter is the less institutionalized personage and the commoner of the two. To him the foreman gives his order, in good English or more likely in the creole dialect, depending upon the linguistic ability of the under-boss and the habits of the foreman, and these orders in turn are passed on and the processes of the job explained to the newly arrived common laborer, in his own language, by the "straw boss" or contractor. Thus the newly arrived Filipino, for instance, gets along until he has learned enough English to take orders directly from English-speaking *lunas*. Some old Chinese laborers appear always to have worked under the direction of a bilingual *luna* of their own nationality and to have left the acquisition of English up to him. This is especially easy to do under the contract system of cultivation. And we must not forget what a great amount of instruction can be given by means of gestures alone!

The interpreter must have a fairly adequate command of English and is often paid by the plantation to handle matters of considerable importance when the creole dialect is not exact enough to convey the full meaning of either party. His influence can be great because he is the go-between of dominated and dominating groups, depended upon by the former to secure favors and by the latter to maintain good relations and morale. In Hawaii, it is interesting to note, the functions of interpreter and of Christian minister and social worker have sometimes been combined. In some situations the interpreter has attained wealth and decisive influence because of his position as middle-man; but such has not been the case in Hawaii, where the number of formal interpreters has been small and their role limited.[16] For, besides the interpreter, neighbors and one's own bilingual children are often called upon to act as middlemen in communication when the immigrant either does not speak English or can not express his meaning adequately in the creole dialect.[17]

At the other extreme from the immigrant who has never had to learn any language but his own is the immigrant who is not

[16]Nevertheless the interpreter in Hawaii deserves a special study by a competent bilingual.

[17]A third figure in linguistic contacts may be mentioned, the *padrone*. His function is that of labor contractor and general buffer between the raw immigrant and his new environment—and, incidentally, exploiter of the immigrant's ignorance. He has a direct interest in seeing that the members of the group he dominates do not speak the vernacular. As soon as they do, they become independent of him. Because of the plantation organization in Hawaii, the *padrone* has had little opening left for his activities and, so far as the present writer knows, is a figure almost absent from the Hawaiian scene, unless possibly in connection with some contract work. It is true that the Japanese laborers had a saying, "He who speaks English is a thief," but the exploitation of their monolingual fellows by bilingual immigrants has been sporadic and uninstitutionalized.

content with a meager acquaintance with the language of his new country. In the typical plantation milieu the imported laborer has little if any chance to rise above the plantation, and has no incentive to learn correctly the current speech any more than his employer has to teach it to him. But in a milieu such as that of Hawaii, where escape from plantation conditions has been comparatively easy and rapid, a portion of the immigrant population will look to mastery of the common language as an aid to economic and hence to social success. Because the Chinese from the time of their arrival turned to shopkeeping and allied occupations, it is not surprising that the first night school for adult immigrants was opened for them—E. Dunscombe's Bethel Chinese School, established in 1869 and continued for several years.[18] This was the first of many night schools and special classes for the improvement of the English of ambitious adult immigrants. A very few of the early immigrants, too, acquired the English language in their own country, and so in recent times have a considerable number of Filipinos. These have been able to skip the makeshift English stage of expression.[19] Some of the younger immigrants, while not trained in the Hawaiian schools, have made such contacts with those who have been that they, too, have not been confined to the use of the creole dialect.

There remains the great middle group of immigrants (together with some native Hawaiians) to whom the creole dialect is useful as a means of communication among the several linguistic communities, and who have not had the opportunity or the desire to learn English well. It is they who gave rise to the creole dialect and who form the bulk of its speakers. Their number at any time can only be estimated and that, far from closely. Possibly they number four-fifths of any first generation (adult) immigrant group, possibly more or less. Included in this group of speakers of a makeshift language, as will be pointed

[18]*Report* of 1878.

[19]"Jose Bulatao was elected first president of Koloa Filipino Civic club, which was formally organized at a discussion meeting held at the Koloa Filipino community hall. . . . Only people who have a grasp of the English language will be allowed to enter the club. The purpose of this organization is to have weekly discussions . . ." ("Jose Bulatao 1st President," *Honolulu Star-Bulletin*, May 17, 1934, p. 7.)

out in detail below, are a considerable number of persons bred in Hawaii. Also, many who can speak fairly good English have frequent occasion to employ the creole dialect.

The creole dialect is essentially two things: an interlanguage and the speech of those whose economic opportunities do not allow them to learn better than a makeshift English. It has been shown why the interlanguage of Hawaii is English. Conceivably the English spoken might be Standard English or a fairly "correct" colonial dialect. But the plantation economy, joined to the overwhelming disproportion between the English-speaking and non-English-speaking groups, made the use of a makeshift English inevitable. The economic and social possibilities of most immigrants do not include positions where the learning of "good" English is obligatory or even very helpful, or possible. Most immigrants arrived as adults, at an age at which learning a new language is commonly considered irksome and difficult. Numbers have not the intellectual ability that makes possible the adequate acquisition of a second language in adult years. But the essential reason for learning only the creole dialect is neither laziness nor dullness of mind but the distinct connection between the work one does and one's opportunity to learn English.

The typical immigrant to Hawaii came to work on the plantation either for a term of years or permanently. His off-duty contacts were chiefly with members of his own ethnic community; this was especially true if those of his nationality were numerous enough to have assigned to them a special camp or section of the mill village. His English was learned partly off the job, in contacts with shopkeepers, peddlers, and neighbors of other nationalities, but even more on the job, from foremen and fellow employees. It was learned in the functional fashion in which all unformalized, oral speech is learned, as an infant learns his native tongue, by a process of trial and error. The immigrant arrived at last at expressions that secured results when used with his English-speaking *lunas* and fellow workmen. Because his boss was as likely as not talking down to him, simplifying his own English and mixing in Hawaiian words and such scraps of the workman's language as he (the boss) might know, and because his fellows were but a little more advanced in their grasp of English, the workman from the start had little opportunity to learn any but broken English. Besides, once he had learned a vocabulary sufficient for the simple needs of the plantation environment and had set this vocabulary to a syntax that depends on word position of the simplest sort, he would very likely follow the line of least resistance and stop learning. If a situation arose in which he had to express himself more adequately than "pidgin English" would allow, he could use the services of an interpreter—official or unofficial—or, later, of his English-educated children. Some workmen, indeed, appear to have come to think that the only English acceptable in dealing with other nationalities, including the Haoles, was the creole dialect. They must have known that among themselves the Haoles spoke a language incomprehensible to the majority of the immigrants, but this was a language which had nothing to do with the processes of intercommunication.[20] Nonetheless, the majority of the immigrants, at least all those who had children in the Hawaiian schools, must have been aware that their English was a makeshift, inadequate speech. (One hears elderly Japanese apologize for their poor English.) But they were also aware that only the exceptional non-Haole could rise

[20]This is illustrated by an anecdote told by a prominent school man, Gus Webling, who during the World War was a timekeeper on a plantation on which a gang of old Chinese laborers was working. An English university man was overseeing the group. The timekeeper, noticing that the usually quiet Chinese were in an uproar, rode up, whereupon the Chinese *luna* (i.e., straw boss) rushed up to him.

Chinese *luna:* "Wats a malla [what is the matter] this Haole? Alla time *huhu* [scold]. Me t'ink so, he like *hakaka* [fight]."

Timekeeper: *"Aole* [no] ; Haole *pololei* [all right]. Me think so you no *pololei."*

Chinese *luna:* "Me long time stop. Me *pololei.* This Haole no use."

Timekeeper: *"Mate* [wait] . Me go speak Haole."

The Englishman complained heatedly that his workmen would not obey his clear orders to cut the cane near the ground so as to obtain the best sugar content near the base of the stalk and prevent fermentation of the stumps, and to cut off the tops of the cane and place these between the rows, where they would be turned under by the cultivators and furnish valuable humus. The more he explained, the angrier the Chinese got, the Englishman said, and it looked as if a fight would start.

The timekeeper turned to the Chinese straw boss.

Timekeeper: *"Luna,* big boss speak, all men down below cutch; suppose too much *mauka* [high] cutch, too much sugar *poho* [lose] —*keiki* [shoots] no use. Savvy? All men *opala* [trash] cutch, one side t'row—byenbye mule men come, *lepo* [dirt] too mucha guru [good]. Savvy?"

Chinese *luna:* "Savvy! Huy," casting a look of supreme disgust at the Englishman, "wats a malla this Haole—he no can talk *haole!"*

very high on the plantation and that, after the rudiments of "pidgin English" had been learned, there was little connection between the command of English and opportunities to advance.[21] Thus the plantation environment furnished neither the opportunity nor the incentive to learn better English.

In such plantation countries as maintained a servile or semi-servile status for the laborers and afforded them little or no chance to rise into the middle class and had no system of free public schools, the use of a makeshift language became fixed at this point. Only a few household servants and the like ever had an opportunity to learn the standard language and had use for it. But in Hawaii the possibility of getting away from the plantation and of engaging in some occupation bringing the immigrant into contact with a widened circle of English-speaking people was always present. To be sure, there was no very definite correlation between the use of good English and the receipt of a larger income off the plantation any more than on it; still, the correlation was there in some measure. A continuous capillarity, to use a figure of speech, drew a small number of ambitious, intelligent, or fortunate immigrants out of the mass of speakers of the creole dialect to use an English which, though not free from foreignisms, was more adequate than "pidgin."

The mass of those who left the plantation were, however, unlikely to escape the makeshift English which they had learned. Some entered occupations depending upon the patronage of, and throwing them among, their own nationality. Even if their patrons were of a different nationality, they might often be "pidgin"-speaking. Others became farmers or fishermen, living within their own ethnic community even more than on the plantation. If employed by English-speaking people, they might still come into but limited contact with their employers, and "pidgin" might still be the most convenient interlanguage and an adequate one. An extension of the vocabulary to cover

[21]Concerning this point, however, Romanzo Adams writes: "I think that to the immigrants there appeared to be an important advantage in being able to use better English. A few men got better positions on this account and some of the older sons also. Probably in 1920 the value of superior English was overestimated by the Japanese but now they are disillusioned." (Communication of December, 1934.)

extra-plantation concepts and activities would be necessary in most cases, but having already adopted the syntax of the creole dialect, the immigrant would naturally stick to it. The average man was not impelled to learn more than the necessary minimum of the English language. His social life was lived for the most part among his own ethnic community;[22] usually only economic activities brought him into contact with English-speaking people; he was living symbiotically in reference to the other ethnic communities and especially to the dominant Haole community. "Pidgin English" was to him, and still is, a mere makeshift, supplementary tool of communication. Thus it has, in this respect, more in common with the trade pidgins than with the creole dialects of countries in which the laborers are socially pulverized and lose their original languages rapidly.

The creole dialect is not only a language of the economically limited but also a lingua franca necessary under Hawaiian conditions. It is used in three classes of communication. Primarily it is a language of command, a corruption of the speech of the ruling class. Its use as a language of command has become traditional on the plantations and in some other employer-employee situations. Schoolteachers sometimes complain that there is no use teaching their students good English while *lunas* resent its use to them as inappropriate; the young workman is thought to be acting smarter than his place warrants. There is no logical reason why orders should not be given to Filipinos today in good English (provided the foreman can speak it), but the Filipino continues to be addressed in "pidgin" not only by old Japanese and Portuguese hands but by Haoles as well. As long as alien laborers are imported to work on the plantations, the creole dialect may be expected to maintain itself. Even among the native-born workmen, broken if not makeshift English may be expected to be more in use on the plantations, with their tradition of stratified classes, than in other occupations.

The creole dialect is, secondly, a medium of communication

[22]Romanzo Adams credits the Koreans with having learned more and better English than other immigrant nationalities, simply because they have been few in number, scattered about in extra-plantation occupations, and thus unable to form self-sufficient communities.

between members of non-English-speaking groups. These are so numerous that the broken English that all have had to learn as workmen is obviously the only feasible language for a common tongue. As each nationality in turn moves out of the segregated plantation camps and mingles with its neighbors, this use of the creole dialect becomes more important. Among those educated in English schools, a tolerably good English takes its place, but among elderly natives and immigrants of the first generation, only the creole dialect is available for the increasingly important inter-group functions of ordinary social intercourse and of buying and selling. In some situations, notably the West Indies and the southern United States, the use of a creole dialect over several generations has knit a heterogeneous mass of imported laborers into homogeneous ethnic units: American, Jamaican, or Cuban Negroes, as the case may be. But as the creole dialect does not have a chance to persist unmodified in Hawaii and is spoken only by the first generation immigrants or at most by their children, both of whom retain a lively sense of their separate nationalities, the unifying character of creole speech has not been possible in these Islands. The quality of unification has been left for the colloquial colonial dialect.

There are limits to the usefulness of makeshift English, or indeed of any sort of English, as an effective interlanguage among the various linguistic communities that make up the population of Hawaii. Numerous individuals, especially those engaged in shopkeeping and kindred occupations, have found it profitable to acquire a smattering of languages other than English. The Chinese shopkeepers who learned both an imperfect Hawaiian and an imperfect English have been mentioned. The older Portuguese and Japanese also sometimes know Hawaiian. Shopkeepers may be found speaking several tongues. A Chinese-Portuguese merchant of the writer's acquaintance, for example, speaks in addition to fluent English some Chinese, Portuguese, Hawaiian, and Japanese, all of which are useful in holding his customers. Isolated members of numerically small ethnic communities have many opportunities to learn the languages of such large and compact groups as the Japanese and Filipinos through mere propinquity, regardless of the commercial value of these tongues. Others have set themselves to learn the more important languages for social or religious reasons. Japanese is the language most frequently learned. The non-Japanese child in the Japanese language school is a not uncommon sight. An English-Japanese-Tagalog wordbook has been published, presumably to help Japanese and Filipinos.[23] Finally, intermarriage, while in the long run contributing to the crowding out of other languages by English, frequently makes it possible and desirable for one or both of the spouses to learn the other's tongue and, in some cases, for their children to be trilingual.[24]

The third use of the creole dialect is as a means of communication between parents or others of the immigrant (or corresponding native Hawaiian) generation and their children and other young folk of the same ethnic group who do not speak the parental language fluently. The only English which the parental generation is able to speak and usually to understand is commonly "pidgin"; their children are often unable to express themselves fully and readily in their parental tongue because they use it little outside the home and, for the most part, are

[23]Published about 1927. I could not secure a copy in 1934, so cannot give further particulars. [Neither was I successful in locating a copy of this work, despite an extensive search made especially in Hawaii. The closest thing to it that I found was an English-Ilokano-Visayan dictionary, combined with an English grammar and reader (see Alverne, *Manual* . . . in the Bibliography).—*Ed.*]

[24]A study by the writer in 1933 of about sixty-one junior high school students in Hamakua District showed several cases of more or less command of a third language by one or both of the parents (usually the father). Of the students themselves, one Japanese boy in a Portuguese community knew Portuguese, one Korean boy in a Japanese village knew Japanese, while one boy of Portuguese-Puerto Rican blood knew both Portuguese and Spanish. Among the fathers: two Filipinos knew Spanish; two Chinese, one of them married to a native, knew Hawaiian; three Japanese also knew Hawaiian; another Japanese knew Filipino and Portuguese; a Korean knew Hawaiian and Filipino; a Portuguese married to a Puerto Rican knew her dialect of Spanish; another Portuguese knew "Porto Rican" and Filipino; a third (a bank teller) knew "Porto Rican," Hawaiian, Japanese, and Filipino. Of only two mothers listed as knowing a third language, one Filipina knew Spanish and one Puerto Rican knew Russian. In all, thirteen out of sixty-one fathers and two out of sixty-one mothers were stated to be trilingual or more. What youngsters of fourteen or fifteen report must be taken with a few grains of salt, but their statements, allowing for all exaggeration, do show a fair amount of trilingualism among the men and a little among the women and children of a typical plantation community.

accustomed to thinking in English.[25] The children grow up in an environment where "pidgin English" is used by their parents in conversing with folk of other nationalities, so that it is now, and has been for at least a decade, unusual to find a child unacquainted with "pidgin" or even with more acceptable English by the time he enters school. Therefore the typical course, at least in many communities, is at present for the child to begin speaking a makeshift English—and in any case the language of young children is inadequate and makeshift to a considerable degree—and thence to pass to the ability to use a more adequate speech more nearly approximating Standard English.[26] At the same time the children retain the use of the creole dialect in some situations, a very important one being in addressing elderly folk of their own nationality. Used to speaking English among themselves—which, even though it may be somewhat broken, is much more adequate than that used by their parents—and often unaccustomed to any but the simplest forms of their parental language, children fall into the habit of addressing their parents in "pidgin English," often mixed with their parents' language. It is easier to understand than to express oneself in a language, and the second generation very commonly state that they can understand their parents' speech but can not respond to it adequately. Likewise the parents understand their children's creole speech but prefer to answer more adequately in their own tongue.[27] What is true between parents and

[25]Many people have the impression that the average youngster thinks in his parental language while speaking English, but this is contradicted by the statements of several dozen persons of the "second generation," and of several teachers, as well as by the objective evidence of sentence construction.

[26]In some localities, teachers (surreptitiously) give some instruction to the lowest grades in creole or extremely broken local dialect.

[27]"I know English more than my parents. Because they were born in Japan, and do not understand English so well, I talk pidgin English to them. They understand better that way. I often talk mixed language to them. When I tell them anything that happened in school, or is making a long speech to them I use half Japanese and half English. When you speak you hardly know that you are talking half English and half Japanese. That is because you are more interested on the thing you are talking about than the kind of English you are speaking. I'd like to talk all Japanese to them, but I am not so good in Japanese, and can't talk well. I start to use Japanese, and end it by using English. I'd like to talk all English to them, but they do not understand. . . . We have a hard time speaking good English because we do not use them carefully at home." (From an essay by K. H., a female eighth grade student at Honokaa, 1933.)

children is in general true also between elderly and young persons of the same nationality, though a young person is likely to be more formal in his speech and to use his national language when speaking to his elders outside the family circle. It must not be overlooked that a considerable number of those bred in Hawaii, even of the third generation, are still tolerably adequate in the use of their parental tongue and need not have recourse to the creole dialect in conversation with their elders.

The limits of the usefulness of the creole dialect will be treated fully from another angle in the following chapter, in which the persistence of the several foreign languages will be discussed. It may be pointed out here, however, that a homogeneous linguistic group maintaining an ethnic spirit and community life, as most of the immigrant groups (and the native Polynesian group) in Hawaii have done, will need to use the creole dialect only as a lingua franca to supplement, not to supplant, its vernacular. Such a group will often endeavor to make its children speak the parental language in communicating with members of their own group and will be largely successful in maintaining the use of their language for several generations. In the camps, villages, and ghetto-like sections of the cities, where a population is found wholly or almost wholly of one ethnic community, there is little reason to hear "pidgin" often spoken. If it were not for the influence of the English language schools upon the children, it would be heard much less than it is.

Yet even in such a community, in conversations in the alien language among first generation immigrants, English and Hawaiian loan words from the creole dialect are heard. The English words in particular are very likely to be adapted to the phonetic system of the foreign language in question. Sometimes the substitution of an English or Hawaiian word or phrase is unnecessary and arises only from its frequent use in the creole dialect. An example is *banbai*, "by and by," for *ato de*, among the Japanese. Sometimes there is a word already in the foreign language which is little used because the thing for which it stands is little known in the mother country, so the English word is adopted in Hawaii, as *fensu* "fence," for the Japanese *kakine*.[28]

SUMMARY

The so-called "pidgin English" of Hawaii occupies a place on the borderline between the mixed dialects of foreign groups under the usual conditions of immigration to America, and the true creole dialects of servile plantation countries; but social conditions in Hawaii have been such as to make it classifiable as a creole dialect. That is, it arose chiefly on the plantations of Hawaii and primarily as a language of command, as a means of communication between employer and workman. Because of the heterogeneity of the population, it is also employed in most communication between the elder members of different non-Haole groups. It also functions as a medium of communication between the parental generation unable to speak adequate English and children unable to speak the parental language adequately. The chief cause of the creole dialect is thus seen to be the economic position of the mass of the immigrant population, a position which makes it both impracticable and unnecessary for them to learn anything better than makeshift English.

Historically, the creole dialect arose from the somewhat amorphous *hapa haole* speech of the whaling days and shows great Hawaiian influence. The Portuguese appear to have been the most influential nationality in spreading its use. The Chinese influence is not easily determined but seems to have been slight.

---

[28]It is desirable that a study be made of borrowings from the English and other languages by each of the major languages of Hawaii, and of other local influences upon them. The present writer is familiar with several dozen English loan words used by Hawaiian Japanese. See: George Wolfe, "Notes on American Yiddish," *American Mercury*, XXIX, No. 16, 473-479; Johanna Hamilton, "Zur Sprachbeeinflussung in anderssprachiger Umgebung," *Sociologus*, IX, No. 4, 473-479; "Naturalization of Tongues," *The Interpreter*, VIII, No. 4, 7-15; H. L. Mencken, *The American Language*, 3rd ed., *passim*. [Now also see Joseph Kess, "English Influences in the Phonology of Japanese as Spoken in Hawaii" (M.A. thesis, University of Hawaii, 1965); Denzel Carr, "Comparative Treatment of Epenthetic and Paragogic Vowels in English Loan Words in Japanese and Hawaiian," *Semitic and Oriental Studies*, 13-26. The latter is reprinted in *Language Learning*, XIV, Nos. 1 and 2 (1964), 21-36.—*Ed.*]

The Japanese influence was also slight, considering the size of the group. The Filipinos are contributing to it, but many of this nationality are able to use better than makeshift English. The chief contribution, however, was that of the English-speaking Americans and British who simplified their speech to meet what they considered their workmen's limitations. The creole speech of the several nationalities can be distinguished, but there are common elements that make it one "pidgin English."

Chapter 5

WHY THE IMMIGRANTS' LANGUAGES HAVE NOT BEEN DISPLACED

In most countries where a creole dialect has arisen, the dialect has supplanted the language or languages which the imported laborers have brought with them, and that rather speedily. So in Mauritius there is left no Malagasy; in Brazil, Surinam, the West Indies, and the Southern States of America, none of the West African languages. The retention of the language of the dominated group beside the makeshift language is more characteristic of the trade pidgin situations than of the creole dialect situations. When, in a situation where a creole language has arisen, the language of the dominated group has not been lost, we have to look for special circumstances that have maintained it. Thus, in parts of Mexico and some other Spanish American countries, Spanish has impinged upon the American Indian languages under plantation conditions. But the Indian tongues have been maintained by sheer force of numbers and by the communal village organization of the Indians. As peons of the Spanish-speaking white and mestizo landlords, the Indians are obliged to learn their masters' language. But they have not been completely uprooted from their native environment, as were the

111

Negro slaves; they have the reservoir of village life, the traditions of their tribe, mutilated though they may be, to fall back upon. The same phenomenon is found in Melanesia, where tribesmen are drawn into terms of plantation labor. When their terms are up, they return to their villages and to their native languages, which have been in abeyance on the plantation, where Beach-la-mar is used.

A kindred phenomenon is seen in connection with the immigrants' mixed dialects. The immigrant under conditions like those of the United States, Canada, and Argentina may for a few generations live symbiotically, surrounded by the native population, whether in a city ghetto or in what are in effect rural ghettos.[1] His English or Spanish, as the case may be, is imperfect and very simplified; his native tongue, Italian, German, Yiddish, or Slavic, is retained for some years through conversation with his fellow immigrants and through such institutions as the foreign language press, the foreign language church, the foreign language school, and the foreign language club. In time, however, his native tongue takes on more and more features of the language of the adopted country and degenerates into a mixed speech (i.e., a language with a mixed vocabulary, like Pennsylvania Dutch) or disappears altogether.

Why, since the makeshift language of the plantations of Hawaii arose in a creole environment and has been classed as a creole dialect, has it not supplanted the Japanese, Chinese, Portuguese, and other immigrant tongues? The answer (generally speaking) is that the plantation environment in Hawaii has never been a perfect type of the species; that the immigrants, like the East Indians indentured to the British Caribbean lands and Mauritius, came under conditions approaching in many ways those of free immigration. In such an environment as they found themselves, of semi-restriction yet freedom from ethnic pulverization, they were, indeed, perhaps

---

[1]Ghetto is used with a more extensive meaning than its commonly accepted meaning of a restricted area of Jewish settlement. It is used to denote an area inhabited by any ethnic community living symbiotically, encysted within the dominant population of a country. See Louis Wirth, *The Ghetto*, chapter on "The Sociological Significance of the Ghetto."

more apt to retain their languages than under conditions of free assimilation.

For some individuals, even of the first generation, the creole dialect *has* very largely displaced their native tongue, and even more have the immigrant languages been displaced by the colloquial dialect of the younger folk, which is part of the same language continuum as the creole dialect. (Of course the earlier immigrants were exposed only to the first crude "pidgin.") Immigrants can be found who are fluent in Island "pidgin" but slow in their native tongue and who lard their native idiom with expressions from the "pidgin." But this is also common among free immigrants, who are not under plantation conditions.

Most individuals on the plantation, however, as well as in other parts of the Hawaiian milieu, have retained their vernacular and are more at home in it than in the "pidgin." Why is this so?

For the aboriginal Hawaiian group, the condition of proximity to native conditions and society has always helped maintain the use of their native tongue. The Hawaiian contract laborer on a sugar cane plantation was in touch with his relatives and friends; his language was accorded some prestige because of the peculiar situation in which an *ali'i* of his race was the nominal sovereign of the white capitalist who exploited his labor and of the manager who directed it; he heard Hawaiian from the pulpit of his church and read it in his newspaper; often his children learned to write it in the schools; frequently his Haole *luna* could speak it after a fashion.

In the second place, the conditions under which immigrant labor was introduced into Hawaii were not so bluntly and brutally those of domination and submission as on plantations in many other parts of the world where creole dialects arose. The religious and social conscience of some of the planters and many of the officials and other people of Hawaii encouraged a concern with the well-being of the laborers. The treatment of Chinese coolies in Hawaii compared with that of their compatriots in Cuba, Peru, and some parts of the United States shows this concern from the negative side; the extension of all the privileges of education to the children of the immigrants and the attention of religious and social workers to the imported laborer even of pre-annexation years shows this concern from the positive side. The involuntary servitude of the contract laborer, which in any case need not have been for a period longer than three years, was done away with in 1900. Even before that date the laborers, with the exception of the Chinese and South Sea Islanders, were drawn from countries which would not hesitate to inquire into too flagrant ill-treatment of their nationals—as indeed the Japanese government did inquire into reports of ill-treatment of Japanese laborers.

Most important of all, the imported laborers were not brought in as a pulverized mass of individuals from several tribes, but instead they were limited to men of a few nationalities, who found themselves together in a situation in which community life of a sort was possible. If the plantations did not at first directly encourage ethnic community life among their employees, they did not discourage it. Later, they directly encouraged it and, incidentally, the maintenance of the national spirit, as by their subsidizing Japanese language schools and Buddhist temples. In rare cases there was strong encouragement to retain the national culture, as among the Germans at Lihue. Escape from plantation conditions was not very hard; at any time within a very few years after the arrival of any immigrant group, some members of that group could be found in other occupations and a few even in preferred positions in the professions and in commerce. In such positions they received recognition from the Haole employing group. While the plantation environment has since about 1870 lain as the foundation of Hawaiian life, it has borne an increasing superstructure of life not greatly different from that of the immigrant in any urban part of America—or, in a few cases, not much different from that of the immigrant in rural America.

The nature of the immigrants must not be left out of account. With the exception of the South Sea Islanders and perhaps some of the earlier Chinese, they were not ignorant, blackbirded victims of the demand for servile labor. Even those who came during the era of contract labor came in much the same spirit as the indentured servants of colonial British

America, hoping to make their term of contract the first stepping stone to a more secure and remunerative economic life, perhaps even to modest wealth. Some were not too badly disappointed. Many immigrants were literate, some even educated; several groups possessed a strong national spirit and pride. There were limits to the domination which could be exercised over such men. Among the Asiatic groups, most individuals were in touch with their homeland and many expected to return. So, to sum up, while a plantation system with all its chief earmarks, including, for fifty years, labor under legal constraint, has been present, that plantation system has been and increasingly is maintained under limiting and modifying conditions which have taken from it several of the harsher features usually accompanying its operation, and have made it like the conditions of free immigration obtaining in the United States and similar countries.

Thus conditions have been favorable for the maintenance of ethnic solidarity and morale among most of the groups coming into Hawaii as plantation laborers (as well as among the native Hawaiians) and, hence, for the retention of their languages. The competition of these languages with English affords one of the most interesting chapters of the linguistic history of Hawaii. This chapter, however, belongs to the wider field of general linguistic competition rather than to the restricted field of the development and fate of the creole dialect, for all immigrant languages (and Hawaiian) have been in competition with and have to a considerable extent held their own against every form of English, whether it be Standard English, the creole dialect, or the intermediate colloquial dialect of the younger non-Haoles. The general rules may be laid down that, in situations like that of Hawaii, the vernaculars of the alien groups will be kept up within the respective groups for a longer or shorter period, depending upon many circumstances; that a makeshift dialect will for the most part be used as the means of communication between the several groups; but that this makeshift dialect will tend to pass into a more formal speech—still imperfect as compared with the standard language—as an interlanguage, until finally this more or less standardized lingua franca becomes the primary tongue of nearly the whole body of inhabitants. Expanded, a consideration of the development and interaction of the various languages of Hawaii could run into several monographs, but there is room here for only a cursory treatment of the matter.

Certain factors are favorable and certain others unfavorable to the retention of their native tongue by immigrants and by small native populations who occupy an analogous place, as do the native Hawaiians. I shall enumerate these theoretically and then inquire how some of them have applied in the case of each of the nationalities of Hawaii.

(1) The size of the ethnic group and of its communities is of prime importance. A person in a large ghetto is encouraged to retain the use of his language longer than his brother who lives apart from the immigrant group. A nationality that is large enough to maintain a complex economic and social life within itself will keep its native language longer than a small group that can not afford such a self-sufficient life, other things being equal. Thus, through mere force of numbers, the Japanese tongue will probably endure in Hawaii for a considerable while after the Korean has passed.

(2) Closely associated with the size of a group is its geographic isolation. In Hawaii that isolation is seen chiefly among rural Hawaiians, as in parts of Kona, in Waipio Valley, in Kaupo District, and on Niihau. It is also important among the Japanese of Kona. Obviously isolation is favorable to the perpetuation of a tongue.

(3) The age and sex composition of the group is significant. A group composed largely of men (as that of the Filipinos at present) will not have the same interest in preserving its language that a society of parents will have, for the latter feel themselves links in the chain of generations of their nationality. On the other hand, single men are not subject to the numerous contacts with the language of the land that children have, and through them their parents, and thus are not as likely to adopt the native tongue as are married people with families. Such is the case among elderly Chinese and Korean bachelors, who may be compared with the married Portuguese of the same age.

(4) The social and economic status and ambitions of the group determine in part whether its members will drop the use of their language in order the better to climb the ladder of success in native (American) society, or will keep their language because they have no great hopes of rising and being assimilated. (5) Or, on the contrary, a group of some status will cling to its language because it finds it useful in commercial life. This is rather marked in the case of the well-established Chinese community, which is largely a petty bourgeois mercantile community. In the case of the Chinese, the rise in status seems to have had something to do with increasing their ethnic pride and their interest in their own tongue. (6) The commercial usefulness of a language depends upon the proximity of the immigrants' mother country and the commercial and cultural contacts possible with it. Contrast the trade and the movement of passengers between Hawaii and Japan or China or even the Philippine Islands with that between Hawaii and Portugal or Puerto Rico.

(7) The strength of national feeling and the social organization of an immigrant people have much to do in determining their attitude toward their language. A strong national feeling is favorable to the retention of a language. One may compare the Japanese with the Portuguese. The national characteristics of both groups appear to be equally tenacious, but the attitudes of the two toward the preservation of their national individuality as expressed in the use of their respective languages are widely different.

(8) Upon national feeling depends much of the attitude toward permanent settlement and assimilation. The Japanese language schools, it is said, arose from the dismay of the Japanese who expected to return to Japan at finding that their children were losing their mother tongue.[2] Groups that expect to remain unassimilated, such as Westerners in China, will take great pains to preserve the use of their language among their children; groups that expect to become assimilated will not care about its use.

[2] U. S. Department of the Interior, Bureau of Education, *A Survey of Education in Hawaii,* pp. 108-109.

(9) With the preceding factor is associated the attitude of immigrant and native toward intermarriage. Where national feeling, race pride, or religious separatism holds back intermarriage, the immigrant does not encounter one of the forces most solvent of his language. Especially when intermarriage takes place between immigrants of different stocks, the native language is extremely likely to be used.

(10) Closely dependent upon the strength of the national sentiment is the maintenance of the foreign language through its use in immigrants' churches, as well as (11) in clubs and associations (*tongs, Turnvereine,* mutual aid societies, etc.). So also are (12) the existence of the foreign language press and (13) the foreign language school.

(14) But the last two depend also upon the degree of literacy and the respect in which literacy is held. An illiterate group, though it may be proud of its language, can not expect to maintain its tongue in a literate society such as that of Hawaii. The superior literacy of the Oriental immigrants, as compared with the Filipinos and especially the Latin immigrants to Hawaii, clearly has an effect upon the greater effort put forth by the former groups to keep up their languages among the Hawaiian-born generation. The reading habits of the literate members of a group, and the amount and type of literature upon which they can draw, also count.

(15) The appearance of the foreign language school is also connected with the degree of familism among an immigrant people. The stronger the feeling of family unity in an ethnic group, the more likely will the parents be to strive to preserve it by having their children speak the mother tongue.

(16) The habit of learning new languages, which in turn seems to be dependent upon dialectal variety in the immigrants' homeland or upon the existence of a foreign language of culture in that land, plays a part. This is probably important among the Filipinos of Hawaii.

(17) The attitude of the native population toward the use of an immigrant tongue is significant. If the foreign speech is hardly tolerated, the immigrant is likely to use it as little as possible, unless an unusual resistance to assimilation develops; if

it is tolerated (as in Pennsylvania among the Germans), it may persist for generations. Sometimes the native population may even encourage the foreign language. Thus the Isenbergs—German-born, it is true, but closely connected with the Anglo-Saxon Haoles—supported the use of German on their plantation. On the other hand, the interaction of American and Japanese attitudes toward the preservation of the Japanese language has caused more conflict than any other linguistic problem in Hawaii.

How did these factors operate in the case of the several ethnic groups in Hawaii?

Chinese. The respect of the Chinese for literacy is proverbial. Nevertheless the peasants who were drawn to the Hawaiian cane fields were of an economic level whose respect was perforce ideal rather than practical. Moreover, men were given the first chance to learn their letters, and literacy among women was not especially esteemed. Table 12 shows the change in literacy (in both Chinese and English) among the age and sex groups of the Chinese for the censuses from 1896 to 1930. Probably about one-half of the men were illiterate when they landed.

True literacy in Chinese is hard to gauge. Ability to scrawl "some tens of characters" needed to keep laundry accounts or write out restaurant orders is literacy in the formal sense. Perhaps the subscription to the Chinese language newspapers is the best way of estimating literacy in the sense of ability to read ordinary writing. In 1933 Chock Lun, a journalist, estimated the subscription list of the three semi-weekly papers published in Hawaii at about 3,000, among an adult Chinese population of 14,500.[3]

The first Chinese newspaper, the weekly *Hawaiian-Chinese News*, was not established until about 1886, after a decade of large-scale immigration had passed. Its next competitor, the *Chinese Times*, did not appear until 1892. The mortality rate among Chinese newspapers has been considerable. Generally the

[3]*Ayer's Directory* for 1931, however, gives 3,784 as the sworn circulation of the *Hawaii Chinese News* (weekly) and 7,960 as the publisher's report of circulation of the *Liberty News* (three times a week). These figures seem much too large.

TABLE 12

ILLITERACY AMONG THE CHINESE IN HAWAII, 1896-1930,
BY AGE AND SEX GROUPS

Groups	Percentages				
	1896[a]	1900[d]	1910[d]	1920[d]	1930[d]
Total Chinese	51.53[b]	40.0	32.3	21.0	15.7
Total Males	49.84[c]	37.7	30.2	20.8	16.7
Total Females	75.05[c]	63.4	43.8	21.7	13.9
10-14 years		13.4	3.8	0.7	0.5
15-19 years		32.5	9.0	1.7	1.2
20-24 years		44.7	19.9	5.4	2.3
25-34 years		43.5	29.9	12.9	6.1
35-44 years		37.3	36.6	21.1	14.8
45-54 years		40.4	39.3	29.9	28.8
55-64 years		46.8	47.1	41.4	39.9
65 and over		44.4	54.7	48.2	49.0

Data from Hawaiian Census of 1896, pp. 95, 97, Table VII; U. S. Census of 1910, Vol. III, p. 1174; U. S. Census of 1930, *Population—Hawaii*, Table 9.

[a]In the census of 1890 (p. 34), 13.27 percent of the Chinese (foreign-born) were returned as literate. ". . . The intention has been to make the expression, 'Able to Read and Write,' apply to Hawaiian, English, or some European language only"; but doubtless some of the 13.27 percent were literate only in Chinese.

[b]Over 6 years of age able to read and write any language.

[c]Approximate, being the percentages obtained by dividing the number able to read and write by the number of *foreign* Chinese. Of 9,010 Chinese males who could read and write, 485 were literate in English, 213 in Hawaiian, and 8,843 in "any other language." For the 354 literate Chinese females, the corresponding numbers were 42, 13, and 324.

[d]Figures for totals for persons 10 years of age and over.

Chinese community has supported from three to five papers, corresponding usually to the shades of political opinion among the immigrant generation.[4] At the present time the newspapers appear nearly to satisfy the Chinese demand for reading matter; no popular magazines are current among them as among the

[4]The Chinese press in Hawaii awaits a competent historian and analyst. The present writer's information is drawn from the lists of publications in the *Hawaiian Annual*, 1878 to 1897, and the *Honolulu Directory*, 1899 to 1933.

Japanese, nor can one purchase Chinese books, with a few cheap exceptions, outside the newspaper offices.

The Chinese drama may have contributed slightly to the maintenance of the Chinese language in Honolulu, although the stage language is very different from the colloquial.

The Chinese, being for the most part unmarried men, turned for social life to that decidedly Chinese organization, the *tong* or club. The *tong*, being common, has helped maintain the solidarity of the Chinese community and consequently the use of the Chinese language. The concentration of the Chinese in and about Honolulu was also favorable to this solidarity.

As soon as there were enough Chinese students, private schools for instruction in both English and Chinese were established, sometimes under Christian auspices. The first, with an enrollment of fifty boys and two girls, was begun in 1880 at the Fort Street Chinese church; a Chinese girls' school followed in 1882; and at Wailuku and Kohala bilingual schools were established in 1887.[5] By 1890 three small language schools conducted by Chinese masters had been established.[6] But it was only with the upsurge of Chinese nationalism in the second decade of this century that the Chinese language school became an institution of importance. Like the newspapers, the schools have in several cases been started to express a political view; thus the Mun Lun School (1910) was founded by the Constitutionalist Party and the Chung-Shan (formerly Wah Mun) School (1911) by the Kuomintang. Other schools, however, do not reflect partisanism.[7]

The Federal survey made in 1920 showed about 1,150 students enrolled in Chinese language schools, or about 21 percent of the enrollment of Chinese in the English language schools. Enrollment has been steadily increasing, and in September, 1934, it was reported as 3,372, or close to 40 per-

---

[5] *Report* of 1882, p. 38; *Report* of 1888, Appendix B.

[6] *Report* of 1890.

[7] Conversation with Kum Pui Lai; Kalfred D. Lum, "The Education of the Chinese in Hawaii," in *The Chinese of Hawaii*, pp. 18-20. Of the eleven schools in Honolulu in 1929, two were founded in 1910, one in 1911, two in 1917, one in 1925, two in 1926, and three in 1928 or 1929.

cent of the number enrolled in the English schools.[8] This increase in a group whose student population is mostly of the third generation argues a tenacious national spirit and an appreciation of the cultural value of the mother tongue, and of its commercial value also. The already mentioned concentration of the Chinese in trade in Honolulu is favorable for the retention of the language in the schools. A considerable number of Chinese are doing, or hope to do, business between China and America; others have settled in China in business or the professions; probably over one hundred are now students in Chinese colleges and high schools. The increasing wealth and prestige of the Chinese have given them pride and assurance in their ethnic group and interest in their ethnic culture, while political events of the past twenty-five years have heightened their interest in Chinese things. But whether instruction in the language schools is efficient enough effectively to prepare the Hawaiian-born youth for appreciation of Chinese literat re and success in Oriental business has not been tested. From the present writer's own observation, it appears that the conscientious Chinese language-school graduate does have a tolerably good grounding in the written language.

Instruction in the language schools has usually been in Shekki, the standard sub-dialect of Chung Shan Cantonese, which is the lingua franca of the Chinese groups in Hawaii. Some standard Cantonese is also taught in the higher grades, but the *kuo yü* or official (Northern) Chinese, only in the University of Hawaii—and even there some local Chinese have sought to have Cantonese taught in its stead. The greatest dialect cleavage is between the Hakkas and the rest of the Chinese, but this does not seriously affect the instruction in the language schools.[9]

---

[8]*A Survey of Education in Hawaii*, p. 112; *Reports* of 1920-1932; "Chinese Language Schools Have Enrollment of 3,372," *Honolulu Star-Bulletin*, November 24, 1934. The 1934 survey, made by the Overseas Penman Club, showed twelve of nineteen schools and 3,106 of the 3,372 students to be in Honolulu. The latest official survey, that of 1932, gave the enrollment in Chinese language schools as 2,479, or about 31 percent of the enrollment of Chinese in English schools.

[9]The material in this paragraph was mostly secured in interviews with James Chun; Chock Lun; and Tin Yuke Char. Instruction in one school has been in the Hakka tongue.

Opposition on the part of the Americans to the use of a foreign language has been mostly centered upon the Japanese language. Even during the foreign language school controversy of 1919 to 1927, attention was only very incidentally directed to the Chinese schools. The perpetuation of Chinese culture and the Chinese language were not considered of political importance by the Haoles, but the Chinese schools would have suffered along with the Japanese had the legislation been effective.

As soon as the Chinese began to engage in trade, those so employed had to learn something of either the English or the Hawaiian language, or both. Yet, considering their length of residence in Hawaii, their concentration in the towns and cities, and their occupations there, the Chinese do not appear to have put forth any unusual effort to learn English. (English has never been a lingua franca between their dialect groups.) Although the Chinese and the Portuguese immigration covered about the same period, in 1930 two-ninths of the Chinese but only one-ninth of the Portuguese could not speak English (see Table 13). This is partly explainable on the basis of age and sex distribution, as 6,601 of the Chinese were over forty-four years of age, many of them old bachelors, but only 3,715 of the Portuguese. Even more is it explainable in terms of parent and child association, for the Portuguese, being mostly married people, came more in contact with the English-schooled youth. Nevertheless, the figures in part reflect the self-sufficiency of the Chinese ethnic community life and the closeness of the ties between the Island Chinese and their mother country.

Considering the length of residence of the Chinese in Hawaii, this ethnic group has displayed strong solidarity and tenacious attachment to its language. It seems likely to continue to do so for at least another generation.

Japanese. The now very efficient public school system of Japan evidently had not begun to function widely among the early immigrants to Hawaii who, contrary to what one would expect, displayed as much illiteracy as the Chinese (see Table 14). Close to one-half of the immigrants before 1900 must have been illiterate. Of the immigrants to the continental United States and Hawaii, fourteen years of age and over, 24.6 percent

TABLE 13

PERSONS IN HAWAII 10 YEARS OF AGE AND OVER UNABLE TO
SPEAK ENGLISH, 1910-1930

	Non-English-speaking Population					
	1910		1920		1930	
Race	No.	% of whole racial group	No.	% of whole racial group	No.	% of whole racial group
All Races	84,177	56.6	69,493	37.1	66,822	24.5
Hawaiian	8,941	42.9	3,693	19.7	1,467	8.3
Caucasian-Hawaiian	233	4.3	66	0.9	56	0.6
Asiatic-Hawaiian	199	9.2	153	4.2	55	0.8
Portuguese	4,380	28.9	2,009	11.2	1,060	5.1
Puerto Rican	2,236	67.3	1,339	35.1	972	21.0
Spanish	925	73.3	551	35.0	106	11.4
Other Caucasian	962	7.7	105	0.6	82	0.2
Chinese	11,456	63.1	6,907	38.1	4,528	22.4
Japanese	49,750	79.0	41,730	54.2	28,150	29.8
Korean	3,335	81.7	2,062	54.5	1,327	29.5
Filipino	1,760[a]	58.2[a]	10,832	60.4	28,993	54.0
Negro and All Other			46	9.7	26	4.8

Data from U. S. Census of 1910, Vol. I, p. 1266; U. S. Census of 1920, Vol. III, p. 1189; U. S. Census of 1930, *Population—Hawaii*, Table 10.

[a]Filipino combined with Negro and All Other.

are recorded as illiterate. Although Ichihashi doubts these figures, he offers no proof of their inaccuracy.[10] The difference in literacy between the sexes is very marked.

The devotion of the Japanese to education, both in their own language and in English, may not be greater than that of the Chinese, but because of the large size of the Japanese group it is more noticeable. Their language schools, for reasons soon to be discussed, serve a much greater proportion of their youth than do the Chinese language schools; they support ten Japanese or bilingual newspapers, besides religious organs and a creditable

[10] Yamato Ichihashi, *Japanese in the United States*, pp. 76-78.

TABLE 14

ILLITERACY AMONG THE JAPANESE IN HAWAII, 1896-1930,
BY AGE AND SEX GROUPS

Groups	Percentages				
	1896[a]	1900[c]	1910[c]	1920[c]	1930[c]
Total Japanese	46.4[b]	46.2	35.0	20.8	12.7
Total Males	41.6[b]	40.3	27.8	15.1	9.0
Total Females	69.1[b]	70.8	55.0	29.3	17.2
10-14 years		10.8	1.5	0.6	0.2
15-19 years		45.0	13.6	3.2	0.9
20-24 years		48.6	26.7	10.9	1.9
25-34 years		46.0	38.2	20.7	9.4
35-44 years		45.5	41.4	28.7	19.3
45-54 years		48.1	44.5	34.1	27.9
55-64 years		35.9	44.3	39.5	34.0
65 and over		—	—	43.0	39.6

Data from Hawaiian Census of 1896, pp. 95, 97, Table VII; U. S. Census of 1910, Vol. III, p. 1174; U. S. Census of 1930, *Population—Hawaii*, Table 9.

[a]In 1890, 2.49 percent of the Japanese were returned as literate, supposedly in English or Hawaiian, but a number surely in Japanese.

Of 10,597 literate Japanese males in 1896, only 285 were literate in English and 68 in Hawaiian; of 1,297 literate females, 28 in English and 6 in Hawaiian.

[b]Over 6 years of age.

[c]Figures for totals, for persons 10 years of age and over.

monthly magazine;[11] they maintain four bookstores in Honolulu and one in Hilo, while books and popular magazines in Japanese can be purchased in numerous shops. All these evidences of the reading habits of the Japanese strike the casual observer and no doubt reinforce in the Japanese themselves a sense of the literate habits of their nationality, and of the need of maintaining a knowledge of their own language.

[11]The newspapers are distributed, two in Kauai, two in Maui (one carrying a Filipino as well as an English section in 1931), three in Hilo, one in Kona, and two in Honolulu. Shunzo Sakamaki in "A History of the Japanese Press in Hawaii" (M.A. thesis, University of Hawaii) estimated their combined circulation in 1927 to be 30,925 copies. Ayer's figures for eight of the ten in 1931 give a circulation of 39,897 copies. The adult Japanese population in 1930 was 62,816. The *Dobo* (Buddhist monthly) circulated 1,500 copies in 1931, and the monthly *Jitsugyo no Hawaii*, about 5,000 in 1927; small church organs circulated extensively.

The first Japanese language paper in Hawaii was the mimeographed *Nippon Shubo*

Japanese national spirit has, until the recent rise of Chinese nationalism, conformed more nearly to the Western sentiment of patriotism than has the ethnic pride of the Chinese. The Russo-Japanese War excited that spirit among the settlers in Hawaii, and it has been fostered by the Buddhist missions. Indeed, for a while the activities of some of the Buddhist clergy were so opposed to assimilation that the priests were vigorously assailed by both the American and the Japanese press.[12] This nationalism, joined to the rivalry of America and Japan in the Pacific, has colored the development of the Japanese language in the Hawaiian Islands.

While religion among the Chinese has had little to do with the retention of their language, the Buddhist churches have been a strong force among the Japanese. Buddhist priests ministering and preaching in the Japanese language are important personages in most Japanese communities. As educated men not entirely dependent upon a schoolteacher's small salary, they are easily eligible teachers for the language schools. Although the first Japanese language schools were founded by Christian ministers (in 1896 and 1897), the strongest impetus to the growth of these schools came from the Buddhist missions, particularly from the Hongwanji, and many language schools have been administered wholly or partly in connection with the Buddhist temples.[13]

The language schools themselves are one of the most interesting and important institutions in Hawaii, both because of their present educational value and moral and social influ-

---

in 1892. The turnover of Japanese language papers has been great; since 1899 some fifty publications have appeared, some of them of course old papers under new names. Sakamaki's otherwise excellent study—which deserves imitation in the other fields of the foreign language press of Hawaii—is deficient in its treatment of this turnover and the reasons for it.

Most of the newspapers now contain English sections, and at least the *Nippu Jiji*, the *Hawaii Hochi*, and the *Hawaii Mainichi* are making a bid for the patronage of the younger Japanese effectively literate only in English. The *Hochi* in particular, because of its outstanding editorial policies, may attract readers of other nationalities and so make the transition from a foreign language publication to an ordinary American newspaper.

[12] K. K. Kawakami, *Asia at the Door*, p. 233, quoted by Ichihashi, *op. cit.*, p. 223; interview with Eisaku Tokimasa, Japanese *kamaaina* Christian minister; files of the *Nippu Jiji* for the period of the language school controversy.

[13] *A Survey of Education in Hawaii*, Chap. III.

ence, and because they were the storm center of a protracted controversy (1919 to 1927) which greatly affected the attitudes of the Japanese and American groups toward each other and which confirmed the Japanese in appreciation of their ethnic solidarity. Briefly stated, the attitude of the Americans (Haoles and those with like views) immediately after the World War came to be that the language schools in general were detrimental to the health and learning capacity of the students who also attended the English schools,[14] and that in the Japanese schools the emphasis upon the Japanese language, and still more upon Japanese history, manners, ethics, and political ideals, was distinctly dangerous to the state.[15] A few went so far as to resent the speaking of Japanese at all by the American-born generation;[16] if the parents could not understand their children's English, that was the parents' fault for not learning the language of the country in which they had made their homes. The majority, however, had a more sensible grasp of the realities of a plantation economy and were opposed to the Japanese language schools on political rather than on linguistic grounds. That the feeling against the language schools was decidedly political, based on apprehension of Japan, was shown by the scant attention paid the Korean and Chinese schools and by the lack of protest against the use of other languages not taught in the schools.[17]

Many Japanese were opposed from the beginning to any legis-

[14]This was not proved so far as the quality of school work is concerned. See Henry Butler Schwartz, "A Study of the Effect of Attendance at Language Schools Upon Success in the McKinley High School," *Hawaii Educational Review*, October, 1925, pp. 30-31, 40-41; also Percival M. Symonds, "The Effect of Attendance at Chinese Language Schools on Ability with the English Language," *The Journal of Applied Psychology*, December, 1924, pp. 411-423.

[15]*A Survey of Education in Hawaii, loc. cit.*, also pp. 42-44.

[16]In about 1927, as the present writer and a Part-Hawaiian schoolteacher were walking past two Japanese teachers in the public schools, they heard the latter conversing in Japanese.

"Look at those Japanese, always talking their own language. Why can't they speak English? It's only the Japanese who stick to their own language that way," said the Part-Hawaiian.

"But," this writer countered, "you and your friends talk Hawaiian among yourselves."

"Oh, that's *different.*"

[17]Personal observation; the general tenor of newspaper articles; also Symonds, *loc. cit.* [Now also see Kum Pui Lai, "The Natural History of the Chinese Language School in Hawaii" (M.A. thesis, University of Hawaii, 1935).—*Ed.*]

lation affecting the language schools, holding that it was an affront to their nationality as well as a potential danger to the maintenance of the language schools. When it became apparent that the legislation was indeed designed practically to eliminate rather than to regulate the schools, the majority of the Japanese community came to support either actively or tacitly the fight against the legislation, headed by Fred Makino of the *Hawaii Hochi*. The legal battle ended in a victory for the Japanese, and the language schools of all three Oriental groups were safe. The Japanese had got rid of the obeisance to the Emperor's picture and some other features objected to by the Americans; the revised textbooks containing American and local instead of Japanese material had been widely adopted; while at last some members of the American community were coming to recognize the stabilizing influence of the language schools in maintaining the familial and social morale of the Oriental groups.[18]

The controversy for several years split the Japanese into two factions, one wishing to conciliate the Americans by agreeing to the legislation, the other "to stand up for their rights," that is, for the independence of their ethnic group from cultural control by the Americans. Rival language schools were established in several communities. The Americans were suspicious of the motives of the Japanese and doubted the loyalty of the litigants to American institutions; the Japanese were exasperated by the dominating attitude of the Americans. Harsh language was used on both sides, but rather more by the Americans. This controversy is the only instance in Hawaiian history of a conflict having difference of language as its ostensible cause.[19]

The *Survey* of 1920 estimated that about 20,200 children, or 98 percent of the enrollment of the Japanese in the public schools, were attending the language schools. The estimate of the Department of Public Instruction for 1925, when the litigation was going on, was 75 percent of the enrollment of Japa-

[18]Romanzo Adams, "Functions of the Language Schools in Hawaii," *The Friend*, XCV, 178-179, 197-198.

[19]For a history of the Japanese language schools in Hawaii, see Koichi G. Harada, "A Survey of the Japanese Language Schools in Hawaii" (M.A. thesis, University of Hawaii); see especially pp. 59-76 for a summary of the language school controversy.

nese in the public schools. By the end of 1931 the proportion was about 87 percent. No other group has been so successful in retaining the bulk of its youth in language schools. At the same time it is noticeable that the Japanese enrollment is slowly declining, while the Chinese is increasing. No study has been made of the effectiveness of the teaching of the schools in Hawaii, but Ichihashi states concerning the schools in the United States that, "generally speaking, these schools have been unsuccessful in their primary function—that of imparting a knowledge of the Japanese language to American-born children of Japanese descent—although they have done remarkably well in some other respects, in particular, in teaching proper conduct and behavior. . . . Bilingual success is yet to be at all generally achieved."[20] The present writer's own observation is that average graduates of the eight-year course can read and write *hiragana* syllabary pretty well, but they do not know enough ideographs to read an ordinary newspaper article. The language school does, however, undoubtedly help maintain the level of spoken Japanese at something better than a broken and ungrammatical lingo, and exceptional individuals, thanks to it, become really literate in Japanese.

The speech of the language schools is a compromise between the standard Tokyo dialect and the Japanese speech of Hawaii, the latter being a mixture of elements from the several local dialects that may be called the Hawaiian colonial dialect of Japanese. An interesting by-product of the mixture of dialects in Hawaii is the aspiration of the Okinawans, who speak decidedly variant dialects, to use standard Japanese. Thus the Okinawan, to become a fully functioning member of his prefectural group, of the greater Japanese group, and of the whole Island community, has to be trilingual.

Several factors besides the press, the schools, the temples, and the national spirit favor the retention of the Japanese language by the second generation. The Japanese constitute the largest group in the Islands and are so widespread that hardly a locality does not have enough Japanese to keep up their

[20]Ichihashi, *op. cit.*, pp. 331-332.

distinctive social life, with such institutions as the *kenjinkai* (prefectural associations), the young people's associations, the language school, and the Buddhist temple. While not a wealthy group, the Japanese have sufficient income to support these institutions and to maintain a considerable cultural life. Although there is a large preponderance of males, there are between 23,000 and 25,000 families and little outmarriage, so that the need for keeping Japanese as a language within the family has been keenly felt. Until recently the Japanese have not felt themselves established in Hawaii, and the permanent or temporary removal of Japanese to the home country is still sufficient to make it worthwhile to maintain home ties. Every year a number of Japanese children and youths go to Japan for education. Considerable commerce is carried on between Japan and Hawaii, and some Hawaiian-born Japanese hope to earn a livelihood in this field.

The language schools and young people's associations have for many years presented amateur theatricals, which call for a correct speaking knowledge of Japanese. Troupes from Japan also tour the Islands and are keenly appreciated even by persons of the third generation. Since 1931 Japanese talking pictures of a standard which compares favorably with that of American pictures have been shown and, according to some observers, are of considerable importance in helping the Island-born Japanese to maintain a good speaking knowledge of their parental language.[21]

Probably because their concentration in large numbers in ghetto-like districts, little in touch with English-speakers, makes acquaintance with that language superfluous, especially for women, the Japanese in Hawaii have been slower to learn English than have the Japanese on the West Coast. They do not, however, lag markedly behind the other Island groups.[22] The

[21]Walter Mihata, who is connected with the distribution of these pictures, estimates that they are seen and heard by about 15,000 Japanese, mostly of Hawaiian birth. The silent pictures, too, contributed to keeping up the Japanese tongue, for they were accompanied by a running fire of explanations and impersonations spoken by a monologist called a *benshi*.

[22]Millis, *The Japanese Problem in the United States*, quoted by Ichihashi, *op. cit.*, p. 213; also see Table 13. Since about 1890, of course, all Island-bred children have passed through the English language schools.

TABLE 15

ILLITERACY AMONG THE KOREANS IN HAWAII, 1910-1930,
BY AGE AND SEX GROUPS[a]

Groups	Percentages		
	1910	1920	1930
Total Koreans	25.9	17.3	17.6
Total Males	23.8	15.7	18.5
Total Females	46.1	22.4	15.7
10-14 years	4.5	0.4	0.1
15-19 years	15.0	3.1	none
20-24 years	22.2	15.6	0.8
25-34 years	23.6	11.6	15.6
35-44 years	29.6	16.4	19.3
45-54 years	37.8	23.8	24.5
55-64 years	—	37.9	35.4
65 and over	—	—	50.6

Data from U. S. Census of 1910, Vol. III, p. 1173; U. S. Census of 1930, *Population—Hawaii*, Table 9.

[a]Totals include those 10 years of age and over.

Japanese language, at least as a spoken tongue, will probably be one of the last, if not the very last, to be displaced by English.

Koreans. The Koreans differ from the other two Oriental groups in being few and scattered; they resemble them in their respect for literacy (being upon arrival the most highly literate of the three groups, probably in the syllabic writing only), and in national spirit and strong familism. (Illiteracy among the Koreans in Hawaii is shown in Table 15.) The Koreans make up for their paucity of numbers by an almost fierce national pride and separatism and by their organization in clubs (usually concerned with aspirations for Korean independence) and in Protestant churches. Their language schools have declined, doubtless because the small communities could not afford their support. In 1920 the *Survey* estimated Korean language school attendance at 800, although only 729 Koreans were enrolled in the English schools; in 1932 there were only 522 students, 24 percent of the English school enrollment.[23] The Koreans have

[23]*A Survey of Education in Hawaii*, p. 112; *Report* of 1932.

maintained at least one newspaper since 1909 or 1910 (now the weekly *Korean National Herald*), and for about thirteen years had a *Korean Pacific Magazine.*

Although the Koreans arrived within the present century and include a large number of unmarried elderly males, according to the census of 1930 they spoke English in the same proportion as the earlier established Japanese. This is undoubtedly due to the scattered distribution of their small group. To the same cause is attributed the unusually good mastery of English which the Korean students are often said to have.[24]

There is very little or no commercial contact between Hawaii and Korea, and few Koreans have wealth enough to allow them to visit their homeland. Korean students do not return to Korea to continue their studies. It is probable that, in spite of the nationalistic spirit of the Koreans, theirs will be the first Oriental language to succumb before the English tongue in Hawaii.

Portuguese. The Portuguese in several respects form a contrast to the three Oriental nationalities. Literacy is not valued by the Portuguese peasantry, and Portugal is one of the least literate of European countries. Some decades ago it was said that "there is many a family in which the parents not only do not encourage the children to write and read, but deliberately forbid it, considering that the drawbacks of education exceed its advantages."[25] In 1890, at the time of the Portuguese immigration to Hawaii, 67.6 percent of the Portuguese males and 83.5 percent of the females over seven years of age were returned as illiterate, and the percentage has not fallen greatly since. In 1917, of men and women applying for marriage licenses in the Atlantic islands, only 38.9 percent of the former and 45.12 percent of the latter signed their names.[26] Illiteracy among the Portuguese of Hawaii is shown in Table 16.

[24]Romanzo Adams, *The Peoples of Hawaii*, rev. ed., p. 46.

[25]Bell, *Portugal of the Portuguese*, p. 71, quoted in Donald R. Taft, *Two Portuguese Communities in New England*, p. 83. [For a more current account of Portuguese in Hawaii, see Edgar C. Knowlton, Jr., "Portuguese in Hawaii," *Kentucky Foreign Language Quarterly*, VII, No. 4 (December, 1960), 212-218.—*Ed.*]

[26]Taft, *op. cit.*, pp. 79-80.

TABLE 16

ILLITERACY AMONG THE PORTUGUESE IN HAWAII, 1890-1930,
BY AGE AND SEX GROUPS

Groups	Percentages				
	1890[a]	1896[b]	1910[c]	1920	1930
Total Portuguese	70.38	72.16	35.4	18.9	9.7
Total Males		69.7	33.3	16.8	7.9
Total Females		76.3	37.7	21.1	11.5
10-14 years			4.1	1.2	0.4
15-19 years			16.6	4.3	1.3
20-24 years			22.2	5.9	1.5
25-34 years			37.1	11.2	3.8
35-44 years			59.8	27.7	9.2
45-54 years			75.2	52.8	23.4
55-64 years			78.6	68.4	48.1
65 and over			84.4	78.2	66.4

Data from Hawaiian Census of 1890, p. 34; Hawaiian Census of 1896, pp. 95, 97, Table VII; U. S. Census of 1910, Vol. III, p. 1173; U. S. Census of 1930, *Population—Hawaii*, Table 9.

[a]Over 6 years of age.

[b]Over 6 years of age. Percentages of illiterate males and females obtained as for Table 12.

[c]The Portuguese were not separately returned in the census of 1900.

This illiteracy and lack of attention to education has affected the linguistic development of the Portuguese in various ways. A group lacking, as it does, strong attachment to its literary tongue will not go to much trouble to preserve its spoken tongue. If its language survives, the survival will be because of its use within the family and because of lack of enterprise in learning the native language, rather than because the group has willed that its mother tongue survive. On the other hand, it is probable that the group's level of accuracy in the use of the native language will not be so high as that of groups which place a higher value upon book learning. The Oriental groups have a much better school record than the Portuguese, and especially the latter's contemporary and comparable nationality, the Chinese, has a larger proportion of educated persons. It is very likely, but not certain, that the level of English among the

Chinese who speak that tongue is higher than among the Portuguese who speak it.

The Portuguese have never set themselves in earnest to build up a language school system, although there were sporadic attempts to maintain schools between 1889 and 1913, and a professor of Portuguese history and language was sent (bootlessly) to Hawaii by the Portuguese government in 1917.[27] The Roman Catholic churches, which most of the Portuguese attend, have been served by priests from the Low Countries and have a polyglot congregation, so that th church societies such as that of the Holy Name are not wholly Portuguese in membership and have not the conservative effect upon the use of the immigrant tongue that the Korean and Chinese Protestant churches have—let alone the Buddhist temples. Three mutual aid societies have done much to maintain the Portuguese ethnic spirit, but what direct influence they have had upon the conservation of the language is not known.

The decline of the Portuguese language is partially reflected by the history of its press. The first newspaper was *O Luso Hawaiiano*, a weekly, established in 1886. It merged in 1891 with the *Aurora Hawaiiana* (1888) to form *A União Lusitana-Hawaiiana*. A few competitors entered the field and died, leaving only two small Hilo papers, *A Setta* and *O Facho* (both about 1905). *O Luso* (*A União*) was closed about 1923; *A Setta* about 1920; *O Facho*, which had in 1923 about 750 subscribers, was the last to go, about 1927.[28]

The Portuguese have been more scattered through the rural and plantation districts than have the Chinese, yet they have not been concentrated anywhere in such numbers as the Japanese. In the cities, assimilation, both racial and social, with the Haoles has been easier for them than for any other group except the Caucasian-Hawaiians. As their sex distribution has been from the beginning the most nearly normal of any immigrant group (it is now entirely normal), there has been no isolated

[27]*Report* of 1920, pp. 26-27; newspaper files, 1917.

[28]*Hawaiian Annual; Honolulu Directory; Ayer's Directory*. [For a history of the Portuguese press in Hawaii, now see Edgar Knowlton, "The Portuguese Language Press of Hawaii," *Social Process in Hawaii*, XXIV (1960), 89-99.—*Ed.*]

body of old men to keep up the exclusive use of the mother tongue. The Portuguese are noteworthy for their intermarriages; and intermarriage both presupposes and encourages the use of a common language—English. For these reasons only 5.1 percent of the Portuguese in 1930 were unable to speak English, while of the comparable Chinese 22.4 percent could not speak English.

Commercial relations with the Portuguese islands are non-existent, and extremely few Portuguese revisit them, because of the great time and expense incurred as compared with that necessary for a trip to the Orient. Feelings of attachment to and pride in their mother country seem to be singularly lacking in the Portuguese.

For all these reasons, the Portuguese language seems likely to pass from general use with the death of the last of the largely illiterate immigrant generation.

Puerto Ricans and *Spanish*. Both these groups are in some respect miniature editions of the Portuguese. There are two very important differences, however: these two groups are considerably later arrivals and they are very small, scattered, and disorganized. There exist among them no organizations of any kind (unless possibly the Puerto Rican Civic Club) which tend to conserve their native speech. Even the factor of family organization and needs is absent, for both groups outmarry remarkably—the Spanish more than they inmarry. Illiteracy among the Spanish was somewhat less than among the Portuguese, and among the Puerto Ricans somewhat greater, but in all three groups there has been no feeling for the glories of the mother tongue (see Tables 17, 18, and 19). The only reason that the Spanish and Puerto Ricans have not become wholly bilingual seems to be their lack of education and of economic opportunity and ambition. This is particularly noticeable among the Puerto Ricans; although they came to Hawaii six to thirteen years before the Spanish, 21 percent of them were unable to speak English in 1930, as against 11.4 percent of the Spanish (see Table 13).

Few Puerto Ricans and Spanish have learned to speak good English, and probably for some years their level of English will

TABLE 17

ILLITERACY AMONG THE SPANISH IN HAWAII, 1910-1930,
BY AGE AND SEX GROUPS

Groups	Percentages		
	1910	1920	1930
Total Spanish	49.6	31.5	16.4
Total Males	40.5	24.0	12.6
Total Females	62.1	40.3	20.6
10-14 years	12.9	5.6	1.8
15-19 years	56.8	19.5	5.0
20-24 years	—	29.4	4.8
25-34 years	61.5	40.5	14.0
35-44 years	58.7	54.0	—
45-54 years	59.2	43.1	—
55-64 years	—	—	—
65 and over	—	—	—

Data from U. S. Census of 1910, Vol. III, p. 1173; U. S. Census of 1930, *Population—Hawaii,* Table 9.

TABLE 18

ILLITERACY AMONG THE PUERTO RICANS IN HAWAII, 1910-1930,
BY AGE AND SEX GROUPS

Groups	Percentages		
	1910	1920	1930
Total Puerto Ricans	73.2	46.7	32.0
Total Males	70.2	45.6	31.6
Total Females	78.2	48.2	32.5
10-14 years	25.5	6.0	2.9
15-19 years	61.0	19.5	7.8
20-24 years	80.5	37.5	13.1
25-34 years	79.7	59.1	26.9
35-44 years	82.1	69.0	54.4
45-54 years	84.1	76.4	70.0
55-64 years	85.6	85.6	79.8
65 and over	—	—	86.2

Data from U. S. Census of 1910, Vol. III, p. 1173; U. S. Census of 1930, *Population—Hawaii,* Table 9.

TABLE 19

ILLITERACY IN PUERTO RICO, 1899 and 1910

	1899	1910
Both sexes	79.6	66.5
Males	75.9	62.3
Females	83.2	70.7

Data from U. S. Census of 1910, Vol. III, p. 1204.

be low; but neither will the Spanish language be likely to continue in use among the second generation.

Filipinos. The three factors most affecting the linguistic assimilation of this nationality are its large size, its short residence in Hawaii, and the attitude of transiency held by a large number of its members. The failure of many Filipinos to regard Hawaii as their home and to look forward to settlement here is largely the result of their abnormal age and sex distribution: according to the 1930 census, 74.4 percent of the Filipino population were males fifteen years of age and over, and about 53.6 percent were of the most footloose age, twenty to thirty-four years; only 34.9 percent of the males were married—and most of their wives were still in the Philippines. The great majority of the Filipinos, especially since the Great Depression reached Hawaii (1930), have not been able to regard themselves as permanent settlers in the Hawaiian Islands; therefore they have not had any reason to give up the use of their native tongue. Furthermore, the large number of Filipinos to be found in most localities and their social isolation from the rest of the population have made it possible for them to maintain the use of their own languages. Their short residence has not allowed most of them time either to learn the English language well or to become part of the Hawaiian Island community.

Protestant missions working among the Filipinos have used their languages, but the only institutions arising among the Filipinos themselves which have perpetuated the use of their

TABLE 20

ILLITERACY AMONG THE FILIPINOS IN HAWAII, 1920-1930,
BY AGE AND SEX GROUPS[a]

| Groups | Percentages | |
	1920	1930
Total Filipinos	46.7	38.5
Total Males	44.0	37.8
Total Females	62.1	43.8
10-14 years	7.3	1.0
15-19 years	38.0	23.7
20-24 years	44.3	36.8
25-34 years	47.9	40.5
35-44 years	56.0	45.2
45-54 years	64.9	54.6
55-64 years	65.7	62.7
65 and over	—	69.9

Data from U. S. Census of 1930, *Population—Hawaii*, Table 9.

[a]Totals include those 10 years of age and over.

vernacular are clubs and the Filipino language press. The former, because of the prestige and status which membership and office-holding give to individuals, have been important. The latter have been of little importance, and only by the use of extraneous methods such as popularity contests have the newspapers been able to maintain their subscription lists at the survival point. Mortality has been great among them. The first to appear was probably *The Sword*, issued at Hilo by Pablo Manlapit in 1913. At present there are eight Filipino papers, mostly in the Ilocano tongue, published in Hawaii. In appraising the Filipino press, the illiteracy of nearly half the Filipinos must be borne in mind (see Table 20).[29]

[29]Much of the information about the Filipinos was gained from Roman R. Cariaga in an interview in 1934; some data on the press is from the *Honolulu Directory*.

Cariaga wrote a thesis called "The Filipinos in Hawaii" (M.A. thesis, University of Hawaii) in 1936, which was published a year later as *The Filipinos in Hawaii: Economic and Social Conditions, 1906-1936.—Ed.*

Certain circumstances make it probable that those Filipinos who do remain as permanent settlers in Hawaii will lose their languages rather speedily, in spite of the large size and the isolation of their nationality. They have settled in a community which uses the English language more and in a purer form than did the Hawaii of 1852 to 1910, to which the other groups emigrated. The Filipinos are divided into two main language groups, the Ilocanos and Bisayans, which must use an inter-language. Both Tagalog and English are now in use as lingua francas, but English has the advantages of superior prestige in Hawaii and of general use in the community. Whether because of differences of language among themselves or because some Filipinos have learned Spanish and English as interlanguages, the Filipinos are generally credited with the ability to "catch on" to English better than members of other nationalities in the Islands. The Filipinos appear to have as a distinct social trait a love of novelty not apparent among most other ethnic groups in Hawaii. The younger Filipinos speak English among themselves as something smart to do, something which shows their clever-ness and assimilative ability. Some immigrants have already learned English in the Philippines. There are not the same strong commercial and cultural bonds between the Philippine Islands and the Hawaiian Islands as between Hawaii and China and Japan. It is not surprising, therefore, that Filipino periodicals appear entirely or partly in English and that the home language is becoming English.

Other immigrant groups. The experience of the other groups of European immigrants has not differed greatly from that of isolated immigrants in other parts of America. Members of most of them—the Russians are perhaps an exception—were able to find a place among the English-speaking Haoles, at least in their second generation. Thrown into close contact with Anglo-Saxons, often educating their children in select and private schools, they were not in great contact with the creole dialect and would make a conscious effort to avoid its use. The children of the German, Scandinavian, and French settlers speak just as good English as do the children of the Americans and British.

The Russians and the Germans are the only groups that were able to retain their linguistic individuality for any length of time. Unfortunately the present writer has practically no information about the Russians except that they once maintained a tiny language school. The Germans settled in large numbers on the Isenbergs' plantation at Lihue, where employers as well as employees were German-speaking and German-reading. The Isenbergs maintained an efficient school, at first purely German and later bilingual, from 1882 to 1918. Another language school, connected with the German Lutheran church, was maintained in Honolulu from 1901 to 1917. German newspapers were subscribed for and the German ethnic spirit fostered. Only the violent war spirit of the Americans and British during the World War practically extinguished German separate group life and completed the decline of the German language in Hawaii. Because the Germans are Haoles, the children and grandchildren of the immigrants skipped the creole dialect stage and speak Standard English.[30]

Hawaiians and Part-Hawaiians. Not an immigrant but an aboriginal group, the Hawaiians were exposed to the creole dialect on somewhat the same basis as the immigrants. They, like the immigrants, were largely a dominated group. They had often to learn English in the situation of plantation laborers under English-speaking foremen; their culture, like those of the immigrants, has been succumbing before American culture. Therefore, especially since the passing of the use of Hawaiian as a language of instruction, the use of the vernacular has been declining. The decline was noticeable in 1893: "Lately they [the natives] are losing the ability to speak Hawaiian well, by reason of their minds being directed in school to English."[31] But at that time some nine-tenths of the pure Hawaiians and six-tenths of the Part-Hawaiians were still literate in the native

[30]*Report* of 1920, p. 26; Bernhard Hörmann, "The Germans in Hawaii" (M.A. thesis, University of Hawaii), esp. pp. 95-97, 100, 116-117, 120, 139, 150; Kuykendall and Gill, *Hawaii in the World War,* pp. 435-440.

[31]Testimony of Chief Justice A. F. Judd, p. 1650 of the "Blount Report." See for other material on language conditions of that date, pp. 221, 269-270, 507, 1633, 1648, and for 1884, p. 91.

language.[32]   With the passing of the generation which had learned its Hawaiian in the schools as well as in the family, the decline has been both rapid and on a large scale. This is mirrored in the collapse of the vernacular press. Since the turn of the century some two dozen Hawaiian publications have appeared, usually for only a short time; by 1920 most of them had gone; and in 1934 only two small newspapers were left, *Ka Hoku o Hawaii* (Hilo) and *Ke Alakai o Hawaii* (Honolulu), and perhaps one or two religious publications.[33]

Until 1882 the Hawaiian group was the largest in the country and until about 1910 had the advantage of relatively large numbers. Now it is but a small group relative to the others and, in addition, is distributed rather evenly throughout Hawaii, a condition not conducive to group solidarity.

Even more important as affecting the loss of the language is the intermarriage of the Hawaiians with other groups and the growth of Asiatic-Hawaiian and Caucasian-Hawaiian groups, the members of which frequently grow up speaking English as their home language. The larger the Part-Hawaiian groups have grown, the more rapid progress has monolingualism made among them, to the detriment of the Hawaiian language.

In spite of all these handicaps, the Hawaiian tongue is still far from extinct. Two forces have been most influential in keeping it alive and still considerably removed from the state of a mere patois: politics and the Protestant and Mormon churches. Even at the present time a candidate's chances of being elected are stronger if he can make a good campaign speech in Hawaiian, and twenty years ago it was practically necessary for him to be able to do so. The churches have for many years been the chief centers of Hawaiian cultural life, and the Hawaiian in which services are conducted is naturally the best that the minister and congregation can use, drawing its sustenance from the Hawaiian translation of the Bible.

The social, and to some extent the spatial, isolation of some of the pure Hawaiian population has also played a considerable

[32]Hawaiian Census of 1896.
[33]*Honolulu Directory* and *Hawaiian Annual.*

part in keeping the vernacular alive. The sentimental attachment of the native and some of the Haole population to the language has been a minor factor. Besides, if the Hawaiian language should disappear, what would the song writers do! There appears to be in Honolulu a movement for the preservation of the native culture which, among other things, is paying attention to the teaching of Hawaiian (in George Mossman's school, as well as at McKinley High School and the University of Hawaii).[34]

But as a literary tongue the Hawaiian language seems to be doomed. Very little interest is taken in it except by elderly and middle-aged persons; only an unexpected strong nativistic movement could save it. On the other hand, as a household tongue, a patois, it seems likely to endure for at least two generations more.

The quality of the English which has taken the place of the native language on the tongues of the Hawaiians differs with their economic level and social connections. On the whole it has been pretty much on the creole dialect level for the pure Hawaiians; but for the Part-Hawaiians, especially those with Haole fathers, it has been more nearly standard. A considerable proportion of the Part-Hawaiians and some pure Hawaiians speak as good English as is heard anywhere. This is a direct consequence of their having usually been reared in an extra-plantation environment.

SUMMARY

It has been seen that circumstances in Hawaii have been favorable for the retention of the identity of the several immigrant groups and of the native Hawaiians, and consequently of their languages, until the present time, and that the identity of several of these groups will probably continue well into the future. By the time the first group will have lost its native

---

[34]In this connection, the work of such scholars as Samuel H. Elbert, Mary Kawena Pukui, and Samuel A. Keala should be mentioned. See, for example: Elbert and Keala, *Conversational Hawaiian*; Pukui and Elbert, *Hawaiian-English Dictionary*; Pukui and Elbert, *English-Hawaiian Dictionary*; and Pukui and Elbert, *Place Names of Hawaii.—Ed.*

tongue (if no further immigration upsets the development), creole dialect will have passed into a colloquial colonial dialect of American English, and an increasing number of the non-Haole population of Hawaii will be speaking either Standard American English or a passable form of the colloquial dialect. Thus, because the ethnic communities of Hawaii have not been living in a typical plantation area, the creole dialect has subsisted as supplementary to the immigrant tongues and to the Hawaiian, instead of supplanting them.

Chapter 6

HOW A COLONIAL
DIALECT AROSE FROM
THE CREOLE DIALECT

In Chapter 3 it was seen that the Hawaiian language declined in importance and in number of speakers before the English language. From the *hapa haole* of whaling days, and influenced by several other languages, a creole dialect suited to plantation economy arose, as was traced in Chapter 4. In Chapter 5 the reasons for the persistence of the various non-English tongues in the face of the competition of English, both "pidgin" and standard, have been described. This chapter will show how the creole dialect, after having failed to drive out its competitors, is also failing to maintain itself as a stable type of speech, and is on the contrary passing into a colloquial colonial dialect of the English language.

Much misapprehension of the problem of the nature of English speech in Hawaii and of the allied problem of how to improve its quality is caused by the use of the term "pidgin English" to cover all deviations from that somewhat indeterminate ideal, Standard English. In other words, "pidgin English" is used to cover almost the whole extent of the language mastery continuum of the alien groups in Hawaii. It is not unknown for a youngster to hold as "pidgin" slang of the purest American water, simply because it deviates from the standard set up by his teachers. Most deviations from "good English" are "pidgin English"; ergo, any deviation from "good English" must be "pidgin English."

I propose to show that this continuum of so-called "pidgin English" should be split in two, the ruder, makeshift half deserving the name of creole dialect which has already been assigned it, while the other more refined and adequate half has passed beyond that stage. It may be objected that such a division is almost impossible to make, that the popular nomenclature is right at least in calling attention to a continuum of English which departs markedly from any standard of English usage. But the continuum of deviations from Standard English extends beyond the continuum generally termed "pidgin." Furthermore, even within the "pidgin" continuum, a division must be made if the problem of speech change is to be analyzed. The contention of this writer, that the speech of the majority of Hawaiian-bred Islanders is not creole speech, is based on the definition of the creole dialect as a makeshift language. As spoken by many, probably by a considerable majority, of these younger people, the so-called "pidgin" is no longer makeshift, at least to any great extent, and should no longer be classified under creole dialect or be given the same name as makeshift speech receives.

But where shall a line be drawn between makeshift and non-makeshift speech, between adequate and inadequate mastery of a language? Whole populations speak creole languages among themselves and originate a folk literature in them, as do the Haitians, Mauritians, and Southern Negroes. Is their speech inadequate? The adequacy of a speech must be measured, in part by the range of ideas which can be expressed in it, in part by mutual intelligibility when it is juxtaposed with the standard language of large masses of the population.

Expression of ideas is chiefly a matter of being able to handle a large vocabulary. Given a large enough vocabulary or the possibility of its invention, any type of speech is able to stand any strain of expression placed upon it. The syntactical structure of the language does not matter. The Taal of the Boers was originally the despised colonial dialect of uneducated farmers, men who had neither subtle ideas nor the vocabulary to express them had they possessed any. Now, Afrikaans under the pressure of a new nationalism and widespread education has discovered new riches of expression, and its simplified syntax, at one time as condemned as the "pidgin" syntax of the Hawaiian schoolboy, is boasted as superior to the more complex structure of Holland Dutch.[1] If it is true that just as subtle, complex, and abstract ideas can be communicated in Afrikaans as in Dutch, the former tongue, which at one time possessed something of the nature of a makeshift language, is just as efficient an instrument as the latter. And theoretically any makeshift language can similarly be expanded to take on the stature of an adequate language. Probably Haitian Creole French is to some extent going through such a process of expansion. Such, however, is not usually the fate of makeshift languages, which normally are designed to express the simplest ideas, and which have alongside them standard languages, rich in prestige, which those who wish to express complicated ideas will learn to use.

There is also the factor of mutual intelligibility. While the makeshift tongue is still less adequate an instrument of expression than the mother, standard tongue, if the former is so different from the latter as to be hardly understood, either because of its poverty of vocabulary or because of its structure of sound and syntax, then its makeshift character is accentuated.

In short, a makeshift speech, and creole speech in particular, unless and until it makes for itself an exceptional place as an accepted language through enlarging its vocabulary and fixing (relatively speaking) its structure, exists only in reference to a previously existing, more flexible, richer, more exact language from which it has in most part been formed. If a speaker of the speech continuum which comprises both the standard and the

---

[1]T. J. Haarhoff, "Afrikaans in National Life," in *Coming of Age*; Adriaan J. Barnouw, *Language and Race Problems in South Africa*.

creole language is unable, because of his scanty vocabulary and defective command of syntax, to understand the speech of a man who uses the accepted standard language and in turn to make that man understand him with tolerable ease, we consider him as using a makeshift speech. This is the condition in which most of the first generation of immigrants to Hawaii find themselves. They can understand many complicated matters if great pains are taken to explain them in the roundabout and inexact language which a scanty vocabulary makes necessary; but even simple matters put in straightforward English are unintelligible, and many ideas quite transcend the possibilities of their creole speech.[2] But if, on the contrary, the speaker of the speech continuum in question can understand anything within his intellectual capacity which is said in ordinary standard speech, and can reply so as to be readily understood, no matter how faulty his language, he has passed beyond the confines of creole, i.e., makeshift, speech. That is the situation of most of the people educated in the English schools of Hawaii. This is not to say that their speech is free from limitations, that it is entirely adequate to communication with the speakers of Standard English. But the speech of all meagerly educated and of all young people is to a certain extent makeshift speech. The persistence of creole elements in the dialect of the Hawaiian-bred generations does not make it creole dialect. We must compare the speech of the average English-educated person with, on the one hand, the speech of his "pidgin"-speaking parents and, on the other, with the speech of persons of the same age and economic levels in America—not with the speech of, say, Haole university graduates—in order to get a clear picture of the advance in the adequacy of English used.

At this point a name must be found for the speech in question. That it is a local dialect is evident. It is confined to the Hawaiian Islands, and though on the whole it is confined also to certain nationalities and classes, it is beginning to tinge the speech of the whole English-speaking community. Its chief features are common to people of all descents who speak it,

[2]See Margaret Mead, *Growing Up in New Guinea*, pp. 304-306, for the limitations of Beach-la-mar pidgin.

much more so than the chief features of the creole dialect are common to people of all nationalities who speak the grosser half of the continuum. Probably its features are more fixed than those of the creole dialect. "Pidgin English" having been discarded, no succinct term for it is apparent. Reinecke and Tokimasa in their article[3] termed it "the English dialect of Hawaii"; T. T. Waterman has referred to it as "Insular English."[4] It may perhaps, without fear of confusion with a wider range of speech, be referred to in this study as "Hawaiian Island dialect" or simply "Island dialect."

That it is a colonial dialect is also evident, though not so clearly. As will be shown in the following analysis, it draws from several American and British sources and is besides influenced by several foreign languages; thus it has the melting pot characteristics of a colonial dialect. It possesses features which are, on the whole, those of Standard American English rather than an extension of any local American dialect and possesses other features which are quite distinctive of Hawaii alone. It is the result of a transplanting of American and other English-speaking stock to a new environment, a semi-tropical American colony. It possesses all the characteristics of a colonial dialect as defined in Chapter 2. Therefore it may, in contradistinction to the creole dialect, be referred to as the *colonial dialect* of Hawaii.[5]

Before analyzing further the structure and functions of the colonial dialect, let us return to see why the creole dialect has failed to hold its own, failed to become fixed as the common speech of the Island population, and why the colonial dialect is taking its place.

In many countries the creole speech has persisted for centuries and has taken on a fixed structure and vocabulary which allow a literature of a sort to be produced in or translated

[3]"The English Dialect of Hawaii," *American Speech*, February and April, 1934, pp. 48-58, 122-131.

[4]"Insular English," *Hawaii Educational Review*, February, 1930, pp. 145-146, 161-165.

[5]Either "the colonial dialect," "Hawaiian Island dialect," "Island dialect," "the local dialect," "the colloquial dialect," or any like term may be taken as a reference to the same entity, the better-than-makeshift speech of the younger folk of Hawaii.

into it. But it is obvious that these countries are among those which do not supply education for the creole-speaking masses. The tribal Bush Negroes of Surinam, the Haitian peasantry, and the blacks of Jamaica and those on the South Carolina Sea Islands who spoke the Gullah dialect are examples of populations which had no opportunity to speak anything other than a creole language, and so have done the best they could with it. In countries where the population is given some educational and economic opportunities and where contact with people speaking a standard language is possible, the creole speech will begin to lose its distinctive features and become more and more like the standard language. Such is the case in Mauritius,[6] and probably if literature were available, it would be found that such has been the case in other British plantation colonies. Such is the case in Hawaii.

Two elements enter into the transformation of the creole dialect, the same that were given as determining the formation of the creole dialect: the extent of economic opportunities and the extent of educational facilities. The latter factor is to be taken in its broadest sense, as including not only the schools but also the English language press, the radio, the talking pictures, and advantages of transportation which break down the isolation of remote non-English-speaking communities and encourage conversational contacts with those speaking good English.

It has already been pointed out that Hawaii afforded opportunities outside the plantation. These have been discussed in detail by Andrew W. Lind[7] and need not be reviewed. Suffice it to point out that they have been varied and abundant, and have brought with them many of the social advantages incident upon attainment to the ranks of skilled labor, the merchant class, and the professions in any part of the United States, this in spite of and to some extent qualified by the racial stratification existing in Hawaii. It has also been pointed out that the

[6]Otto Jespersen, *Language,* p. 228; communications from Mauritian school officials.

[7]"Occupational Trends among Immigrant Groups in Hawaii," *Social Forces,* December, 1928, pp. 290-299.

majority of the first generation immigrants were unable to aspire to a very high economic position; nevertheless, the number of those succeeding was sufficient to arouse a great deal of emulation among the Hawaiian-bred generations. But increasingly the preferred occupations have been open only to those who have a command of fluent and fairly accurate English. This is the more true now that the opportunities of the entrepreneur are diminishing and the average ambitious non-Haole must look for success and prestige to the professions and to white-collar positions with the already established firms rather than to founding a business of his own. Among the occupations within the reach of an industrious and able non-Haole, the English requirements are growing steadily higher. It is obvious that a good grasp of English is necessary in the learned professions and in teaching, as well as in certain types of office and clerical work. But in many personal service occupations and skilled trades as well, a fluent and considerable, if not grammatically perfect, knowledge of English is advantageous and sometimes necessary. The demand for adequate English goes hand in hand with economic and social rewards for its command—up to a certain point.

Without the facilities for education afforded by a free public school system supplemented by a number of fairly inexpensive private schools, the economic opportunities would have been much smaller for the non-Haole population, and only a favored few, able to afford private education, would have been able to learn enough English to enable them to fill preferred positions. Hawaii, by carrying out the American ideal of offering to all a free primary education and to some a cheap secondary education, has made it possible for the youth to learn with considerable accuracy and fluency a speech approaching Standard English, even though many are unable to use it as a ladder in attaining a higher economic level.

The influence of the schools can hardly be overestimated. In many country districts the schoolmaster was the only person able to use English with some approach to adequacy. The linguistic limitations of the teaching force have been touched upon. It is evident that many of the Hawaiians and Part-Hawaiians and some of the Portuguese and others among the early English language school teachers did not speak the English tongue correctly. But they did at least speak it with comparative adequacy; they were not speaking "pidgin." They insisted upon a certain minimum of intelligibility and accuracy in the speech of their pupils, and though this minimum in some cases was low indeed, it was at least a step above the makeshift language of the parents and at best within reasonable reach of Standard English. Thanks to the schools, districts with a very small, sometimes a negligible Haole population have been able to produce young men and women who have succeeded in the professions and business. The whole influence of the school system has been toward raising the standard of the English spoken in Hawaii. The date by which any linguistic community has entered an appreciable number of its children in the schools is the date that marks the beginning of the transformation of that community from a group speaking the creole dialect to a group using the colonial dialect. As soon as all of a group has passed through the English schools, the hold of the creole dialect on that group will be almost wholly broken.[8]

The transformative power of the schools was strengthened by their use as an agent of Americanization (or, before annexation, the practically synonymous Hawaiianization). The "American" language[9] has constantly been held up by many teachers and other Americans as the only medium of communication appropriate and indeed possible for good American citizens. Its mastery therefore has been emphasized as a patriotic duty as well as an economic asset. It is not unusual at the present time to find Japanese and other Island-bred schoolchildren who assert that English is the only language which they ought to use; the use of their parental language appears to them as a necessity forced upon them by disagreeable circumstances. This senti-

[8]For the processes by which the schools helped create the Island dialect, see pp. 267-284; for some limitations of the schools, see pp. 304-308.

[9]A House Resolution introduced in 1921 by Representative Kupihea requested Congress to substitute in the Organic Act "American language" for "English language" as the official language of the territory. (See Hawaiian *House Journal,* April 22, 1921.)

ment might not necessarily do more than substitute a makeshift English for an adequate foreign language, but the requirements of the higher grades of the schools have largely averted this possibility.

Since about 1922 the radio and since 1929 the talking pictures have supplemented the schools in teaching the people of Hawaii oral English. Their influence is so recent that it cannot yet be appraised. All that can be said is that thousands of people whose ears have been attuned only to the creole dialect and to the Island dialect now have to understand the various American and British accents heard over the radio and especially at the talkies.[10] It is anticipated that these instruments will be of great service in standardizing the speech of the larger countries. Although in Hawaii their influence will therefore be felt most forcibly among speakers of the colonial dialect, they can still be of some slight use in encouraging the learning of better English by those speaking the creole dialect.

The increased mobility of the population is also a factor of some importance in breaking down the creole speech. The young people who speak the creole dialect are very frequently those who have lived all their lives in some isolated place such as the Hawaiian beach villages of West Hawaii and Puna, or have been restricted to a narrow circle of their own nationality as so many young women have been—taken from school at fifteen or younger, kept at home in a plantation camp, married young, and then still kept at home. The accessibility of places and the mobility of the population of Hawaii in 1900 and in 1934 may be compared to show how much less likely isolation has continuously become.

Lastly, it must be borne in mind that the number of English-

[10]A clipping from the *Honolulu Star-Bulletin* (some time in 1933) illustrates amusingly the impact of outside pronunciation upon speakers of the colonial dialect.

"Members of the cast of 'The Office Girl' speak their lines in polished English fashion. . . . And in this connection, we overheard an amusing conversation between two Honolulu oriental youths as they were leaving the theater. One of them made this remark to his companion:

"'Gee, the skinny fella could dance good, eh? But, e-e-e, the funny kind talk those fellas got! Hard to understand, eh? Must be foreign, those guys.'

"Apparently these fans did not realize that they had been listening to English.— J.P."

speaking people with whom communication is possible and even necessary has been increasing rapidly. A Hawaiian, for example, or a Portuguese, upon completing six years in an English language school in the early 1890's, would be in contact with only a narrow circle of English-speaking folk, and they would for the most part speak "pidgin"; thus he would be under constant pressure to slide back into the use of makeshift English and would forget much of what he had learned. The Hawaiian or Portuguese youth who today completes eight years of school is thrown, much of his time, into contact with people who speak fairly good dialectal English or even Standard English, and although he may at times speak very pronounced "pidgin," he is much less likely to relapse into makeshift English of the baldest sort than was his father in *his* time.

Notwithstanding the influence of the school system and of the economic opportunities and social mobility of Hawaii in breaking down the use of the creole dialect, it is still not unusual to find Hawaiian-born Islanders who have passed through the English schools speaking a makeshift English, usually along with their parental tongue. Why is this possible? The reasons have for the most part already been mentioned casually from a negative angle in the discussion of the passage from creole to colonial dialect. The continued influx of immigrants, going first to the plantation with its linguistic traditions and affording in due time a continuous supply of schoolchildren accustomed to their parental language and "pidgin," is the most obvious cause of the maintenance of the creole dialect. Hawaii has never had the leisure to digest linguistically its immigrant population.

The necessity of communication between parents and children, and between young folk of one nationality and old folk of another, has already been discussed at some length. If the children do not have an adequate command of their mother tongue, they must communicate with their parents in makeshift English, and so they fix in themselves the habit of its use. The necessities of communication with parents and older people is the excuse most frequently offered by the young for their use of imperfect English. It is, of course, possible to keep "pidgin English" and Standard English compartmentalized as separate languages, as some Haoles do, but when the language of one's associates is dialectal English strongly affected by the "pidgin," this is difficult to do, and there is a constant temptation to revert completely to makeshift English.

In spite of the economic opportunities of Hawaii and the demand for a knowledge of English which accompanies these opportunities, there remain many jobs which require but a meager command of any language. In many cases these occupations are filled by those persons whose meager educational background or restricted environment have already made it difficult for them to learn English adequately. In spite of a number of years in the schools, many persons learn little and forget part of that little. Their occupational duties do not demand or encourage even adequate, let alone grammatical, English, and in some cases definitely discourage its use. In contact with immigrants who can speak nothing better than very makeshift English, sometimes working under foremen or employers who prefer to speak the creole dialect because of its master-to-servant connotations, they slip into a type of English but little removed in lack of suppleness and accuracy from that spoken by their parents before them. Thus the creole dialect is perpetuated in the second and third generations by the uneducated, the intellectually lazy, the isolated, and some of the economically and socially unfortunate.

SUMMARY

The term "pidgin English" is used to cover almost the whole language mastery continuum of the alien groups in Hawaii. But much of the so-called "pidgin" has passed beyond the makeshift stage and has become a fairly adequate colonial dialect. (Degree of intelligibility and accuracy as compared with the standard language may be taken as the criteria of the dividing line between makeshift and non-makeshift "pidgin.") The Island dialect was refined from the creole dialect chiefly because of the educational facilities and economic opportunities of Hawaii, a country of marginal colonial type, with many American institutions and economic characteristics. The increase in the number of English-speaking persons has also diminished the field of the creole dialect. Nevertheless, the environment is not favorable enough to the use of adequate English for "pidgin" (creole) to disappear entirely from use among those born in the Islands.

Chapter 7

THE NATURE, FUNCTIONS, AND PROBABLE FUTURE OF THE COLONIAL DIALECT OF HAWAII

NATURE OF THE COLONIAL DIALECT

A general idea of the nature of the Hawaiian Island dialect and of the reasons for its formation has been given in the preceding chapter. In this chapter its nature will be more carefully examined and some of its functions pointed out.

The Island dialect, it has been shown, fits the definition of a colonial dialect—which is a local dialect. But it has not been emphasized sufficiently that the dialect in question is also to some extent a class dialect, being chiefly confined to a certain part of the population of the Hawaiian Islands. In their article, the present writer and his collaborator defined it thus:

> The Hawaiian Island Dialect is the variety of American English spoken by a majority of the English-speakers of Hawaii up to forty years of age; these are for the most part bilingual and comprise the bulk of the product of the public schools of Hawaii since its annexation to America. This class includes those who immigrated in childhood, the second generation or children of immigrants, the third generation of some groups, most of the young native Hawaiians, a few *haoles* or *whites* (not of Latin descent),

156

and, allowing for their national intonation, some adult immigrants, most of them Filipinos.[1]

The majority referred to is of course that part of the younger non-Haole population who have improved their speech beyond the makeshift stage, but not to such a point that it would be acceptable as Standard American English. This excludes most of the Haoles, for an unusually large proportion of the civilian Haole population is well educated and speaks careful English; some, of course, speak with traces of various dialects current outside Hawaii. A few of the Hawaiian-born Haoles do speak the local dialect, and it is a common observation not only that many of the local Haole youth are acquiring the intonation and certain other features of the dialect in their playground associations, but that even newcomers to the Islands are likely to drop into certain Island habits of speech, especially if they are isolated in the rural districts. A considerable number of the Haoles can use the dialect, or rank "pidgin" for that matter, when they wish to do so. The vocabulary of all Haoles is, moreover, sprinkled with localisms and with Hawaiian loan words. It is likely that in the course of time certain expressions thoroughly peculiar to the local dialectal speech will find a place in the standard speech of the Islands alongside the unavoidable localisms and loan words which are now part of both dialect and standard speech.[2] But, for the present, the dialect is quite distinctly a speech of non-Haoles, a speech which follows racial and social if not economic class lines. The younger generation with which the present writer comes into contact in the schools does not always differentiate between its own speech and that of its parents (though it is coming

[1]Reinecke and Tokimasa, "The English Dialect of Hawaii," *American Speech,* February, 1934, pp. 51-52.

[2]An example of such a localism is *gulch,* which covers what would in the western United States be called "canyons." Other thoroughly typical localisms are *calabash cousin* (distant relative) and *Waikiki itch* (athlete's foot). The loan words are so numerous as to need no illustration. As an example of the receptivity of the local standard speech to dialectal influence, we may take the popularity of the slang phrase *go for broke,* i.e., act recklessly. *Yama beer* (home brew) was dialectal slang at first, but is now good journalese.

increasingly to do so), but it does differentiate between its own speech and that of the Haoles.

Almost unnecessary to say, the number of speakers of the local dialect can only be approximated in a very rough fashion by examining the age distribution of each nationality. In his article referred to above, the present writer estimated it at 200,000 to 225,000 out of a total population of about 380,000.[3] A more detailed estimate on the basis of the 1930 census statistics gives of the 301,514 returned as English-speaking at that date from 130,000 to 160,000 as the probable number of dialect-speakers; about 55,000—perhaps too generous an estimate—as speaking Standard English or an approximation thereto; and the remaining 85,000 to 115,000 as users of the creole dialect, or as speaking English with a decided foreign accent. Of the total, 55,036 are non-Haole children five years or less of age, and their allocation makes considerable difference in the figures. Of these children, the present writer has surmised that at least one-half learn the local dialect at home from parents or elder brothers and sisters, and the rest learn creole dialect from parents. The basis of the following estimate of dialect speakers is so nearly guesswork that the writer is almost ashamed to present the figures which form it.

	Approximately
All races (excluding Other Caucasians), birth to 5 years x .5	27,418
All races (excluding Other Caucasians), 6-9 years	34,390
Hawaiians, 10-34 years, x .9	8,803
Hawaiians, 35-54 years, x .1	531
Caucasian-Hawaiians, 10-54 years, x .5	3,282
Asiatic-Hawaiians, 10-34 years, x .8	3,438
Asiatic-Hawaiians, 35-54 years, x .5	274
Portuguese (excluding foreign-born), 10-29 years x .9	8,993
Portuguese (excluding foreign-born), 30-64 years x .1	354
Puerto Ricans, 10-24 years, x .75	1,732
Spanish, 10-24 years, x .75	352
Chinese, 10-29 years (excluding foreign-born), x .9	6,939
Chinese, 30-44 years, x .2	798
Japanese, 10-29 years, x .5	24,191
Japanese, 29-44 years, x .1	2,244

[3]Reinecke and Tokimasa, *op. cit.,* p. 52.

Koreans, 10-24 years (excluding half the foreign-born), x .9	1,302
Filipinos, 10-34 years, x .1	4,246
Negroes and Others, over 10 years, x .5	266
Other Caucasians, x .05	2,245
Total	131,898

An analysis of the Hawaiian Island dialect from a purely linguistic point of view does not fall within the scope of this study. For as complete a picture of its peculiarities as is at present available, the reader is referred to the studies by Reinecke and Tokimasa, Mowat, King, and Richmond. At this point, however, enough description must be introduced to show the truly dialectal nature of the colloquial speech of the Hawaiian Islands, to aid in distinguishing it from the creole dialect, and to help cast light upon its origin.

Within the continuum of Island speech marked off as reasonably adequate and hence entitled to the epithet of true regional dialect, there is so much variation that it is hard to say what its characteristics are. For while a university student, for instance, may readily be recognized as an Islander by the cadence and pronunciation of his speech, the sentences which he forms differ remarkably from those uttered by a stevedore or truckdriver, or from those of his younger brother in the elementary grades. Reinecke and Tokimasa described rather loosely the highly colloquial dialect of the comparatively uneducated, or of the better educated in their unbraced hours. For the most part the dialect may be taken as the "common speech" of Mencken, the "popular English" and "vulgar English" of Krapp,[4] a highly colloquial dialect unacceptable as good colloquial American even when certain allowances are made for local peculiarities. But in its higher reaches, where the peculiarities heard may be loosely subsumed under "accent" rather than under syntax and accidence, the dialect is acceptable as good colloquial speech, at least in most situations. While remembering that the dialect forms a very widely inclusive entity, we may concentrate our attention upon the "popular" or "common" speech.

[4]Henry L. Mencken, *The American Language*, "The Common Speech"; George Philip Krapp, *The Knowledge of English*.

Essentially the dialect is American English strongly influenced by the creole dialect or "pidgin English." Most of its sentences take essentially the usual English syntax. Americanisms and typical American vulgarisms and grammatical errors are found in large numbers, whereas typical Briticisms are not at all common. (This reflects the numerical predominance of the Americans and, still more, their educational and general cultural predominance.) Some of the sentences, however, take a highly concise "pidgin"-like form, in which the word order is not truly English in the whole sentence and in which much of the sense depends upon the tone of utterance. This is combined with a general lopping-off of particles, articles, and unimportant words generally. Thus the sentence, "Nine lose already" (i.e., "I've lost nine already") borders upon the pure creole dialect. "Last year a Rockne was changed" (i.e., "Last year he changed his car for a Rockne") illustrates what may be dubbed median dialect, differing from both "pidgin" and the more circumlocutory and exact Standard English. "*Only what* the Filipinos know is *to fool around* young women," with its two dialectal idioms but falling within the general syntax of English and not distinguished by the cutting out of any element, is another step nearer Standard English. Finally, "Are 'you going?" uttered with stress on the second and a rise-fall intonation on the third word of the question (while in normal American conversation the last word would receive the stress and be spoken with a rising intonation), betrays its dialectal character only to the ear.

Because the colonial dialect forms part of the same speech continuum with the creole dialect, it is difficult to single out any speech element and say, "This is 'pidgin,'" or, "That is dialect." The aggregate of the speech elements, not any single element, is what matters in drawing the distinction between the two forms of communication. Nevertheless, there are some forms which the casual hearer can recognize as confined to one or the other. A short time ago, the present writer heard a Korean woman describe the reputation of a physician: "All same too muchie good speak" ("They say he's very good"). Such a locution would never occur in the Island dialect. "Everybody speak him *toooo* good" would be a more likely form in which the most careless speakers of the dialect would express the idea. It is doubtful if even so extremely lopped a sentence as, "Bell us no?" ("That's the bell ringing for us, no?") could be paralleled in "pidgin" as spoken by the older generation. While the dialect differs as markedly from the Standard English as the creole dialect does, the two unorthodox forms of speech differ just as markedly from each other.

For the most part, however, dialect speakers have come to the point where they are aware of many complicated idioms of English grammar. It is in trying to handle these idioms, of which the "pidgin"-speaking immigrant is still unaware, that the younger folk fall into many errors, some of which have become fixed in the dialect. These give it, especially in writing, an aspect of foreignness, just as one would expect of a language largely but still imperfectly apprehended by people of foreign background. Such a form as "We *went and see,*" quite unacceptable as Standard English, is beyond the capacities of the creole dialect, but the combination of preterit plus *and* plus infinitive (or present) is characteristic of Island English. Examples might be multiplied indefinitely.[5]

The dialect has its own chromatic accent, intonation, and general tempo of utterance, all very distinct from those of any other dialect of English which the present writer has heard spoken, and somewhat distinct from those of the Island creole. It has its own syllabic and word stress for a considerable number of words and, partly due to this stress but in larger part to inability to pronounce English sounds, its own pronunciation of very many words. Certain sound substitutions are very common in Hawaii. The same substitutions, Olive Day Mowat has shown, occur in several large cities of the United States

---

[5]Jespersen has pointed out (*Language,* p. 234) that slang is different from make-shift language, the former being the result of verbal exuberance, the latter of verbal poverty. Therefore, makeshift language can have no slang, but locutions from makeshift language can be adopted as slang by speakers of a fuller dialect. The Hawaiian Island dialect, though inferior in richness of slang to the speech of most parts of the mainland, does possess a considerable slang vocabulary. *Go for broke* (act recklessly), *catch the cream* (get the best of anything), and *suck wind* (go hungry) will suffice as examples. (Some of these are from a collection of Kamehameha Boys' School locutions compiled by Kilmer Moe about 1931.)

containing a large foreign population, but no study has been made to show the relative frequency of given substitutions in Hawaii and elsewhere, or the causes of these substitutions.[6] Distinctive misapprehensions of the English vocabulary and syntactical forms, and solecisms in the use of words and grammatical forms, are far commoner in the dialect than are new coinages and added meanings. The rich heritage of Hawaiian and other loan words has saved the Islanders the trouble of many coinages. Nevertheless there are some. *Papaia-bird* (the linnet), *Hilo grass* (Paspalum conjugatum), *banana wagon* (a yellow station wagon), *calabash cousin* (a distant relative) are examples. The passion fruit or *lemiwai* is sometimes called *poker* or *poka* in Island pronunciation—it is said, from the sharp *pock!* or popping sound heard when the brittle rind is broken. Taken all together, these peculiarities of accent (in the broadest sense), pronunciation, syntax, and vocabulary suffice to mark off the Hawaiian Island colonial dialect from the English spoken in any other part of the world. The dialect, at a grade above the "pidgin" creole, is recognized both by its speakers and by others as a distinct form of English speech.

One element of the dialect has been reserved for discussion here, so important is it in illuminating the origin of the dialect; that is the strong influence which youthful speakers have had upon it. Almost all the present speakers of the dialect are children, youths, or middle-aged people, not elderly people. Probably a majority of them are under the age of twenty. The

---

[6]The processes by which such a word as the technical term in the game of marbles, *slynopau* [ˌslainʌ'pau], arose are clear: *Slide* was pronounced *sly* through failure to articulate the final *d*; the youngster was in effect calling out, "Slide, no *pau*," ("The marble has slipped from my hand accidentally, I'm not *pau* or through my play, I'm entitled to another shot"), and because of the strong stress placed upon *pau*, the *o* of *no* has become [ʌ]. But what of such a sound substitution as that found in the use of *slumper* for *swamper* (assistant)?

Concerning the relative frequency (but not the causes) of these substitutions in Hawaii, now see Etta Cynthia Larry, "A Study of the Sounds of the English Language as Spoken by Five Racial Groups in the Hawaiian Islands" (Ph.D. dissertation, Columbia University, 1942).—*Ed.*

For a description of suprasegmental features in the English of Hawaii, now see Ralph Vanderslice and Laura Shun Pierson, "Prosodic Features of Hawaiian English," *The Quarterly Journal of Speech*, LIII, No. 2 (April, 1967), 156-166.—*Ed.*

children's influence must of necessity be very great. Although in learning a new language the reactions of adults are much the same as those of infants learning to speak,[7] there is some difference between the influence of adults and that of children upon the forms of speech. Roughly speaking, the creole dialect was the product of adults, chiefly of adult males, while the colonial dialect is largely the product of little children and adolescents. Certain vocal peculiarities mark the speech of children, among them exuberant, explosive utterance, loudness of voice, excessive prolongation of vowel sounds to show stress of feeling, and in general a lack of the restraint found in adult utterance. These appear in some degree in the colonial dialect.

It has been shown that the dialect owed its origin to the economic possibilities and necessities of Hawaii and to the educational opportunities which went hand in hand with the economic development. These were the *raisons d'être* of the dialect; but the milieu in which it arose was primarily the school. (This is not to deny that the shop, the office, and other places of employment helped form the dialect.) The problem of how the children of Hawaii have come to speak the dialect is closely bound up with the problem of when the dialect was formed.

It may almost be said that, just as the day when the first members of a nationality began trading with or working for an English-speaking Haole was the day on which that nationality began acquiring the creole dialect, so the day on which its first members began attending an English school was the day on which it began to acquire the colonial dialect. But this statement must be somewhat qualified. The first students to learn English were Hawaiian, and within a generation of the advent of the missionaries there were also Hawaiian teachers of English. The Hawaiian school child, habitually using his vernacular, learned English quite as a foreign language; he received his knowledge of that language filtered through his own Hawaiian verbal categories and often through his teacher's as well, exactly as the American student today usually receives his high school

[7]Discussed by Jespersen, *op. cit.*, Book II.

French. It was into such an atmosphere of language-learning, accentuated by the rapid change made in the language of instruction during the 1870's and 1880's, that the Portuguese and Oriental children from 1880 on were introduced. In the schools, we may suppose, an English strongly colored with Hawaiianisms was spoken—when the teacher was about and could forbid the use of the vernacular. The newcomers received their English filtered through the Hawaiian speech processes as well as through their own parental languages, which were for a considerable time the only ones that they heard at home. As time wore on, two developments occurred: in the homes "pidgin English" began to be heard, and on the schoolgrounds the linguistic processes of the immigrants became important enough, through the increase in enrollment of foreigners, to influence in turn the native children. Unfortunately, there is no way of determining for any of the nationalities when either development became important; we can only guess. For a while, however—and this is the qualification to the statement at the beginning of this paragraph—the children were reabsorbed into communities where the parental language was almost the sole means of communication, and where the English spoken (if not "pidgin") remained colored almost wholly by the original language of the student. That is, there were Portuguese graduates, Chinese graduates, and Hawaiian graduates of the English language schools, but they spoke Portuguese-English, Chinese-English, and Hawaiian-English respectively, not yet a composite dialectal Island English.

Probably not before 1890 was "pidgin English" spoken extensively enough in the homes for many children, with the exception of the Haoles and some Caucasian-Hawaiians, to have had an opportunity to learn English before entering school. It is unusual for parents to use in their homes a language which they have acquired, usually imperfectly, in adult life. Therefore, for every nationality there was a period during which its children entered the schools for the most part ignorant of even the scantiest English. The Minister of Public Instruction reported in 1886:

The Hawaiian with his twelve-lettered alphabet, the Chinese boy who knows not the sound of *r*, the Japanese whose vernacular has no *l*, the German and the Portuguese who are ignorant of the vocal or aspirate *th*—all these nationalities go to the same school on Monday, the opening day, not one able to communicate with the other, and the teacher speaking an entirely different language from any of his pupils.[8]

Apparently even after the "pidgin" was in widespread use, the parental tongue continued to be the home language of children as well as of parents. The *Survey of Education in Hawaii* made in 1920 stated that:

Investigations which have been made disclose the fact that when children of the islands enter school at 6 or 7 years of age, not more than 2 or 3 per cent can speak the English language. The teachers, therefore, from the very first, before they can begin where teachers in the States begin, must establish a working vocabulary to serve as a medium of communication between teacher and child. In many instances it is weeks before the teacher can make herself understood.[9]

This statement, however, may be taken as highly exaggerated. For the *Survey* further stated: "Enrolled in the schools of the islands, public and private, there are only about 2,400 children with whom the English language is native; 1,500 of these are in private schools and 900 in public schools."[10] But the *Report* of the Department of Public Instruction for 1920 gives the number of Anglo-Saxon children in the private schools as 1,267, or 16.75 percent of the total, and in the public schools as 1,186, or 2.9 percent of the total. It is absurd to believe that none of the other Haole children, none of the Part-Hawaiian and Chinese and Portuguese children, could speak good English when they entered school about 1920. And many more children of several nationalities, as any Islander can recall, spoke passable dialect or at least fluent "pidgin." Indeed, Romanzo Adams observed as early as June, 1924, that:

[8]*Report* of 1886, p. 7.

[9]P. 37.

[10]P. 38. It is the writer's opinion that all estimates in the *Survey* must be taken with caution.

It appears that at the present time nearly all Honolulu children and considerable numbers in the country districts enter school with some knowledge of English. They get it from older brothers and sisters or from the play group. . . . Where the various language groups live apart from each other there is less progress.[11]

"One very observant principal in Honolulu," wrote Adams, "told me that there had been clearly observable improvement in the language status of beginners in the last five years." Even so, for some time previous to 1920 there must have been a considerable number who entered school able to converse in English. Of those speaking dialectal English, a good many are between the ages of thirty and forty. Therefore, it is the present writer's deduction that the use of the English language at home and on the playgrounds of many neighborhoods became fairly general in the second decade of the present century, and that by 1925 the children were (with allowance due their age) as a general thing speaking the Island dialect rather than very broken creole. This estimate allows about one generation (1876 to 1900) for the formation of the creole dialect and its diffusion to the point that the average child would have more or less opportunity of hearing it from neighbors and possibly from elder children who had passed through the English schools, and another generation (1900 to 1925) for the schools to have bred a generation of young people to whom English was no longer a foreign language and who would use dialectal English in conversation with the younger children. The use of the Island dialect must have been under way by 1900 and well established by 1910.

The process by which a child came to speak dialectal Island English may be presented in a generalized and somewhat hypothetical manner. Presuming him to be the eldest of his family, the child entered school in the latter years of the nineteenth century, perhaps including in his vocabulary some English loan words in use by his parents and their circle, but with no

11"English in the Public Schools," *Hawaii Educational Review,* May, 1925, pp. 193-194.

conception of the structure of English. He was obliged to guess at the meaning of the teacher's language from the context of the situation[12] or, if unable to do so, to get help from an older child of his own language group—at so early a stage we find the interpreter, though a very immature one. Soon he came to master orally related phrases and whole sentences. This was the point at which his father in the cane field had stopped learning English. But the school child was impelled to go further. In the classroom, no matter if the teacher's knowledge of English was itself imperfect, formal accuracy was aimed at though, alas, rarely hit. The child was taught to read and write. His conversation in classroom situations vis-à-vis the teacher was restricted so as to be tolerably correct. These situations, however, occupy only a small part of the day and are felt to be artificial.

Did the play groups on the schoolground and off reinforce the learning of the English language in the schoolroom? If the student were thrown almost entirely among those of his own language group, probably not. In several schools, chiefly in isolated native communities, the students were drawn from one non-English-speaking nationality. In other schools, however, the student body was very mixed in composition. Nor must it be overlooked that in many Caucasian-Hawaiian families English was, from about 1870 on, being learned side by side with Hawaiian, and that in 1880 perhaps one-tenth of the children enrolled in school (half of them Haoles and half Part-Hawaiians) were already bred to speak English. Though a small minority except in a few select schools, in the schools which they did attend these English-speakers formed a nucleus using the most practicable common language on the schoolground. Members of different groups had to communicate in an interlanguage, which was naturally the tongue taught in the classroom. This was, however, at first interspersed extensively with Hawaiian words, as is evidenced, among other things, by the considerable number of Hawaiian words still used as technical terms in the game of

[12]Bronislaw Malinowski develops the concept of understanding the situational context in order to understand the language used, in Supplement I of *The Meaning of Meaning,* by Ogden and Richards, p. 307.

marbles.[13] The English used was affected by the syntactical and phonetic systems of the languages spoken by the more numerous nationalities and by the "pidgin English" which the child, after a few years in school, was able to understand when he heard it spoken in his neighborhood. Always, however, there was a reference to the richer vocabulary, the more nearly standard syntax, learned in the classroom. Some students, under unfavorable circumstances of late entry, few years' attendance, cultural isolation, or plain lack of capacity, were unable to master English well enough to read and speak it acceptably; they remained at the "pidgin English" stage. But others, probably a majority, were, after leaving school, thrown into situations where their tolerably adequate knowledge of English was useful and maintained. This knowedge was not necessarily dialectal in the sense of approximating the present Island dialect; it was perhaps still English with a marked Chinese, Hawaiian, or other foreign accent. But in some cases it represented a compromise between two or three foreign influences, and it may be regarded as early dialect proper.

The hypothetical first child of a family to enter the English school was in turn able to give linguistic help to his younger brothers and sisters and playmates. At first he was likely to do this only in school situations, while at home and in play groups of his own nationality he spoke only his parental tongue. But as his knowledge of English became wider and more adequate and came to include terms which he was unable to translate into his parental tongue, he was more and more likely to use English in these situations as well. Probably at first his English was far from pure, but it was macaronic, the parental language being interspersed with and corrupted by English words, phrases,

---

13This is a game early introduced and, not being an organized sport like the various ball games, retains its early nomenclature which grew up on the schoolground. Perhaps the game of top-spinning is in the same category. Among the terms used are *muka,* to move one's hand ahead unfairly when shooting a marble; *bua,* a small marble made of clay; *malua,* to put a marble on a *hupupu; hupupu* (fr. Haw. *ho'opu'upu'u*) or *opupu* (fr. Haw. *'ōpu'upu'u*), a small mound of dirt; *kini,* a small steel marble, like a ball bearing; and in top-spinning, *mala,* a term applied to tops which cannot spin because they have become tangled or have been struck by another top. There is also the term *ka,* to turn a rope for skipping.

sentences, and finally longer scraps of discourse. Adams in 1924 noticed that on the playgrounds of the Japanese language schools (where Japanese ought to have been spoken), the general talk was mainly in Japanese, but the technical terms of baseball, etc., were English.[14]

As year after year the student body moved up a grade and some families came to have several children entered at the same time at various levels, a schoolground dialect and universe of discourse grew up. (This can be attested by any teacher of several years' experience.) As the composition of the student body shifted from Hawaiian and Part-Hawaiian to include a large proportion of Portuguese, and then to become one-half Japanese, and as several minor nationalities entered, making the use of English still more imperative, the dialect became composite and relatively homogeneous in structure. This dialect, containing many childish misapprehensions of English and many expressions which have arisen in the environment of the lower grades of school—they may be called puerilisms—was the English which most of the students carried with them when they left school. In many cases it was not improved beyond its schooldays level. If it was improved, the basis of the youth's speech was still this dialect.

By 1910 a considerable number of Hawaiians, Portuguese, and Chinese, who had carried their schoolroom-learned knowledge of English with them into the homes they had founded, in turn had their own children, the "third generation," in the schools. Parents who could speak English, whether learned in school or the creole dialect of the fields and markets, found it necessary to use that language in communicating with some of the children who had acquired the habit of thinking in English and who preferred to speak the language of their school-ground environment. By 1920 the "second generation" parents were numerous enough to be reckoned with in the formation of the dialect, and a few of the "third generation," even among the Japanese, were learning English from both parents and elder

---

[14]So cumulative has the use of English been that a decade later English not only is spoken most of the time on the Japanese school grounds, but is even used in addressing the Japanese teacher in the schoolroom.

brothers and playmates in the home and play groups.[15] But not until about a decade later were the second generation bilingual homes numerous enough, especially among the Japanese, to be a conspicuous factor in the acquisition of English by the children.

The successive influences of the more numerous nationalities can be deduced from Table 9, which gives the school enrollment by descent. The Chinese and Haoles have been predominant or numerous in only a few schools. The Hawaiians (and later the Part-Hawaiians), the Portuguese, and the Japanese in turn have exerted most influence upon the dialect. Especially since 1910 the Japanese pupils have modified the original Hawaiian-Portuguese-English complex very considerably. Certain Japanese idioms are present in the dialect but not in the creole speech.[16] The lesser national groups seem to have had only the influence which comes of the addition to the student body of students of severally incomprehensible speech. The Filipinos, if they remain settled in large numbers, may however come to have considerable influence; already young people sometimes affect the Filipino "accent" as something different and smart. Meanwhile the Japanese, as formerly the Hawaiians, dominate the field of dialect usage, particularly in the most easily affected department, that of intonation and stress.

Mention has been made of the fact that some Filipinos, skipping the "pidgin English" stage, learn the Island dialect.

---

[15]Students emphasize, often vividly, the influence of their friends in teaching them strongly dialectal English. Two extracts from the papers of intermediate school students illustrate their analysis of the matter.

"Another reason why so many of us use pidgin English [i.e., dialectal English] is because, when we were young pidgin English was our good English. We heard our friend speaking it, so we followed without thinking about the future. Now that we are big we can't break the habit of using pidgin English." (N. A., female freshman, Honokaa School, 1934.)

"A child at the age of four, starting to learn to speak, hears his elder brothers and sisters, and also his neighbors speaking Pidgin English. A child at this age does not know whether Pidgin English is wrong or correct, so long if the Pidgin English he uses means what he want he uses it and thus form a habit." (T. F., male freshman, 1934, Honokaa School.)

[16]Two may be cited: *cut the neck*, or *cut the neck off*, for *cut the head off*; and the use of *no?*, an anglicization of *ne* (eh?), at frequent intervals between phrases to hold the attention of the listener.

Formerly the young adult immigrant had as a general rule only those who spoke makeshift English to associate with, but the Filipinos often associate socially and in sports with Island-born persons, from whom they acquire the dialect. True, they usually speak it with a marked Filipino accent, and one may perhaps refer to a Filipino-English mixed dialect as distinct from the Island dialect; but the difference is often slight between the two varieties of speech.

Among all nationalities are found a large number who speak the dialect with enough trace of their ancestral tongues to be distinguished as belonging to a certain linguistic community. This number, however, is constantly diminishing. Some localities, too, especially those which have had a population strongly Hawaiian or Portuguese, may be distinguished to a very slight degree by the influence of one national speech. Local differences are due to other reasons as well: to the degree of contact with influences found most strongly in the cities, to the length of residence of the groups living in each locality, to educational and cultural facilities. Thus the speech of Honolulu is commonly considered better than that of most rural sections, because there have been more Haoles in Honolulu, the urban dwellers have on the average resided in Hawaii longer and spoken English longer than the rural dwellers, the occupations there demand the use of better English, and probably the city schools are better than the rural.[17] Similarly, Hilo is said to have better English than the rural districts of Hawaii County. From school to school, also, the level of English varies, depending upon the skill of the teaching force and the economic and cultural status of the strata from which the students come—and upon the prejudices of the observer.

So much has been said recently about the influence of the non-white teachers in the formation of their pupils' English that

[17]"One principal was most emphatic in her opinion that the so called pidgin English of Honolulu was entirely different from that of our local plantations. She felt that the Hawaiian predominates here while Oriental idioms are more noticeable in Honolulu." (From a letter from Bernice E. L. Hundley, Supervising Principal of Kauai, March 4, 1934.) Other persons, however, are just as emphatic in denying any difference in kind, and most or any difference in degree, between urban and rural dialectal English.

attention may at this point be recalled to the composition of the teaching force, 1890 to 1934, as shown in Table 10. From this it is to be seen that, until the Island dialect was in pretty general use, only Haole and Hawaiian teachers were employed in numbers large enough to have much influence upon the children's speech. Even the Portuguese influence from the teacher's desk was negligible until about two decades ago, and it never has been great. The influence of Oriental teachers, of which most is heard, could not have been appreciably felt until 1918 at the earliest. Now, with the Japanese, Chinese, and Koreans occupying approximately one-third of the teaching positions, and these chiefly in the first nine grades, their speech influence may well be felt; but that is a matter of the present and future, not of the formation, of the dialect.

More important than the influence of the national tongues upon the Island dialect are the influences of the immediate situation and of the educational level of the speaker. The average person in any community changes from less formal to more formal colloquial speech when he turns from intercourse with intimates in a free and easy situation to intercourse with less intimate acquaintances (especially if they be recognized as well educated or otherwise of high status) in a situation which requires the maintenance of dignity and reserve by the respective parties. Furthermore, the degree of adaptation to the situation which one can make is dependent largely upon one's education in the language spoken. A well-educated person has ordinarily a greater range of command of his oral language than has a poorly educated person; he can play high and play low with it at will, though not so low as he might wish under some circumstances. And when the written language must be used, obviously the educated person has a still greater advantage in understanding and using its more formal and complex categories. Yet all literates, no matter what their degree of education, will endeavor to use their best language in writing. To use the words of a Japanese student: "If a student is writing a story, he will try to use his best English. Also, when talking to some well-educated people he will speak his best and correct

English. But in talking with his friends he will not use good English."[18]

In a milieu such as that of Hawaii, where definite levels of English discourse are more clearly recognized and correlated with class and to some extent with racial differences than in most parts of America, the shift from very informal and careless, not to say vulgar, dialectal speech to what approximates Standard American English takes on a decided social significance. Thus we are led to a consideration of the functions of the Island dialect.

FUNCTIONS OF THE COLONIAL DIALECT

The purely linguistic function of the dialect is simple and easily dismissed; it is to furnish a medium of communication, in accord with the linguistic traditions of the Hawaiian Islands, which will be understood not only by the dialect-speakers themselves but, for the most part, by the speakers of Standard English on the one hand and by the speakers of the creole language on the other—in short, to serve as a liaison between the creole dialect and Standard English.[19]

But a dialect is more than an objective means of communication; it is a mark of locality, often of class, and is the source of a strong emotional bond among its speakers. "The home speech," writes Sapir, is "associated with kinship ties and with the earliest emotional experiences of the individual."[20] The primary home language of most English-speaking persons in Hawaii, it is true, has not been the Island dialect but a foreign tongue. But most persons who have learned to speak the local dialect have, as has been pointed out, learned it early in life, from brothers and sisters or intimate playmates, either in home

[18]From an essay by I. N., male freshman, Honokaa School, 1934.

[19]The use of the local dialect is often justified on this ground. To quote young people who use it:

"I associate with many people of different nationalities and many of them know but little of the english language. In order to make them understand what I say, I have to speak pidgin english." (S. Y., male, Honokaa.)

"He [a student] gose home and talk to his mother in Japanese language, but when he dosen't know how to explan in Japanese he would explan in English and Japanese language, that form a pidgin English." (K. O., male, Honokaa.)

[20]"Dialect," *Encyclopaedia of the Social Sciences*, V, 125-126.

surroundings or in school and playground surroundings, whose emotional impress upon the child is almost equally deep. The standard language, on the other hand, is commonly learned (if at all) later in life, in the somewhat artificial surroundings of the classroom. It is not often the speech of one's intimate associates; so, however desirable it may be culturally, it has few emotional connotations.

Normally, whoever speaks one's language is accepted as belonging to one's group, as a person whom one can meet and converse with freely. Even though he may differ from one in class, manners, and tastes, one's initial reaction toward him is usually to accept him as a member of the we-group—to be sure, often a very unintimate we-group. This tendency is especially marked wherever several language groups occupy the same region. When the speakers of a dialect actually, through the circumstances of their education, race, and social position, do form a we-group, their language becomes a doubly strong emotional bond. Not only are their words the same, but their universe of discourse and their emotional background are the same. Such is the situation in Hawaii, where the dialect is spoken by the "New Americans" who have shared the same schooling, who occupy on the whole a like economic and social position, and who are marked off by differences of "race" from the majority of those speaking the standard tongue. Though the generalization is not by any means wholly true, the Haole is thought of as speaking Standard English, the non-Haole as speaking dialect. "A haole," wrote a Japanese student a few years ago, "is a person who speaks a beautiful language." And while racial lines are not drawn so closely and invidiously in Hawaii as in most parts of the world, the non-Haole is generally strongly aware of the gap in appearance, manners, and often in economic status and opportunities, between himself and the Haole. The dialect is, then, a mark of the we-group for the younger non-Haoles. As a class dialect and a local dialect in one, it emphasizes doubly the consciousness of kind.

Parenthetically it may be remarked that this function of the Hawaiian Island dialect is not likely to be one of the functions of the creole dialect, which is learned late in life and then as a makeshift speech. The father has only a utilitarian attachment to his form of "pidgin," as his emotional attachment is to his native tongue.

This does not mean that the speaker of the local dialect is necessarily conscious of his attachment to his own form of speech. As far as he thinks of it consciously, he is apt not to prize it. For reasons that will be dwelt on below, he has had drilled into him in school and elsewhere the excellence of "good English" and the defects of "pidgin," until he is likely to feel somewhat apologetic for retaining his dialect. He therefore frequently holds forth on the need for overcoming the use of "pidgin" and sometimes insists that his younger sisters and brothers and his children speak better English than he has used. Comparatively few arrive at the point of consciously justifying their dialect and pointing out that most Americans and British have their own dialects and "speak just as bad English as we do."

This depreciation of the dialect by its speakers, by the very persons to whom it is an emotional bond, arises from the low estimation in which the dialect is held by most of the influential people of Hawaii, the educated and refined people, those most patently American, and in particular by the school teachers. And this low estimation springs from a three-fold root: the mere fact of its being dialect, its origin in the creole "pidgin," and its present social and racial associations.

Most dialects in countries where there are standard literary languages in use suffer from discrimination. Sapir writes:

The speakers of local dialects begin to be ashamed of their peculiar forms of speech because these have not the prestige value of the standard-ized language; and finally the illusion is created of a primary language, belonging to the large area which is the territory of a nation or nationality, and of the many local forms of speech as uncultured or degenerated variants of the primary norm. . . . In the main, markedly dialectic peculi-arities have been looked upon as symbols of inferiority of status. . . .[21]

[21]*Ibid.,* pp. 124, 126.

And in this case, the local dialect *is* quite patently an uncultured and degenerated variant of a primary norm, namely, American English.

The makeshift "pidgin" was even more manifestly so, and therefore was regarded with amused contempt by those who spoke acceptable English. Now the products of the American schools speak a dialect called by the same name and sharing many of the characteristics of the old "pidgin," and their speech too is regarded with contempt, but not so much with amusement. They, it is often felt, are blamable for not learning Standard English, which they are presumed to have had the opportunity to learn.

Meanwhile, those who speak Standard English or some dialect different from that of Hawaii feel proud of their ability, sometimes hard won, and of their connection with outside linguistic traditions, and are correspondingly contemptuous of the speaking of Island dialect. In part their attitude arises from a real appreciation of the English tongue, reinforced by a realization of the difficulties that language has had in establishing itself in Hawaii and of the danger that it faces of being greatly changed. Those who did not originally speak Standard English, or whose ethnic communities do not, feel the superiority which most persons feel upon standing out from their fellows as masters of a difficult accomplishment. But, as a large proportion and probably a majority of the speakers of Standard English are Haoles, there is added to their sentiment of superiority a feeling that the dialect is properly the speech of a different race, of folk of an inferior social status, and of very imperfectly assimilated Americans.

The contempt in which the larger part of the speakers of Standard English hold the local dialect, and their attitude of superiority, have caused several connected. though not wholly consistent reactions among the speakers of the dialect, who may be said on the whole to stand very much on the defensive regarding their speech. The dialect-speaker usually first becomes aware of differences in English speech level in the classroom, where his English is contrasted with that of his teacher. There he learns that the teacher disapproves more or less strongly of some of the locutions which he has been using in innocence of their not being universally acceptable. The further he goes in school and in life outside school, the more carefully is he taught to draw distinctions between the acceptable and the unacceptable in his speech in situations where he must communicate with educated people. As he usually desires to carry on intercourse with them to his own advantage and to avoid the stigma of inferiority which his use of "pidgin" places upon him, he comes as near speaking Standard English as he is capable of doing. And this is, up to a certain point, approved by his associates. They do not desire that one of their number be placed at too great a disadvantage in his intercourse with others, and they feel that "good English" is the speech best fitted for intercourse on a certain level of communication.

Those who can to a considerable extent adapt their speech to the situation, who comprise the great middle mass of dialect-speakers, often feel some superiority to the least educated of the dialect-speaking population, those who are least able to make of their speech a flexible instrument. No matter with whom they converse, the latter speak in nearly the same broken and extreme dialect, and they suffer socially as a result of their lack of social adaptability as expressed in speech.[22]

The great middle mass of dialect-speakers, who are able to adapt their speech fairly well to their surroundings, feel that the habitual use of careful, near-standard English among themselves is presumptuous, snobbish, a dissociation of oneself from one's class. This is most keenly felt among the group in which the individual is most subject to the influence of his fellows in points of behavior: the adolescents and older children in school.[23] Among them the boys are commonly said to be more subject to group pressure than the girls, the latter being more

[22] Small children, too, are usually lacking in speech adaptability, but as they learn more choice English and come to recognize differences in social milieu, they normally learn to discriminate in both speech and society.

[23] Apparently Deborah N. C. Woodhull was the first person to discuss in print this commonly remarked fact; see *Report* of 1926, pp. 45-49.

It is noteworthy that students of the English standard schools are commonly reproached for being "stuck up" because of their superior linguistic level, and because of the preponderance of Haole children among them. For this reason these schools, although apparently valuable in raising the standard of spoken English, are not favored by a considerable element both of teachers and of laymen.

likely to form small cliques whose approbation means more than general disapproval; but this has not been tested by comparison of the spoken English of boys and girls.

The following quotations from essays by students of Honokaa Intermediate School (January, 1934) illustrate the attitudes of adolescents generally.

If we speak good English our friends usually say, "Oh you're trying to be hybolic [i.e., to act high and mighty], yeah!"

They usually make us blush and we fill [feel] out of place among them. (N. A., female.)

Almost everytime I use pidgin english is because I don't want people telling bad about me. Sometimes when I used good english some people say, I act as if I know everything or acting fresh.

Sometimes when we [are] in a crowd of people some people tease us saying, "black haole." (M. A., female.)

One day when a boy and I were talking. We were not speaking good English, so, another person heard the boy speaking poor English. The person tried to correct the boy, but what did the boy do? Correct himself or not? What do you think his answer was? The boy's answer was, "I talk how I like, you no boss me, you not my teacher." (S. Y., male.)

I think those who laugh at people trying to use good English are jealous of them and are trying not to let them talk good English because they themselves cannot talk good English. (K. H., female.)[24]

As the individual grows older and leaves the school environment, he finds it necessary in many cases to have more regard for the standards of a small occupational or social group, or for the standards of his employer, than for the standards of his general social class. The general level of his speech therefore approaches more closely Standard English. As the need for "good" English is more common in cities and large towns than in country places, the English is more nearly standard in the cities than in the country; at least that is the impression it makes upon the casual observer, who no doubt picks his company more in Honolulu or Hilo than in a rural village. But whether in city or village, in school or out, the general principle

---

[24]The reasons which the students gave in these essays for using "pidgin" were: to go with the crowd without being teased; because "good English" sounds queer to them and is more difficult to speak; because old people and foreigners cannot understand anything but "pidgin"; because they grew up using it; because it is the general speech of their district.

holds, that dialectal English of some grade or other is considered the only appropriate speech among the "New American" population, and that one risks ridicule and the unpleasant feeling of "being different" if one does not use it.

A small number of "New Americans" are, however, because of the occupational and social level to which they have attained, conceded the right to speak Standard English in any company. Usually they may be recognized as Islanders, but only because of certain nuances of intonation, a very few peculiarities of pronunciation and grammar, and perhaps the use of a few localisms not current among Haoles. But even professional men revert to dialect in some situations. Thus a young physician practicing in a country town, though he received his university and part of his high school education in the United States and has studied in Japan, has quickly fallen back into the Portuguese-influenced speech of his native district. He feels that it puts him on a more intimate footing with the other young men of his set, although he would not be criticized much if he spoke careful Standard American English.

While too careful a use of English is considered snobbish, too careless speech, even among one's own nationality, is considered somewhat unbefitting educated non-Haoles. In public situations one has his dignity to uphold. Thus a teacher is under obligation to speak good English in the classroom, and on the playground and in other more informal contacts with his students, it is not considered altogether becoming for him to drop to their usual level of English. But in really intimate situations with friends of his own social group and age, where he does not have his dignity to think of, he may freely speak the most broken dialect.

Thus the average person of the second or third generation reaches, in the English language, a practical bilingualism of standard speech and dialectal speech or, more often, of an upper and a lower level of dialect. So do all persons use several levels of speech, but in America the difference between formal and intimate speech is not usually on so wide a level of dialectal difference as in Hawaii.[25] As has been pointed out, this

---

[25]In Europe, however, a contrast like that found in Hawaii is normal in many countries. (See Sapir, *op. cit.*, p. 124.)

bilingualism in the English tongue usually goes with knowledge of a foreign language, so that the individual is practically tri-lingual. Occasionally, too, there is so great a difference between the careless colloquial and the more formal levels of his parental speech as he speaks it that he may be said to be quadrilingual in his everyday conversation.

As a reverse phenomenon to the use of "good" English in some situations by dialect-speakers is the use of the dialect by some of those brought up to speak Standard English, in an attempt to attain intimacy with those who naturally speak the dialect, to become at least temporarily part of their we-group. If this is done naturally and with discretion, it is approved by the users of dialect. But for an adult outsider to use the dialect requires tact, lest he be thought to condescend. An anecdote will illustrate. At a rural hotel, a Haole salesman was drinking and talking with a group of Japanese. The more convivial they grew, the more he dropped into extreme dialect, until finally a Japanese exclaimed, "Why the hell don't you talk English?" The Japanese probably felt that the Haole, by speaking "pidgin," was putting them in the same class as their elders who can understand no other sort of English, or was implying that they were beneath the use of correct English.

As yet, although resenting the superior attitude of some critics of the Island dialect, most dialect-speakers are quite on the defensive. Some would like to speak more nearly standard English (or claim to wish so) and deplore the pressure of ridicule applied within their group. The majority, at least so far as its expressed opinion goes, still believes that the better one's English, the better are one's chances of rising in the world. Few have reached the attitude of the lad whose essay is quoted here.

> Most of us use "Pidgin English" because it is the simplest way for us, while talking to each other. By simple I mean that we don't have to bother whether the verb is right or wrong.
>
> Pidgin English, I believe, is not harmful because no matter how much we use it if we are ambitious enough we are most likely to be or get what we are aiming for.
>
> People may say that if we use good english we can have good jobs, but I

think it as a "hash" saying. The only persons that can have good jobs are the rich fellows. By rich fellows I most likely mean the "haoles."

When we students use good english we are sure that we will be called "haoles." And of course we hate to be called "haoles" because of many reasons.

If we use "Pidgin English" the teachers should keep their mouths shut and mind their own business. If the teachers lectures the pupils during school hours they are making more enemies day by day. Pupils may promise to speak good english before the teachers but after they are with their pals they will use "Pidgin English" so what's the use of lecturing the pupils.[26]

It is the present writer's belief that, because the ideas expressed above have some social and economic justification, they will in the future be more widely held.

The use of the Island dialect, it is frequently claimed, is disadvantageous and limiting in several respects. We may at this point examine these disadvantages and limitations.

Because the dialect is regarded with contempt by those who have jobs to offer, those who speak it are at a distinct disadvantage in obtaining certain types of employment. The Department of Public Instruction, for example, naturally does not favor hiring graduates of the University of Hawaii whose English is too dialectal, no matter if they be in other respects well qualified to teach. The more responsible office positions also are frequently withheld from persons whose English is dialectal—perhaps really for that reason, sometimes perhaps because deficiency in English by the group furnishes a good excuse for racial discrimination against the individual. Socially, too, dialectal English is a reason for discrimination against both the individual and the group.

Faced with double discrimination, against his race and against his speech habits, the individual sometimes sets himself resolutely to overcome his more obvious dialectalisms as a means of overcoming in turn racial discrimination; sometimes, perhaps in most cases, he lets the racial discrimination be an excuse for not mending his English.

[26]M. H., male freshman, Honokaa Intermediate School, January 11, 1934.

Rather often it is claimed by newcomers to Hawaii that the dialect is unintelligible, at least when spoken most carelessly. In turn Islanders sometimes complain that mainland English is partially unintelligible to them. The present writer, perhaps unduly influenced by his long residence in Hawaii, is of the opinion that these claims of unintelligibility are often made for rhetorical effect. There are some instances where the use of the dialect—not of the makeshift creole speech, which is another matter—does give rise to slight misunderstandings,[27] but these may be safely dismissed as unimportant. The context of the situation usually supplies the meaning of any localism or unaccustomed intonation.

The true limitations of the dialect-speaker come from the social disapproval with which non-dialect-speakers listen to his speech, and from the consequent fear of expressing himself in their presence. While a person is speaking his own dialect, the English philologist Wyld has pointed out,[28] he usually speaks correctly; it is when he tries to speak another dialect that he makes mistakes, and becomes unpleasantly conscious of them. Several observers besides T. T. Waterman[29] have noticed how keenly many Islanders, whether children or adults, fear to express themselves in formal situations such as a classroom recitation. Thus on the one hand the dialect-user comes to be considered slow or stupid, or at the least to be censured for his lack of self-expression, and on the other, he acquires a feeling of inferiority and perhaps of resentment at the superior attitude of the speaker of Standard English who really knows no more than he. Waterman probably exaggerates the limitations of the dialect and the effect they have upon the Island youth. Many Islanders use local dialect before speakers of Standard English without becoming embarrassed or feeling inferior, and most

[27]To take an instance on a rather high level of dialect: As this writer was standing before the magazine shelf of his school library, he was asked by the librarian, "How many time?" This he interpreted as "How many times have you drawn that magazine from the library?" and both he and the librarian (a university graduate) were embarrassed when the latter had to correct himself, "How *much* time yet?"

[28]Henry Cecil Wyld, *The Historical Study of the Mother Tongue*, pp. 21-22.

[29]T. T. Waterman, "Insular English," *Hawaii Educational Review*, February, 1930, pp. 145-146, 161-165.

speech situations, besides, are within the dialect-speaking group. Many, too, are able to use either dialect or nearly standard English freely and do not suffer. Nevertheless, the use of dialect by persons who have not learned to express themselves with equal ease in Standard English has created a psychological-social problem of real gravity, through the shutting off of the dialect-user from participation in easy social intercourse and from free expression of his ideas.

The retardation of the Hawaiian Island students, particularly in the field of language usage, is well known from a number of tests[30] and undoubtedly is due in some part to language difficulties. It is the present writer's guess that a considerable part of the difficulty in the understanding of sentence meaning comes from the average student's inability to think very effectively outside the syntax and morphology of dialectal English. That is, he usually thinks in English, but not in the sort of English with which he is confronted on the printed page. This hunch, however, remains unsubstantiated by tests. The rather small number of students who in English language situations still think in their parental language has even more difficulty with the categories of English.[31] That bilingualism usually causes some retardation in the learning processes is generally admitted,[32] but what the amount may be in the Hawaiian situation is unknown because of other factors entering into the picture. Retardation here may be caused by the difficulty of passing from a foreign language to English, or from dialect to Standard English, or by the general cultural poverty of much of Island life, or by the students' lack of acquaintance with American culture, or by varying combinations of all these factors.

A danger, which in the present writer's opinion is of more

[30]*Report*, 1925-1926; Ayako Kono, "Language as a Factor in the Achievement of American-Born Students of Japanese Ancestry" (M.A. thesis, University of Hawaii); Eleanor D. Breed, "A Study of the English Vocabulary of Junior High School Pupils" (M. A. thesis, University of Hawaii).

[31]Jane Stratford, "Cross-Section of a High School Student's Life" (M.A. thesis, University of Hawaii), pp. 57-60.

[32]*Psychological Bulletin,*   May, 1929, containing résumés of articles on bilingualism.

importance than is embarrassment in attempting standard speech or retardation in school, is that a linguistic division may be added permanently to the present racial and economic class distinctions. Notwithstanding the unifying role of the public school system, division into social classes is unavoidable under capitalistic economy, and notwithstanding intermarriage, the present racial divisions show every sign of persisting for a long time. While we have economic classes, we in turn have unequal education; this in turn tends to throw those who speak dialectal English into the lower income groups. Because of the economic succession of the immigrant peoples and the superior advantages enjoyed from the start by the Haoles, the racial cleavage follows the economic cleavage too closely for the comfort of foresighted people. At present the dialectal cleavage is being added to the other two. Should the three become stabilized, for the most part overlying one another, the situation will be triply fraught with danger of race conflict. The upper classes, that is to say for the most part the Haoles, will have additional excuse for discriminating against the lower. And, more serious, the groups speaking the dialect will more than ever associate the use of the standard language with "haolefication" and dissociation with their own racial and social class, and will, through their linguistic self-limitation, cut themselves off in large part from participation in the common culture of American Hawaii. The ideal, "All culture to the masses," will be negated in large part by the attitude of the masses themselves.[33]

This danger, while not to be minimized, is not immediately pressing and has several obstacles in the way of its fulfillment. The formation of a middle class of various racial origins is one barrier against it. Another is the continuation of the present policy, emphasized by some educators, of stressing the cultural advantages of learning Standard English. Still another is the gradual passing of the older people whose creole speech has

[33]The writer apologizes for the evaluative nature of this paragraph. He shares the attitude of the large majority, which considers the cultural unity brought about by the understanding use of a common standard tongue to be a great value to a nationality, however divided it may be by racial and economic conflict. He is also of the number who deplore the heightening of economic class conflict by interracial conflict.

acted as a drag upon the improvement of their children's English. Changes in attitude toward labor on the plantations, and the employment of both *lunas* and workmen from the same English-speaking groups, may also discourage the use of extreme dialect. The continued adoption of localisms and other features of the dialect by Haoles will certainly do something to bridge the linguistic gap.

The attitude of the public schools toward the use of the Island dialect is both interesting in itself and of some influence on its development. Officially the Department of Public Instruction has constantly emphasized the importance of the use of good English by all elements of the population. School-teachers in all grades have been encouraged to pay especial attention to the quality of the English used by their students. But the actual practice of the Department has been largely marked by conservative formalism, lack of analysis and imagination, and a negative, ordering-and-forbidding attitude toward the language problem. No analysis of the problem has ever been made.[34] No complete résumé of the chief features of the dialect is yet available.[35]

For the most part, methods adapted to the parts of the United States inhabited chiefly by native-born Americans have been applied in Hawaii. Instruction in formal English expression and in grammar has been from mainland texts, with only the adaptation to local conditions that an occasional clever teacher

[34]An analysis was begun by Deborah N. C. Woodhull (see *Report* of 1926, pp. 45-49) but was not carried through by the Department. The survey of which Myrtle King was the moving spirit is also a step toward analysis.

In recent years especially, the attitude of the Department has changed considerably both in outlook and in practice, as evidenced by two current projects: (1) The Hawaii English Project, for a description of which see Shiho Nunes, "The Hawaii English Project," *Hawaii Schools,* IV, No. 3 (November, 1967), 14-17; and (2) The Hilo Language Development Project, a summary of which is to be found in Robert Petersen, "The Hilo Language Development Project," *Elementary English,* XLIV, No. 7 (November, 1967), 753-755, 774.—Ed.

[35]Except the imperfect one by Reinecke and Tokimasa, and that is due to individual initiative. The survey made in 1933-1934 by Myrtle King (which incidentally revealed remarkable lack of exact observation and attention to detail on the part of intermediate teachers who were asked to analyze the English problem) is under the auspices of the Department, but the credit for it goes chiefly to King. Still, it shows a hopeful turn toward realism by the Department.

has been able to make single-handed. Textbooks adapted to local needs might well have been written by members of the Department after due analysis of the situation, but there has been no move in that direction. The attempts by Olive Day Mowat and T. T. Waterman to emphasize the teaching of phonetics have not been followed up consistently by the Department in the lower grades—the only place where the teaching of English sounds can be made truly effective. A standard of English usage somewhat too formal for the average person in Hawaii or elsewhere to follow has sometimes been set up, but the blame for this no doubt falls upon individual teachers rather than upon the Department.

Although it has been admitted that for many years the children can not be broken of using "pidgin," no dividing line between allowable and unacceptable dialect has been worked out. The local dialect and foreign languages have been lumped together and regarded negatively: "Don't speak Hawaiian or Japanese on the schoolground; don't use pidgin in the classroom." Such has been a very general attitude on the part of teachers. The coupling of dialect and the foreign tongues has done nothing to emphasize that good language is good language, whether it be English or Japanese (for on Japanese has fallen most of the opprobrium). So strong has been the prejudice against the use of a foreign language in the schoolroom that even within recent months a teacher was severely reprimanded by her supervising principal for using Japanese in explaining the meaning of a word to a Japanese child in a primary grade, though the teacher's linguistic method was sound. The students have been taught to regard anything but the teacher's English as bad, not to regard "good" English as good for its own sake; and their reactions have been accordingly negative in many instances.[36] Trained teachers of English have not been secured and kept teaching English in sufficient numbers; there has been an attitude that "any Haole can teach English." Unfortunately, the teachers best equipped to impart good English through their conversation if not through their methods have usually gravi-

[36]See the essay on pp. 180-181.

tated toward the upper grades, where they are the least needed. All in all the activities of the Department of Public Instruction may be summed up in the lines from the *Rubaiyat*: "... great argument/About it and about, but evermore/Came out by the same door as in I went." Of late, the Department is moving toward the adoption of a more realistic and analytical attitude toward the problem of securing the use of a higher grade of English. This attitude, however, has not yet become part of history.

The political necessity of hiring local-born and locally trained teachers will undoubtedly have some effect upon the sort of English used by future products of the Hawaiian schools. In the past, and indeed up to the present time, a very large minority if not a majority of the teachers have been American and British Haoles accustomed to speaking acceptable English from childhood. In the future the majority of teachers, especially in the formative lower grades, will have spoken a foreign language or dialectal English during their childhood and will for the most part be unable to discern and remedy the subtler features of the dialect—at least without having taken thorough courses in phonetics and grammar. As a child's idea of "good English" is largely based upon his teachers' usage, certain dialectal features will probably be perpetuated as acceptable English.

FUTURE OF THE COLONIAL DIALECT

All observers are agreed that the local dialect will continue in some form or other, but beyond the fact that it will continue, they are uncertain. Some expect that those features of the dialect which connect it most closely with the creole speech and earn it the epithet of "pidgin" will be in large measure corrected and will disappear; they say that the trend of English in Hawaii has been toward carefulness and acceptability. Others expect exactly the opposite and claim that the trend of English, especially of late, has been toward carelessness. The latter sometimes reason thus: Children now in the schools, and still more those to be enrolled in coming years, have an increasing number of parents, elder brothers and sisters, and other respected persons to look to, whose English is dialectal, whereas in the past there was not this mass of dialect-users to give "pidgin" respectability and emotional appeal in the minds of the young. Evidently much will depend upon the economic opportunities and social recognition accorded the non-Haole population of Hawaii. If good English continues to give social and economic rewards worth striving for, its mastery will be sought by many; if not, then by only the pertinacious few.

In the present writer's view, the most probable course for the dialect to take during the next few decades is only a continuation of the present situation: the more ambitious and able, and those in particularly fortunate surroundings, will continue to use good dialectal English, and the rest will continue to use poor dialectal English, which will still go by the name of "pidgin" and be regarded with contempt by the more educated. A middle ground of colloquial dialect will be the informal speech of a majority of the Island population and perhaps will come to be commonly recognized as a dialect. Probably it will be somewhat nearer Standard English than is the present dialectal middle ground. The radio and the talking pictures will probably have some influence in raising the level of English spoken. At the same time, an increasing number of Haoles and those assimilated to them will fall into the dialect through association with the rest of the population and because of the leveling of distinctions through the rise of Orientals and Portuguese into the middle class. Thus to some extent the racial class distinctions of the local dialect will be erased, though on the whole they will hold.[37]

In some places the local dialect, under the influence of past or present nationalist or regionalist traditions, has come to be a cherished semi-literary form of speech to be used beside the

[37]The transformation of Hawaiian "pidgin" English in the direction of Standard English in the last three decades seems to have been more rapid and thorough than predicted in this discussion. This has been due, however, to developments which Reinecke could not have foreseen in the 1930's—e.g., the heavy influx of Haoles from the continental U. S. to Hawaii after World War II, post-war advances in communication and transportation, and the advent of statehood in 1959. These developments brought about a far greater increase in income and economic opportunity than could have been predicted while Hawaii operated mainly under a plantation economy.—Ed.

standard speech. It is within the bounds of possibility that the development of regional sentiment in Hawaii might make the dialect to a certain extent a rallying point for local spirit, but this is highly improbable. There is at present no indication of a regionalist spirit in Hawaii of the type that would seek a separate form of speech. Besides, the local dialect wholly lacks prestige. Its only appearance has been in farce such as "Confessions of Joe Manuel of the Raddio Patrol," which appeared in the Saturday editions of the *Honolulu Star-Bulletin* between 1932 and 1933. Finally, the American tradition is very unfavorable to the use of dialect in serious literature. Local writers with a better grasp of the Hawaiian scene than any fictionmonger has thus far evinced may put the dialect convincingly into the mouths of their characters,[38] but there will be no reason to use the dialect in writing, except for local color in fiction, in advertising (and even here the old creole "pidgin" is more effective), in foolery, and in such pseudo-humorous columns as that of "Kahuna Nui" of the *Honolulu Times*.

SUMMARY

The English dialect of the Hawaiian Islands is at once a class and a local dialect, being spoken throughout the Islands by the younger non-Haole population, a group numbering less than one-half of the total population but constantly growing. It forms part of the same continuum of speech as the creole dialect, yet it differs from the creole speech in that it is more adequate, approaches Standard English more closely, and is more fixed. Also it has its own peculiarities of intonation, stress, pronunciation, syntax, and morphology, which distinguish it both from the creole dialect and from any other adequate dialect of English. It is a true local dialect and, from the circumstances of its formation, a colonial dialect.

[38]The few fiction writers who have tried to use dialect in their dialogue, such as Armine von Tempski (see the Bibliography), have not been eminently successful.

For some examples of authentic dialect used in plays written by local writers, see: University of Hawaii, English Department, *College Plays* (10 vols.); and University of Hawaii, Drama Department, *University of Hawaii Plays* (5 vols.).—*Ed.*

The dialect arose chiefly in schoolground surroundings, among a very youthful population, and has been perpetuated as elder children have passed it on to younger children while at the same time themselves maintaining its use. It was probably spoken by 1900 and well established by 1920.

The chief nationalities contributing to its formation were the Hawaiians, the Portuguese, and the Japanese, with the influence of the Chinese doubtful and that of the Filipinos a problem for the future. Since 1910 the influence of the Japanese has been especially strong. Slight local differences are found, depending upon the linguistic groups most numerously settled and the cultural environment of the particular district.

More important than any other factors in determining the type of dialect spoken by a given person at a given time are the social situation in which the person finds himself and the level of his education; in formal situations a person, especially if he is educated, tries to avoid gross dialect.

The dialect functions as a connecting link between the creole and Standard English speech. Much more important, it is a mark of a large we-group (or a number of we-groups) of racial and class origin. Its use is almost obligatory in informal and intimate conversation within the group, and the weapon of ridicule is turned against those who in informal situations affect the use of "good" English. This is particularly true among adolescents and children, for economic and social necessities modify the views of older persons without, however, destroying the validity of the general rule. Thus the use of dialect has come to be largely a matter of class and racial distinction, with attitudes of superiority, contempt, and condescension on the one hand and of group loyalty, defensiveness, and "inferiority complex" on the other. The use of the dialect, while valuable in unifying the majority group of the Hawaiian Island population, is a disruptive force between this group and the Haoles. It handicaps many in their mastery of the English language and shuts them out from full participation in American culture.

The Department of Public Instruction has coped insufficiently with the problem of improving or eradicating the dialect.

The local dialect will probably persist for a long while, perhaps in a form more like Standard English than at present, perhaps less like it, but more probably the former, without, however, attaining literary status. Meanwhile the creole dialect will disappear, but there will continue to be several levels of acceptability and of adequacy within the colonial dialect.

Chapter 8

CONCLUSIONS

The present writer is conscious of having touched upon a number of topics falling under the general head of the history and sociology of language in Hawaii, without having treated them as fully as they deserve. His chief interest has been in the reasons for the formation of the distinctive forms of English spoken in Hawaii and in their functions. He has reached the following conclusions.

THEORETICAL

1. Contact between considerable numbers of two or more linguistic groups in situations unfavorable for the adequate learning of one another's languages normally gives rise to a makeshift or minimum language based on one or more of the languages in contact. Such situations are especially likely if the groups in contact differ markedly in culture and in prestige and power.

2. While the purely linguistic differences between makeshift languages formed in different milieus are slight, if existent at all, such languages may be divided sociologically, on the basis of the

environments which give rise to them, into: (a) trade pidgins, spoken between groups having primarily trade relationships, (b) immigrants' or foreign mixed spcech, the versions of the native language spoken by immigrants until they lose their linguistic identity, and (c) creole languages or dialects, which arise in a plantation environment of masters and very dependent laborers.

3. In most plantation environments, at least of the colonial type conspicuous in the history of the past four hundred years, creole dialects tend to form and to be perpetuated while the plantation economy endures.

4. Creole dialects tend to disappear or to persist only in a modified, no longer makeshift and minimum form when the laboring population is allowed to share in educational and economic opportunities.

5. Immigrant populations cut off from their parent stock, if they retain their language, tend to retain it in a modified form which may be called colonial dialect.

6. The widespread education of a creole-speaking population tends to create a peculiar form of colonial dialect having many vestiges of the makeshift speech.

7. In Hawaii were exemplified the principles laid down in statements 3 through 6 above. That is, a creole dialect (which, however, because of the freedom from many plantation conditions, borders on foreign mixed speech) grew up; a colonial dialect spoken by the children of the plantation immigrant laborers has arisen, and now occupies the place of a true local Hawaiian Island dialect of American English; the languages of the immigrants, insofar as they remain in use, are taking on typical colonial dialect characteristics.

HISTORICAL

1. The history of Hawaii—economic, social, and political—made inevitable the use of English as the cultural and business language of the country.

2. The native Hawaiian language consequently declined in importance, prestige, and purity.

3. A makeshift speech was often used in communication between English-speaking foreigners and native Hawaiians; this

seems to have been a mixture of broken Hawaiian and broken English (sometimes called *hapa haole*), with sometimes the one and sometimes the other element predominating.

4. With the immigration of great numbers of plantation laborers, a makeshift language was more than ever necessary, both as a language of command for the employing Haoles and as a lingua franca among the immigrant nationalities. Upon a basis of Hawaiianized English rapidly grew up a creole dialect known as "pidgin English," spoken by a majority of every ethnic group except the Haole.

5. This creole dialect was the basis from which the children of the immigrants (and natives), educated in the English language schools, derived a form of English also commonly called "pidgin English," but more adequate and more refined than the makeshift speech of the immigrants.

6. The form of English used by a great majority of the younger non-Haoles of Hawaii is a colonial dialect of English. Being at the same time a local dialect and to a great extent a class dialect, it has a two-fold emotional basis.

7. This dialect seems likely to continue in colloquial use for a long time; the creole dialect, meanwhile, is declining in use.

8. The various languages other than English have been maintained, though modified by isolation from their cultural background and by contact with the English, and they seem likely in most cases to remain in use in Hawaii for some while.

The present writer is keenly aware of his deficiencies of training for the investigation of linguistic problems and hopes that some of the questions raised in this study will engage the interest of more qualified students, especially as linguistic phenomena are difficult to record and conditions are changing so rapidly that it will soon be too late to attempt a study of some aspects of speech in Hawaii. He particularly indicates the desirability of investigation in the following fields.

1. The origins, nature, and functions of the creole dialect. (This is the most pressing need, because competent observers of its early stages are already few.)

2. The changes undergone by the foreign languages in Hawaii.

3. The psychological and educational problems of bilingualism in Hawaii.

4. The social phenomena connected with the competition of languages in Hawaii, of which the foreign language school controversy is the most dramatic example.

5. The nature of the colonial dialect of Hawaii: its origins, the influence of each of the major foreign languages upon it, its linguistic characteristics, and comparison with other English dialects.

6. Comparison of the linguistic history of other plantation areas with that of Hawaii.

Appendix

EXAMPLES OF MAKESHIFT
AND DIALECTAL
ENGLISH USED IN
THE HAWAIIAN ISLANDS

1. Excerpts from Beecher and Harvey, *Memoirs of Henry Obookiah . . . Who Died at Cornwall, Conn., Feb. 17, 1818, Aged 26 Years.* The editors promised: "His own ideas, and, in general, his own language will be preserved." [p. 6] Some of his conversations were recorded; the editors may have remembered others imperfectly, but they were probably struck with some of Opukahaia's (i.e., Obookiah's) characteristic inversions. Excerpts from his letters and diaries are also included, and the level of English in these improves from year to year.

I went home, and told the man all what my Uncle had told me. . . . Not long after this I went and told my Uncle what the man had told me, and he would no more let me go back to the man's house, until the man come after me, then he would converse with him on this subject. [p. 7] No, poor boy am I. [This exactly tallies grammatically with what I once heard an annoyed old Hawaiian woman shout: "Dumb are you!"] [1] . . . I was now brought away from my home to a stranger place . . . While I was with my Uncle, for some time I began to think about leaving that Country, to

[1] Unless specifically indicated to the contrary, in the appendix all explanatory notes enclosed in brackets may be attributed to the author.—*Ed.*

197

go to some other part of the globe. I did not care where I shall go to. [p. 9]
. . . and his kindness was much delighted in my heart . . . He asked me
where was I been through all that night before. . . . And I told him what
my object was, and all what the Captain invite me to. [p. 10] She said that
I was very foolish boy. [p. 11] . . . in the evening after the sun-
down . . . [p. 13] I thought that he was quite an old age; by seeing his long
beards and his head covered with gray hairs . . . Did not any body knew it
for it was dark. But friend Thomas he was so full of scare. . . [p. 15] Many
times I wished to hear more about God, but find no body to interpret it to
me. [pp. 16-17] [These examples are from the *Memoir.*]

Owhyhee gods! they *wood, burn*; Me go home, put 'em in a fire, burn
'em up.—They no *see*, no *hear*, no *any thing.* . . . *We make them—Our
God,* . . . *He* make *us.* [p. 21, oral]

When I at home—Torringford—out in the field I can't help think about
Heaven. I go in a meadow—work at the hay—my hands—but my thought—
no there. —*In Heaven—all time—*then I very happy. [p. 38, oral, spring of
1815]

I want to ask the people—what they all waiting for?—they live in Gospel
land—hear all about salvation—God ready—Christ ready—all ready—Why
they don't come to follow Christ? [p. 44, oral]

Torringford, March 2, 1810.

Mr. E. D. Sir,
I here now—this place, Torringford—I glad see you very much. I laugh
Tom Hoboo—he say—"Obooki write me that? Me no write." I want you
tell Tom Mr. S. Mills say if we be good boys we shall have friends. One
morning you know I come into your room in College, and you tell me—
read—you say, *what c.a.p. spell?* then I say, c.a.p. *pig.* I spell four syllables
now, and I say what is the chief end of man. I like you much. I like your
brother, and your friend Mr. Dean. I wear this great coat you gave me to
meeting every Sunday. I wish you would write me a letter and tell me
what Tom do.

This from
Henry Obooki
[The second letter which Opukahaia wrote in English; p. 25.]

Andover, Dec. 15, 1812.

Dear Christian Friend,

I improve this opportunity to write to you. And I saw your beloved book which you sent by Mr. G. and that I very much thank you for it. I am great joy to God to give me such a good friend in this land where we hear the words of God—God is kind to us and to the other—that is to every body else. God will carry through his work for us.

I do not know what will God do with my poor soul. I shall go before God and also both Christ.

We must all try to get forward where God wish us to do. God is able to save sinners if we have some feeling in him. Is very great thing to have hope in him, and do all the Christian graces. I hope the Lord will send the Gospel to the Heathen land where the words of the Saviour never yet had been. Poor people worship the wood and stone and shark, and almost every thing their gods; the Bible is not there, and Heaven and Hell they do not know about it. I yet in this Country and no father and no mother. But God is friend if I will do his will and not my own will. [Part of a later letter; pp. 33-34.]

Opukahaia's written English, as evidenced by his letters and the diary which he kept from about March 5 to August 5, 1816, improved remarkably, but apparently he spoke a somewhat broken English until his death.

2. Letter from King Kaumuali'i of Kauai to Hiram Bingham, dated early in 1820, given on page 113 of Bingham's *A Residence of Twenty-One Years in the Sandwich Islands.*

Dear Friend. I feel glad that your good people come to my islands to do me good. I thank you. I love them. I give them eat, drink, and land to work on. I thank all American folks, they give my son learning. He know how to read, write all America books. I feel glad he come home. He long in America. I think he dead. But some man speak 'no.' I very glad you good people. I love them. I do them good. I hope you do good Hawaii, Oahu and all the islands.

Except this from your friend, Tamoree.

3. A report, probably oral, from Honolii, one of the three Hawaiians of the mission (Opukahaia's schoolmates), given on p. 133 of Bingham's *Residence.*

On Sunday morning the king and queen came into the meeting, with his few people. Then Mr. Whitney read about Jesus Christ on the cross, and the Ten Commandments, and I explain them, in our tongue, and make prayer, and after that, I sit down. I ask the king, 'How you like the meeting?' He say then, 'I like the meeting very well, sir.' Mr. Whitney ask him—'You understand what John tell you about.' 'Yes, sir.' Then he say, 'I not understand what you say before, but little; now I hope I do understand more;—more by and by.' I, John, told the king, 'Your peoples—they have *hulahula* (dancing) on this day?' King say, 'Yes.' Then I ask him, 'Can you wait *hulahula*, on this day? Your people may *hulahula* (dance) on Monday.—This day, it is holy.' And the king say, 'We may stop *hulahula* on another Sabbath day.'

4. Examples of broken English used by Hawaiians about 1874, given from memory by Mrs. Isabella L. (Bird) Bishop in *The Hawaiian Archipelago*.

Too many, too many! too much chief eat up people! You good Queen, you Bible long time, you good! [pp. 60-61] Too old [very old]. [p. 153] "Kaluna . . . frequently brought me guavas on the road, saying, 'eat,' and often rode up, saying interrogatively, 'tired?' 'cold?'" [p. 105] But can't go back, we no stay here, water higher all minutes, spur horse, think we come through. . . . Think we get through; if horses give out, we let go; I swim and save you. [p. 109]

5. Letters written by Hawaiians living on Molokai, available through the kindness of Mrs. George P. Cooke.

Kaunakakai. Sept. 13, 1910.

Dear Brother——
Kahului-
Your letter with best aloha and with two Delegates came to me me ka hauoli nui [much to my pleasure].

We are prepared the lanai [patio] beside the Church—nice lanai—Bipi ume [jerked beef?] ka puaa [pig] already—raw fishes, hee [squid], oio [bonefish], amaama [mullet], dry and raw. Sweet potatoes

I want you do me a favor viz—Can you send me with you from there 150 lbs of Ice—How much's worth of that? the money in my hand for the expenses of this association already. If you send ice—you take money with to pay the ice. We want order in Honolulu, but, too long from there—come early here.

Lahaina Ice work let me if I want Ice but I think—Wailuku Ice works better or Kahului-

Do not doubt to send Ice here with you. & also do not be afraid for money.

Too bad, the Concert very late on Saturday—the Mikahala be Kauna-kakai nearly 10 or 11 o'clock.—

My best Aloha nui to Mrs.———

Yours Servant Brother
[Rev.] I—— D——

Pukoo   July 10th, 1909

To you kind Mr.—— ——. Aloha nui kaua [Greetings]. I am asking you kind. to let me have some work. I am a poor man. I have wife an child. Their is no work up here. Just only four days work as all. I can not live on it, an my wife. That was why I am asking you if you please I am a poor man. I know how to cow boy. I no how to break horses. I have breaking horses mule every time I think I will close my letter with kind love

from
I—— K——

Don't fail to answer by next week.

Pukoo Molokai
June – 13 – 1914

Dear Madame——

Enclosed will find you a few lines. Here I am dropping you a few lines of leting you know for what you sent. I am giving you my best thanks for ever. I am very sorry when I saw them things [gifts, evidently]. I had seven children. My first born was twelve years my next one ten years next eight next 5 years a boy next 4 years next 3 years next one year old Poor children had no father to guide them. Same to me I am in family way and nearly time to give birth. I am a poor women. I do not know. If here shall I get things and living with this children as my husband in jail. He is like a lost sheep from the flock. I wish that you and your husband can do a thing for him. Seven fatherless children and I. Only God will help. My children and I are giving our best thanks to you and best regard. My children are worrying day and night for the father. And I am trying to make them be patience. [*Patient* was originally written, then *ce* written over the *t*.] God will help you and your family. Excuse for my writting

Yours Resceptfully.
Mrs. D—— K. I——

Kamalo Molokai

Dec 17 1910

My dear Mr. & Mrs. ——

        I Received your lett[er] and I am glad to hear you get all that things I am shame to let you know some think but I can not help I want you to keep me againe because I never get no man to keep me now. next eyers [year] Feb then Manuel one eyers Make [meaning, that the period of mourning will be over and she can marry again] then I want Mr—— please to keep me againe till I get man to keep me then pau because my papa to[o] old know [no] work please to that [let] me know if thies think is all right

with my aloha nui

to Mr. & Mrs——

Remaine   Mrs M—— [own name misspelled]

6. Letter from a Hawaiian woman living in Hamakua District, Island of Hawaii.

At Home.

Nov. 2, 1933.

Dear Mrs A. T. Renieck

        Good-morning. Listen Josephine and Samuel still on bed yet. I have three sick children, Josephine, Samuel and my baby. They also throwing blood from the nose.

        In the day they all not very bad but when night comes Gee, I have the hardies time to look after them

        I can't sleep with the cough they get. It seems to me that is a very bad cough. So, excause me from telling you such a big story as this.

        Say, for Mrs Warner's Akulikule lei I'm willing to make it. So, just let me know. How many lei does she wanted me to make for her.

        This is all, with thank's

From Mrs A——.

7. A Chinese merchant's letter, available through the kindness of Mrs. George P. Cooke.

Pahala, Kau, Hawaii

December 16, 1911

Dear Sir: —

        Am perfectly glad to say that we will enjoy again our Christmas soon therefore I am now sending you by the new steamer "Kilauea" one only of Young Pig.

I beg you acknowledge receipt of same and acceipt it in remembrance of your nice Christmas dinner.

Wish to find you in success and with many Merry Christmas and Happy New Year to you and all.

I am

Your very sincerely,
L. C——.

8. An advertisement written in Chinese dialect by George Mellen of Honolulu, head of Mellen Associates, Ltd. Mr. Mellen claims that he follows quite closely the actual conversational style of P. Y. Chong, operator of the Waikiki Lau Yee Chai. Musa-shiya the Shirtmaker, another of Mr. Mellen's advertising creations, however, owes more to Mr. Mellen's originality than to actual Japanese English. The Lau Yee Chai advertisements appear currently in the *Honolulu Star-Bulletin*; this one is dated April 14, 1933, and has the caption "Chart Sui Arp."

Me P. Y. Chong numba one China cook, allsame Big Boss Waikiki Lau Yee Chai, sabe anything me business—cook, waita, dishwashy, no can foolem. Me P. Y. Chong got system.

Sposy got system, money no wasem, catch numba one good wegable, meat, duck, chicky, licy, any kind; numba one cook, no humbug chargy taxedo big gamble style look see.

Me P. Y. Chong sabe plenty good flen cusoma no allsame New Yok big gamble style man, sposy like numba one good looksee placy, no can eat nicy looksee. Me P. Y. Chong no chargy looksee, chargy too cheap numba one hot, clisp kaukau. Sposy you eat 25 cent hundled dollar allsame wely welcome.

Olo China wiseyman say "Sposy follow honest, wely slow, wely hart, bimeby topside mountain numba one clean. Sposy follow humbug wely easy, too quick fall down numba one stink placy." Me P. Y. Chong take hart, take slow, bimeby topside mountain.

9. From the life history of an immigrant, a Chinese woman, as recorded by her daughter, apparently as nearly as possible in

her own words. (Courtesy of the Department of Sociology, University of Hawaii.)

My husband house kau-kau [food] no good—cheap kind and too li-li (little). Elly time I kau-kau [eat] junk kind den keep good kind kau-kau for my mada-in-law and all da man. I no can eat fust—must wait till all sit down den I can kau-kau. Dis place—must hana-hana [work] hard too. If sit down sometime, people speak dis kind daughter-in-law lazy. Den wen my fada sabbee, he too much hu-hu [angry] me. He say I make him shame. In China, life too hard for da wahine [woman]. Lady all same dog. Maybe if mada-in-law allight.

By'm-bye my husband he go Honolulu. Sometime he send letta, sometime he send money. I no can lead, so I take da letta to my fliend and my fliend he lead to me. One time, da letta, he speak for me come Honolulu. I too much happy. My mada-in-law no can bossee me no more. She wild, you know. She scold too much and I no can say one word. Das why I hate her and I want go 'way. No blame me for be too glad. I come Honolulu wid one fliend. Dis fust time I see boat and I li-li scared da water. But I no sick one day. Maybe because I too happy. Sometime plenty lain and plenty wind. Plac, plac, plac—da boat he make . . . o-o-o-o, I tink da boat be bloke. Long time we stay on da water. One day I see some mountain. Das Honolulu, das Honolulu, I tell my fliend. And my fliend he look too; "Yeah, yeah" my fliend he say. He know, because he been come Honolulu, one time before.

Wen I come down boat, one man, he lock me in big loom. He ax wot for I been come Honolulu—if I come stay for hana-hana licee field. I speak "No". Den he ax me if somebody he been sell me das why I come Honolulu. No, I say, I come Honolulu, das why my husband he speak for me come o'er hea. Den make he ax wot da name my husband he get. I speak L—— L——. Den he go. Two-tlee hour pau [passed]. Dis man he come back. Speak all same I can go. Outside door I see my husband. I velly glad—das ony face I sabbee—all face no see before. Dis fust time I been see kanaka [native Hawaiian]—I li-li scared. My husband he speak I pupule [crazy]. Kanaka all same pake [Chinese]—no scared. He hapai [carry] my tlunk and two suit case on top nice car. I ax wot da name he call dis car. He speak das hack. I scared by'm-bye da horse he lun too fast I hold tight da chair.

10. Essay entitled "My Dog," written by "a Chinese boy in the freshman class of one of the high schools of the Territory,"

quoted on pp. 257-258 of *A Survey of Education in Hawaii* (1920). There appear to be no peculiarly Chinese idioms in it; instead, it is full-fledged colloquial Island dialect.

Two years ago I went to my friend's home for a visit. My friend has seven little dogs about one month old. He asked me if I want a little dog. I was surprise of little dog, so I took a male one. I thanked him very much and I went with the little dog. I put him in a little box for him to slept in. He cried during the first night because he was lonesome. I named him Jimmy, and I fed him with rice and meat. He grew very large in four months. He has yellow and white shaggy hair.

I taught him how jumped and played in the grasses, and he could jumped about six feet high. He loved to played with cats and chickens. I taught him how to swim; first he was scared of water. I threw him in the river and let him swam ashore. He has only one master, and he followed me every time when I go some places. I used to go hunting and tramping with him. He grew as a old dog now, and he is still lived.

11. Letter from a Japanese merchant, in decidedly Japanese English.

Dec. 5 1932
Honolulu T. H.

Madamn:—
          Thanking your order, we keep
10 for 5¢ printed postale card
 1 for 5¢ Photo postale card (plain)
 1 for 10¢ Photo postale card (cored) [i.e., colored]
Also, We keeping as follows Books. . . .

12. A wedding address delivered by a middle-aged Japanese, fairly well educated in Japanese and a wide reader in English. It was evidently thought out, if not written, in Japanese and translated with the aid of a dictionary; parts of it are simply Japanese in English words. Dated December 2, 1933.

Mr. Toastmaster, Bride and Bridegroom, Ladies and Gentlemen:
It has inlisted to my deep conscience, as to how much important the necessity of wedded-life, moreover, I feel so much the responsibilities now and than, lies upon us, particularly of the present generation, in order to

face and maintain the present and future *manhood* and *womanhood,* that
so much being discussed among the master brains of the country of to-day,
is no less *the standard of morality.* Indeed it is a pleasure on my part, to
have the previlege this evening, to express my wishes and a word of con-
gratulation in that auspicious, upon the bride and bridegroom, particularly
to my friend Mr. ——— ———, whom had just gone into the bonded-life, an
offspring to the full fledged shareholders toward the beneficient life, that
in order, if I may interpet the occasion.

The evening have bec[k]on me, ladies and gentlemen, that I am very
much and boldly tempted to say, some part of what the orator of the day
might have say about the *personal ovation.* Wed-lock is the noble-bond, an
honorary partners toward the ever kindled light of *immortal streams,*—an
honorary league toward the obligations, where the almighty had given
unreservedly to all living beings, and that previlege is most graciously and
significantly virtuallize by the human beings and its culture. It has been
fairly and distinctively handed over to us,—if we do obey, we will flourish,
and if we do, otherwise, negelect its golden rule, we shall perished. So
notably as it is, the wedded-life, the linking knob toward the immortality,
may I not quoth you from the Japanese saying, as to that particular
linking of soul: *The relation of child to parents is simple, merely of
existance, but to those of wife to husband is perpetual, doubly and trebly,
as well as to pre-existance.* It is that peculiarly ordinated previlege, which I
quoth you in the last clause, of which *wife* to *husband,* is what I meant
that peculiarly confered to upon us human beings, is the fountain of all
virtual ethics, toward all noble deeds,—it creates the longivity and happy
life,—it must be the mandate to mutual respect and reverance,—and it must
be an innate to love and hommage to the place where our berth and life is
given, to live upon:—and above all, of anything else, human's most precious
thing, the *filial piety,* the roads toward obedience to parents, by which, I
am very grateful to say, may upon occasion, we might have been quoted as
singularly champion, hithertofore, what made and fostered, and had been
the back-bone of the Japanese culture for centuries and of to-day. The
basic thing to all worthy deeds. Isn't that something to be proud of to
posses as a nation. Isn't that also something infinitely *American,* and
America needs ever increasingly, and I am proud of that such thing is ever
indigenous in the American soil, increasing in double-fold, by which I think
we are doing greatness in dedicate to the *liberty,* the land which we owe
our allegiance. When the liberty was pronounced to the world, the American people had brought with them, I meant the forefathers of those who
had planted that vision, the immortal spirit, of what the *Anglo-Saxon*

people will ever abide to the golden maxim: *Fear thy God—honor thy father and mother—loyal to thy country*, they did not leave them in their mother-land, but they brought it to this side of the continent, and when they declare the freedom and liberty, it was a declaration of freedom to oppresive and tyranny. It was not their own selfish and meager purposes, it was a road to immortality. Future have much in store to this couple, as the past have already have proven, the first chapters of their susceptible life is closed, but now they are on to their second chapters of the responsible prudence, on a mission toward an American leadership,—leadership not by force or fistic, but by peaceful and gentle mission. Now comes to my second sober mind, that the ladies share to such a responsibility is noteworthy. Let me stressed to you my friend, while we turn over the leaf of American History, among the achievements of the noble-men, provably, not a single item, if not all, can outsted, first without bear in our mind the unforseen force that foreshadow beneath, the priceless and noble deeds of the American mistresses. These mothers of the young nation,then, did not forbade their free-land, just for the simple reason of fortuitous changes, at the reverse erra, but they have kept their promises that this country will ever be the land of everlasting, the land of opportunities and peace. Really they are the undisputed peaceful force behind the liberty, co-partners to the advancement of American-Wit. Now therefore, ladies and gentlemen, there are many epic things to make a nation,—epic things that are first acceptable to our general principal, whether you are Christians, or Buddhists, or Hebrews, and moresoever, the circumstances of this country is made up of compounded nations, but you will find in that epic things that are elementarily acceptable to our own benefits, if you will look into it fairly without favoritism.

There are to night I sees our foreign friends, but you will execuse me for the using of word foreign, I simply meant foreign, allies to our ceremonial customs, and not any more, to which I may add, if I may interpret to you the occasion, something you are accustomed to see time to time, and you may not have the chances to know what it is all about? You have customarilly upon occasion witness among the colorfully decorated tables, particularly on wedding ceremonies, paraphernalias, I believe, those most attract your attention might have turn to the miniature of Crane, that saintly looming before the sunrise; the Turtle laboriously climbing up on the beach rocks, and the aged couple wandering about, the immeasurable-light, under the masterly and age pine trees, the evergreen. The Crane purported to out live 1000 years according to the Japanese traditions, and that of Turtle 10,000 years, and the evergreen for everlasting. Do you suppose that in your mind, is there anything more cunning, primitive loving, and innocent, than those enumerative hypotheses,—a simple aspiration toward longlive, everlasting, in most natural way, in their own terms, rather than a mixture of religious incantation, I am sure you do not have any other than the mutual endorsements, in the name of sacredness in that Esthetics, that have been degenerate from an ancient rites, a single outline toward immortality, which gives the insight in enliven our pathos, that could only be found, in *the modern and recognized and acceptable* religions. Now we are to dedicate upon this holly shrine, the visions and insight, what a personnal achievements may have meant, rather than distroying it. Once more may I quoth you from the Japanese saying:

Toil thy self, thy mind toward the achievement and perfectability of things, but what a pitiful and forlorn, to count the debris of demoralize essance.

In closing my speech let me reiterate the joy of happy union,—the day's union of the best soul to soul, as well as the best of hopes, and the best of rich promises yet to come,—that beautiful and unforgetful attire of the best day will mutually clutch in hand to hand, and reaching for the unforeseen images that shall yet come to true, what makes the life contentment and wholesome, the best of the day shall be the symbol, shall be the perpetual streams of immortal omen. We are to here merely renew the impulses, on our own common course, the vision and inspiration which some of ourselves had drank from the same inspiration of fountain, whence upon a time. Let the vision to immortality, the spirit never to fail, never to mourn, deeper than the million fold of heavenly hue, father than the tiniest star, that looms beyond the countless fellow planet, deeper than the light of all the tinsel shone in one. It was pleasure indeed, best wishes to the bride and bridegroom, I thank you.

13. Part of a news story, "Life of Early Japanese Immigrant Laborers to Hawaii Is Recounted," by Masa Hiraiwa, appearing in *The Nippu Jiji* of October 3, 1934. It is of etymological as well as of general interest. While Mr. Hiraiwa's English is for the most part grammatically correct, it has in places a foreign awkwardness and lack of idiomatic directness and grace, and it contains some Japanisms. This extract is included as typical of much of the writing for the English sections of the Japanese language press.

What do we know about "conpan house," no less the general conditions of those early ancestors of the Japanese who came to Hawaii as immigrant laborers.

Next year marks the 50th anniversary of the first Japanese immigration to Hawaii. Fifty years ago, a shipload of 956 intrepid adventurers came to these shores, subjected themselves to three years of toil as were the Negro slaves in the southern states before there appeared on the horizon—their liberator—Abraham Lincoln.

Let one of the survivors of this first batch of immigrants relate a story of those trying days, days that were days as daylight meant work and more work under lashing, besides.

So, it was no wonder that once the three years were up, there appeared a horde of gamblers, idlers and ill-mannered, happy-go-lucky crowd. They have seen toil, they wanted to "enjoy" life a bit.

In the meantime, the up-and-coming plantations were in dire need of men, laborers to work their fields, to open new lands for sugar cane production as sugar was greatly in demand at that time.

Thus it came about that there was instituted a law requiring all able-bodied men to be gainfully employed. It was intended especially for the idlers.

The men, surprisingly, sought employment rather than go to jail. They had ideas of their own, however, which meant that they could do whatever they pleased, work when they felt like and play at times they tired of working.

This they did by banding themselves into companies or "conpan" as the olden Japanese termed it. "Conpan houses" were those apartment-like structures built to house these "conpan" men.

Many of our fathers have lived in one of these at one time. They leased a tract of land from the plantations, cleared and cultivated it for cane production, living all the time at these "conpan houses." Being sort of independent, they worked when they felt like working, but idled away the time for the most part.

It behooves us to wonder why is it that certain camps at Wainaku and other camps at Kukaiau and Amaulu are called "San-kai-sen," or "Shi-kai-sen" or "Ku-kai-sen."

Heard from the lip of an original settler, these camps are said to have been built for every shipload of laborers that reached here. For instance, the third shipload would settle in camps at all of the plantations and the places where they lived would be called "San-kai-sen." A year or so later, the fourth tide of laborers would arrive in the islands and new camps built to house them would be named "Shi-kai-sen."

14. An essay by a retarded seventh grade student living at Haina, Hawaii, which shows great Japanese influence, although the student probably thinks in dialect. Dated November, 1934.

I wish you come to Haina for look all the mill. There have three house of mill. One is for shimashi [smash] cane juce and will go to the second house. The steam engein will pull the car in the mill and the two hook will take the cane from the car and pull the cane in the carry. The carry will bring the cane in the roller and the roller will shimashi the cane. There have five set of rollers to shimeshi the cane juce.

15. A letter by a Filipino, appearing in the *Honolulu Star-Bulletin,* December 8, 1934. The writer's mastery of English idiom is considerable, and he does not write in so flowery and hyperbolic a fashion as do some Filipinos. Some traces of Island dialect may be seen in his writing.

Sir: As one of the law-abiding citizens in the territory of Hawaii, kindly publish this letter.

On or about 10 a.m. December 2, 1934, I was arrested in Kahaluu, Oahu, and was brought to Kaneohe police station, then to Honolulu police department before Chief Detective Mr. McIntosh. Then said chief told the police to book for investigation. Before booking I asked the said chief to give me meal for I was hungry. Said chief told me "by and by." Until 4 p.m. on said day they gave me cup of tea and two pieces of crackers. In this whole day and one night cup of tea and 2 pieces of crackers only was my meal.

On December 3, I was handed again cup of tea and two pieces of crackers at about 6 a.m. Then they brought me to Pearl City police station where they questioned me until 4:30 p.m. I demanded meal on this day at Pearl City police station including Judge Oliver Kinney, they refused to give me eat. I was almost starved on this day because I did not have any penny in my pocket to buy for something to eat, but however one man given by God's power of sympathy this man is Sergeant Sam at Pearl City police station, offered me ten cents to buy something for meal. And I thanked Mr. Sam for this assistance where I save my life. And by this time I suffered headache all the time and I blamed the police department for refusing my regular meal.

On or about 4:30 p.m. December 3, I was discharged on false arrest through the information of Mrs. Tomas Sigubia, of Aiea, Oahu. Then I demanded transportation back to Kahalu[u]. They refused as there is no free transportation. But, however, they took me up to Aiea where I met some of my friends to take me to Honolulu. Then in Honolulu I will find again another occasion to take me to Kahaluu. I believed that I was discriminated. For the information of the public, may I ask the honor of the editor of this paper to find out if there is any fund given by the government of the territory to supply meal and transportation to those prisoners of the city and county or to the territory of Hawaii?

If there is sufficient fund to provide any prisoners, then I was really discriminated and the only Lone Eagle in the Dark Cell ever since. Hoping that this letter be given space for the satisfaction of your subscribers and the public. In anticipation I extend my hearty thanks for the same.

Very truly yours,
Hilario Advincula

16. A letter written as a school exercise by a Filipino girl in the seventh grade of Honokaa School, December, 1934. Its floweriness is Filipino; its other deviations from ordinary English are Island dialect.

Dear Most Beloving Friend,

I am dropping you a few words for remembrance. And also thanks for your most beloved words in your letter, which I have also read it with pleasure. As for my condition I am in the best health. Hope to hear from you, the words of, "I am fine."

I was glad to hear from you about your living. I am also in the same place as before. I hope that when you come over, you will never forget to drop in. As for me I think I cannot drop in to see you, on account of my mother.

Lately with the most beloved aloha, I shall close my letter.

Your's sincerely
E—— A——

17. A poem, apparently by a Filipino lad, appearing in "Our Own Poets" column of the *Honolulu Star-Bulletin,* October 6, 1934.

THAT PERSISTING SHYNESS
By Juan Romano
McKinley High School

Hark! A cold zig-zagging shock penetrates me,
I become tense, astill with suspense
Blushing as red as a bougainvillea tree.

I sulked away to find myself astray;
Out in an untouching atmosphere,
I've wondered why I am that way
That makes me feel exceptionally queer.

I've always tried and often sighed,
Of the many astounding thrills, I pushed aside,
All because of that persisting timidity in me
That I've not yet found a remedy.

It follows me in all affairs,
(But proud to say not in my prayers)
It rips me from many friendships true,
Leaving me at times lonesome and blue.

But yet came a day, when I pulled myself to say,
That I will conquer this devilish foe, by practicing power;
With faith, practice and eternal steadiness, I'll pray
To turn into a new leaf with a full-blossomed flower.

Finally at this moment I feel like a polished metal,
Because of the skirmishes of shyness I've battled,
But still I have several more to arrest,
So "Down with Shyness" I have sworned to cast,
And may the Lord bless me for the things that I tried to possess.

18. Description of how to make Portuguese sausage, told orally by a seven- or eight-year-old Portuguese child living in Ahualoa, Island of Hawaii, 1933.

They kill the pig and cut the pig and then they take the inside out. She wash the inside. And then she take the parsley and the *sabula* [blood][2] and

[2]More likely *cebola* (onion), as pointed out by Edgar C. Knowlton, Jr., "Pidgin English and Portuguese," in *Proceedings of the Symposium on Historical, Archaeological and Linguistic Studies on Southern China, S. E. Asia and the Hong Kong Region*, p. 231.—Ed.

put 'm inside the stuff they bring outside from the pig and then she tie them so it won't come out and then she let 'm stay there. When it come little bit black all around you fry 'm and eat 'm.

19. An essay by C. K., an Okinawa-ken Japanese girl in the eighth grade of Honokaa School, 1933. It is in exceptionally good English for an eighth grader and represents the highest type of Island dialect—that is, Standard English interspersed with occasional dialectal expressions. There seems to be no specifically Japanese influence, though in one or two places there is a slight awkwardness of expression.

How My Parents and I Talk Together

My parents, though they lived in Hawaii for about twenty years, can not speak English. They can only speak Japanese [Note: In addition to the Okinawa dialect.] and understand only some parts of the English which we speak, and of course they understand the common Hawaiian words which everyone speaks in Hawaii. Because they cannot speak English, we speak Japanese to them. They understand that we cannot speak Japanese very well, so they send us to the Japanese school. Knowing that the Japanese language is still important, they want us to learn how to speak Japanese good by practicing it at home. Therefore I always speak Japanese to my parents, but somehow I never can speak Japanese for a long time to my sisters and brothers. Without knowing, English is out of my mouth quicker than Japanese. Sometimes I want to speak Japanese for a long time, but because I usually speak English, it just comes out of my mouth without knowing. Because my parents can not understand English, they sometimes scold us when they do not understand what we are talking about. They say that even if we say unpleasing words to them, or plan an evil deed, they cannot understand so will not be able to warn us.

Sometimes when my brothers and I are talking excited stories and making lots of noise mother comes in. Thinking that we are quarreling, she begins to scold us. We then begin to laugh, saying that we are not quarreling but having a fine time. Mother begin to laugh out too when she finds out how she misunderstood. She says to us that we can't blame her for scolding us because she cannot understand what we are talking about. "If you don't want to have any scolding, why don't you speak Japanese so that I can understand you? If you do so, father and I can understand you and may appreciate your stories also," says mother. She sometimes gives us lectures saying that though we may be able to speak English well but if we cannot speak Japanese, we will not be able to have a good position. She says, "As you know, there are still many Japanese who cannot understand English. Because of this, in order to have a good position, you must be able to speak Japanese just as well as English. Maybe in the next generation, Japanese language will not be very important as it is now."

By this way, she tells us time and again until we're tired of what she is saying. I think that what she says is right after all, so I am trying to speak better English and Japanese.

20. We now turn to conscious attempts to write in Hawaiian Island dialect. The first example, a story by a Portuguese girl in the seventh grade of Honokaa School (1933), contains also a great deal of unconscious dialect.

Once upon a time there lived two brothers, who lived near the river. Every day they would go for a walk.

One day they took a walk, and saw three beautiful girls.

They went home and sported up themselfs. John was very silly in his work. He was dressing when his brother said, "What I tell little, tell plenty." John said, "OK." They went to the girls' house. John had a girl too.

When they reached there. She welcomed them in. She said, "Please seat down." The two brothers said, "Thank you." They sat down. Jack said, "Ah! I forgot to feed my little chicken." "Your little chicken! you get thousands of chickens." The youngest [girl] said, "Gee! rich men."

Then Jack said, "Ah! I forgot to feed my little cow." "Your little cow! you get thousands of cows." Then the same girl said, "Gee! I'll marry him then."

Jack was glad and didn't say anything. Then Jack just happened to scratch where the fly has flown.

Then the same girl said, "What you get?" "Ah! only one little sore." "One little sore! You get thousands of sores."

"Ah! I no go marry you then."

Jack was angry and went off the house.

When he saw John he said, "What for you been go stay tell that?"

John said, "Well you said when you tell little tell plenty. So I been go stay tell what you said."

21. The following story, by a Japanese lad, James K. Nakagawa, was much more vivid in the original draft, in which dialect was used more freely and the author was not striving so hard to write book English.

Ghosts! Murder!

" 'Ey, you guys, no mo' mo' better stories dan jus' love stories? Come on, somebody, start out with a ghost story—mo' better if get murder stories, because you no hear about murders too much nowadays. But anyhow, start somet'ing peppy," said James, a Japanese boy of fifteen, to a group of Portuguese and Porto Rican men and a few young boys, sitting lazily on a creaking bench on the dirty veranda of Nakagawa's little dingy, poorly lighted and aired store.

"Talk about ghosts," spoke up a middle-aged bachelor, one of the greatest liars in Hawaii, "I had one experience, myself, that would make the ghosts' hair turn white and then to green with fear and dread. Chee, if you was in my boots you would faint entirely. Do you want me to tell you about that ghastly experience? All right, here's the story. One twilight (it was about seven o'clock, I think) as I was riding a horse—whew the dandy horse; she didn't fall down even once with a rider on her back—the lousy horse started to walk lame. At first I thought she might have had some thorn in her hoof; but I kept on going. (I was going up Gama's hill, you know.) Then, all of a sudden, the horse went head over tail and heels over head. As usual, I was off the saddle and on the sloping ground, hardly believing my eyes. The horse went head over tail THREE TIMES! Now, can you believe any such thing happening? No! But it is the fact, because the next day 'John Bull' and I examined the horse minutely and found many bruises. But the oddest thing about it was that horse's tail and mane were knotted together in the queerest fashion. . . . That same day I sold the melancholy beast to an old Japanese laborer for only ten dollars. That beast cost me, I think, about a hundred and fifty dollars. Quite a large s–"

"Say, I t'ot I bin see you on dat horse (was one mare, eh?) was day befo' yesterday," Manuel cut in abruptly. "You an' me was by de fence w'en we bin see 'im on de pony, not right? James. An' I t'ot you bin tell jus' now dat you bin sell 'im to a Jhapaun ole fut [Japanese old fart], not right, eh? James.

"Sure, 'at's right w'at Manuel bin tell right now. You still got de horse, an' you say you bin sell 'im: How much? Only ten plunks," James laughed.

"You young ignorants do not know anything about this matter and you want to butt in. The horse on which I was riding the day before yesterday is a very different one, which I bought later because of the inconvenience of being without a well-to-do horse. Now, you unlearned young scamps, do you have any argument against that? Answer!" Antone said hotly.

"W'at? No talk too damn high-bolic words, when you don' know da meaning of dem," Manuel retorted.

At this point Bascillio, a dark Porto Rican of giant stature but of soft words, said soothingly to all of the boys engaged in the little conflict:

"Come on, boys, no raise scraps now. Let's be friends an' talk stories an' make fun an' not be grumblin' an' grudgin' agains' each other. Maybe w'at Antone bin tell is true; you never can tell. I bin get some experience of dat kine, too."

"All right, then, tell. We will listen," said Antone with conviction.

"All right. If you all agree to keep your mout' shut, I will start right away with de story. W'en I was a lil kid—oh, about the size of Toshino san—my father used to make me work like a dickens. Early in the morning he used to pull me out of the nice, cozy bed an' send me out for cut grass for the horses and cows. Dat kind job summer time all right, but w'en winter time, chee, you no like walk insi' the cold grass after you was in the conforlable bad. But I had to go—whether cold or no cold, freezin' or boilin' hot I had to go pick the grass. Then after school he sent me again. How I hated dat job. If I didn't go, he got out the whip so I had to run. Sometimes I came home after the sun set, sometimes later than that."

[The story was left unfinished.]

22. The confessions of "Joe Manuel of the Raddio Patrol," which appeared in the Saturday edition of the *Honolulu Star-Bulletin* during 1932 to 1933, are in this writer's opinion the best imitation in print of the Island dialect. Although there is perhaps a little exaggeration and concentration of features of the dialect for literary purposes, its very twang is recaptured in some of the best of these sketches. They represent the speech of a Honolulu Portuguese but could, with a few changes, be put in the mouth of a youth of almost any nationality in any part of Hawaii. Their author, I understand, is Harry Stroup, a young Haole of wide associations.

The following sketch, which appeared on November 19, 1932, introduces also a caricature of the speech of the older Japanese and of the Filipinos.

Da Terrific Probslem

Us fellas on raddio patrol get all kine work for do but what I don't like da bess ees dese terrific case wen Japanee and Portugese car bang bang.

Da other day talfone ring and one Japanee he say, herro, herro, prease come Arakea King streets queek my car get bang bang. So queek I make da sireen and go da scene for da accidents.

Firs ting I get by da corner three Japanee and two Portugee come run one time wit one Filipino and all try tell same time what ees da troubles.

What trouble I say and one Japanee he say, arru same my hordo car Waikiki side come King streets. Bime by makai side Arakea streets one stewsbaker Portugee on top go riku herro no stop rook see what prace he go.

I make horn arrusame dooda, dooda but he no one time rooking me for seeing how I going. I make turn arru same rights side, I make turn arru same left side but no can herrupo stewsbaker car bang bang hordo car.

Aw chief da Portugee fella tell dis Japanee he lie like enni ting. I was driving makai on top Alakea and blow my horn three times when he come in his junk and bang my car. Whats da matter dis Japanee more betta take heem poleece stations.

Japanee he tell Potugee fella what for you speak me arru same, you arru same! I tink so more betta you go poreece station. Sure two man go poreece station talk talk Judge I tink so you inside jairu go.

So Filipino boy he speak up an tell. Fleece sir, Mr. fleecemans I am witness for accident. Eef you will give por me one minute I will exflain prom da start and pinish.

Da Portugese gentlemans was coming prom da mauka side of Alakea and da Jafanese from King going Waikiki. In my humble ofinion dey are bote at pault because had dey put on da break dey would escape da bang bang accidents.

I say tanks den I go look da car and find out nobody hurt and only one fender smash da Ford and one fender smash da Studebaker.

So I tell da Japanese and da Portugee more betta dey fix own damage and no make trouble. If you fellas go da deestrick court I tink Judge poot you bote inside jail, I tell.

So da Japanee he look me and tell, Ah, arrigato, tank you meester poreeceman, and da Portugee he look me and tell, O.K. Joe Manuel das how you take side for your fren from Punchbowl. You wait I feex you.

Aw, I say how you going feex me I no broke and beside I got do my dooty by da raddio patrol.

23. The following imitation of Japanese immigrants' dialect is also said to be by Stroup. It is from the *Honolulu Star-Bulletin* about 1929.

Evangelist Speak, Prodigal Son Get Too Muchee
Nice Kind Luau

Parable of Numba One Boy (Good Kind) and Numba Two Boy (Too Much Whoopee Make) Related in Honolulu's Own Vernacular by Earnest Worker.

Unmindful of Chinatown's thousand and one pungent odors and apparently oblivious to the banter of his polyglot audience, a diminuitive [sic] Japanese evangelist stood at the corner of River and Hotel Sts. one evening not long ago, and led his small band of followers in the singing of a well known hymn.

Three women and two men joined him in the singing of the song. Crowded around them were about 30 others who had stopped to listen and to make fun of the preacher. Two or three drunkards on the outskirts of the picturesque crowd added to the merriment by singing "How Dry I Am" in competition with "Yes, Jesus Loves Me," the song chosen by the evangelist.

"Yes, Jesus rub me, yes, Jesus rub me," sang the little preacher and his followers, "Yes, Jesus rub me, for the Bible tell me so."

A friendly cop chased the drunkards away and the evangelist settled down to the serious task of addressing a mixed gathering of Chinese, Japanese, Koreans, Hawaiians, Filipinos and haoles.

He chose as his subject the parable of the prodigal son.

"You tink so the Bible is nothing," the salvationist declared pointing an accusing finger at the crowd, "I no can talk good English but I savvy the Bible he's good." His sincere and earnest demeanor won the attention of the mob and it kept silent as he continued his story.

"One time one old man he got two son, speak inside Bible," he said, "One old son and one young son. This young son he too much pakiki [headstrong]. He speak the old man, 'Give me my share—I like go nother prace. I tired dis prace.'

"So papa he give his share and the old brother his share—all same half half.

"Pretty soon bimeby young son he go nother prace look see. He trow away everythings he got. He lose all money. He make big luau [party], he drink plenty okolehao [native brew], shoots crap, play card, anykine he do. He find plenty wahine [women] make big time—all same haole speak hoopee.

"Dar arri, bimeby money all pau [gone, finished]. Ikane [aikane, friends] pau. Kaukau [food] pau. Everyting pau. He look see jobs but no kind find. Erri prace he go—speak me too sorry dis time, country got dispression dis time, no more hanahana [work] gotch.

"He speak, 'Auwe [alas], wasamatta for me dis time too much pilikia [trouble].' Porice speak no stop dis prace. Erribody speak dis fella no more good. Auwe for dis fella dis time no more luau. He eat any kine kaukau—puaa [hog, pig] kaukau [food] he kaukau [eat]!

"Bimeby dis fella he tink plenty man work my father prace. Papa he got all kine good kaukau, more betta I go home stop. Spose old man he huhu [gets angry with] me I speak him nice ting. Me speak I too much sorry. Maybe bimeby erriting more betta.

"He go home. Father he look see his son all time—he too much like dis boy—bimeby he look see son he come. He run outside quick for see boy. He speak, 'Aroha, me too much grad you come, rong time no see.'

"Father he too much grad. He tell man bring new crothes, new shoes, gold ring—anykine he give dis boy.

"Bimeby papa he tell cook make big luau—kill puaa kill pipi kane (figuratively speaking the fatted calf), plenty kine kaukau he tell him fix.

"He tell erribody come eat. Play music, dance hula—plenty good time.

"Big brother he too much huhu [angry]. He speak father, 'Wasamatta you. I stay home hanahana. No drink okolehao, no make luau, nobody make good time for me.'

"Father tell him, 'Wasamatta you wassamatta me—you wassamatta! Dis boy he bad boy. He go nother prace make haole kine hoopee. He spend all money bimby he broke he come home. He speak he too much sorry. I grad for see dis boy—long time no see. He is prodigal son. We make big luau.'"

BIBLIOGRAPHY

The following bibliography deviates from the original in a number of ways. (1) Whereas the original is classified by subjects and sources—e.g., general linguistic material, material relating to Hawaii (subdivided into government documents, theses, etc.), foreign language schools in Hawaii (government documents, newspaper articles, etc.)—the present bibliography is arranged in a single alphabetical list (with the exception of communications), first by author, then by title, and finally by date in a few cases. (2) Whereas the section on communications (i.e., letters, interviews, and the like) is included as a major division within the original bibliography, it is not so treated in this revision. Instead it constitutes a separate section, which immediately follows the bibliography. (3) Whereas in the original no distinction is made between works actually cited in the text or footnotes and those that are not, in the present revision the distinction is made. Specifically cited works are unmarked, and works not so cited are marked with an asterisk preceding the entry. (4) Whereas the original contains brief prefatory notes at the beginning of the major divisions of the

221

bibliography, this revision does not. (5) Additions have been made to the original bibliography, and these are marked with a dagger. Comments added to original entries are enclosed in brackets.—*Ed.*

Adams, Romanzo. "English in the Public Schools," *Hawaii Educational Review*, XIII, No. 9 (May, 1925), 193-194.

————. "Functions of the Language Schools in Hawaii," *The Friend*, XCV, No. 8 (August, 1925), 178-179; XCV, No. 9 (September, 1925), 197-198.

An able analysis of the social functions of the foreign language schools—favorable to the schools.

————. *The Peoples of Hawaii.* Rev. ed. Honolulu: American Council, Institute of Pacific Relations, 1933.

The *sine qua non* of statistical study of the peoples of Hawaii. See especially pp. 42-43 on pidgin, literacy, and ability to speak English.

Advincula, Hilario. Letter to the editor, *Honolulu Star-Bulletin*, December 8, 1934.

African Education Commission, *Education in East Africa: A Study of East, Central and South Africa.* Study made by the second African Education Commission under the auspices of the Phelps-Stokes Fund, in cooperation with the International Education Board. Report prepared by Thomas Jesse Jones, Chairman of the Commission. London: Edinburgh House Press, 1925.

*Alexander, William De Witt. *A Brief History of the Hawaiian People.* New York and Cincinnati: American Book Company, 1899.

Alverne, Macario Leones (?). (English-Japanese-Tagalog wordbook published c. 1927.) [Not able to verify its existence or to secure further details.]

†————. *Manual for the Progressive Laborer, with Translations in Ilokano and Visayan.* Honolulu: By the author, 1930.

*Anderson, Isabel Chadbourne. *Sentence Mastery.* New York: D. C. Heath and Company, 1932.

A high school textbook. Mrs. Anderson, a teacher at Kauai High School, gives several examples of Island English in the sentences to be corrected, but does not distinguish them from other departures from Standard English.

*Anderson, Izett, and Cundall, Frank. *Jamaica Negro Proverbs and Sayings Collected and Classified According to Subjects.* 2nd ed. revised and enlarged by Frank Cundall. London: West India Committee for the Institute of Jamaica, 1927.

    Contains a brief but good bibliography.

*Andrews, Lorrin, and Parker, Henry H. *A Dictionary of the Hawaiian Language.* Honolulu: The Board of Commissioners of the Public Archives of the Territory of Hawaii, 1922.

    Andrews' *Dictionary* was issued in 1865 and was revised by Parker, 1915-1921. Not very good, but the best available [at the time].

Annual Report of the Governor of Hawaii. See: Hawaii. Governor. *Report.* . . .

Ayer and Son's Directory. . . . See: *N. W. Ayer and Son's.* . . .

*Babbitt, Adeline Emily. "A Vocabulary Study of Preschool Children." Unpublished M.A. thesis, University of Hawaii, 1931.

Baissac, Charles. *Étude sur le patois créole mauricien.* Nancy: Imprimerie Berger-Levrault et Cie., 1880.

————. *Le folk-lore de l'Île-Maurice.* Paris: Maisonneuve et C. Leclerc, 1888.

Ballou, Howard Malcolm. "Bibliography of Books in the Native Hawaiian Language." "Boston and Honolulu, 1908." (Not published.)

    A typewritten copy of this work, which incorporates the following item, is to be found in the Carter Memorial Library in Honolulu.

————, and Carter, George R. "The History of the Hawaiian Mission Press, with a Bibliography of the Earlier Publications," in *Papers of the Hawaiian Historical Society,* No. 14 (Honolulu, 1908), pp. 9-44. (Paper presented to the Society, August 27, 1908.)

    Covers the period 1822 to 1829.

Barnett, A. G. "Colonial Survivals in Bush-Negro Speech," *American Speech,* VII, No. 6 (August, 1932), 393-397.

Barnouw, Adriaan J. *Language and Race Problems in South Africa.* The Hague: Martinus Nijhoff, 1934.

    A very careful discussion of the rise and nature of, and problems connected with, Afrikaans.

*Barrows, Sarah T., and Cordts, Anna D. *The Teacher's Book of Phonetics.* Boston: Ginn and Company, 1926.

    General phonetic differences between several foreign languages and English. For Spanish, see pp. 134-138; for Japanese, pp. 139-144; for Chinese (Cantonese), pp. 144-146. These sections discuss rather simply certain errors that speakers of these three languages represented in Hawaii are likely to make, but some of the authors' statements are to be taken with caution.

*Beals, Carleton. *The Crime of Cuba.* London: J. B. Lippincott Company, 1933.

Beecher, Lyman, and Harvey, Joseph. *Memoirs of Obookiah, a Native of Owyhee and a Member of the Foreign Mission School, Who Died at Cornwall, Conn., February 17, 1818, Aged 26 Years.* New Haven: Office of the Religious Intelligencer, 1818. [150th Anniversary Edition edited by Edith Wolfe. Honolulu: Woman's Board of Missions for the Pacific Islands (the Hawaii Conference of the United Church of Christ), 1968.]

    Contains excerpts from Obookiah's diary and reports of his conversations; the first record of the English of a Hawaiian.

Bell, Aubrey Fitz Gerald. *Portugal of the Portuguese.* New York: C. Scribner's and Sons, 1915.

*"Bilingualism," *Encyclopaedia Britannica,* 14th ed. (1929), III, 562.

Bingham, Hiram. *A Residence of Twenty-One Years in the Sandwich Islands; or, The Civil, Religious, and Political History of Those Islands: Comprising a Particular View of the Missionary Operations Connected with the Introduction and Progress of Christianity and Civilization Among the Hawaiian People.* Hartford: H. Huntington and New York: S. Converse, 1848.

    The preface to the first edition is dated June 7, 1847.

Bishop, Artemas. "Address. A Brief History of the Translation of the Holy Scriptures into the Hawaiian Language," *The Friend,* August, 1844, pp. 74-75. (Paper read before the Sandwich Islands Bible Society, June 12, 1844.)

Bishop, Isabella L. (Bird). *The Hawaiian Archipelago. Six Months among the Palm Groves, Coral Reefs, and Volcanoes of the Sandwich Islands.* 4th ed. London: G. P. Putnam's Sons, 1893. (First ed.; London: John Murray, 1875.) [Now reprinted: *Six Months in the Sandwich Islands* (Honolulu: University of Hawaii Press for the Friends of the Library of Hawaii, 1964).]

    The author traveled in Hawaii during Lunalilo's reign.

Blount Report. See: U. S. Senate, Committee on Foreign Relations.

Bloxam, Andrew. *Diary of Andrew Bloxam, Naturalist of the "Blonde" on Her Trip from England to the Hawaiian Islands, 1824-25.* Bernice P. Bishop Museum Special Publication 10. Honolulu: Bernice P. Bishop Museum, 1925.

*Boehm, Max Hildebert. "Isolation," *Encyclopaedia of the Social Sciences* (New York, 1930-1935), VIII (1932), 350-352.

*————."Nationalism: Theoretical Aspects," *Encyclopaedia of the Social Sciences,* XI (1933), 231-240.

Brauns, Ernst Ludwig. *Praktische Belehrungen und Räthschlage für Reisende und Auswanderer nach Amerika.* Braunschweig: H. Vogler, 1929.

Breed, Eleanor D. "A Study of the English Vocabulary of Junior High School Pupils." Unpublished M.A. thesis, University of Hawaii, 1928.

    Great retardation is shown in the vocabulary of Washington Junior High School students in Honolulu, especially after the eighth grade. This is attributed to the fact that 73 percent of the students come from non-English-speaking homes.

*Briggs, L. Vernon. *Experiences of a Medical Student in Honolulu, and on the Island of Oahu, 1881.* Boston: David D. Nickerson Company, 1926.

†Bright, William (ed.). *Sociolinguistics: Proceedings of the UCLA Sociolinguistics Conference, 1964.* The Hague: Mouton and Company, 1966.

*Brinton, Crane. "Equality," *Encyclopaedia of the Social Sciences* (New York, 1930-1935), V (1931), 574-580 (esp. 578, col. 2 to 279, col. 1).

*Brodie, H. H. "An Attempt to Find a Natural Correlated Method of Teaching English Wherein the Child Expresses His Child Life and Activities," *Hawaii Educational Review,* XIII, No. 2 (October, 1924), 27-28.

    Brodie explains his methods at Eleele School, reputed to have the best English of any school on the island of Kauai.

Brookes, Edgar H., *et al. Coming of Age: Studies in South African Citizenship and Politics.* Cape Town: Maskew Miller, Ltd., 1930.

    Contains essays by T. J. Haarhoff and R. F. Currey.

Brown, Lawrence Guy. *Immigration: Cultural Conflicts and Social Adjustments.* New York: Longmans, Green and Company, 1933.

    Valuable chiefly for the quotations from Thomas and Znaniecki, *The Polish Peasant in Europe and America* and H. A. Miller, *The School and the Immigrant.*

Brunner, Edmund de S. *Immigrant Farmers and Their Children.* Publication of the American Institute of Social and Religious Research. Garden City, N. Y.: Doubleday, Doran and Company, 1929.

*Buller, J. P. "Fundamental Requirements of a Good Command of English," *Hawaii Educational Review,* XIII, No. 4 (December, 1924), 77-78.

    A discussion of the language difficulties of Oriental students, especially at McKinley High School in Honolulu.

*Bureau of Public Instruction. See: Hawaii. Public Instruction.

†Cariaga, Roman R. "The Filipinos in Hawaii." Unpublished M.A. thesis, University of Hawaii, 1936.

†————. *The Filipinos in Hawaii: Economic and Social Conditions, 1906-1936.* Honolulu: Filipino Public Relations Bureau, 1937.

†Carr, Denzel. "Comparative Treatment of Epenthetic and Paragogic Vowels in English Loan Words in Japanese and Hawaiian," *Semitic and Oriental Studies: A Volume Presented to William Popper on the Occasion of His 75th Birthday, Oct. 29, 1949* (University of California Publications in Semitic Philology, No. 11), 1951, pp. 13-26. (Reprinted in *Language Learning*, XIV, Nos. 1 and 2 [1964], 21-36.)

*Census of the Hawaiian Islands. See: Hawaii. Public Instruction. *Census.* . . .

Chen, Ta. *Chinese Migrations, with Special Reference to Labor Conditions.* Bulletin of the United States Bureau of Labor Statistics, No. 340. Washington: Government Printing Office, 1923.

See especially Chapter VII, "Chinese in Hawaii," pp. 11-127.

"Chinese Language Schools Have Enrollment of 3,372," *Honolulu Star-Bulletin,* November 24, 1934.

Chock Lun. "Chinese Organizations," *The United Chinese News* (Honolulu), January 6 to June 16, 1934.

See especially articles of January 20 and 27 and February 3 and 10.

Churchill, William. *Beach-la-mar: The Jargon or Trade Speech of the Western Pacific.* Carnegie Institution of Washington, Publication No. 154. Washington, D. C.: Carnegie Institution of Washington, 1911.

*Coelho, F. Adolpho. "Os dialectos românicos ou neolatinos na Africa, Asia e América," *Boletim da Sociedade de Geografia de Lisboa,* II, No. 3 (1880-1881), 129-196; III, No. 8 (1882), 451-478; VI (1886), 705-755. [Also published separately in Lisbon, 1881-1883.]

*Colket, G. Hamilton. "Japanese Schools in Hawaii," *The Friend,* XCIII, No. 10 (October, 1923), 243-244.

A history of the Japanese language school controversy up to that date—favorable to the schools.

*Coman, Katharine. *The History of Contract Labor in the Hawaiian Islands.* Publication of the American Economic Association, Third Series, Vol. IV, No. 3. New York: Macmillan Company, 1903.

Coming of Age. See: Brookes, Edgar H., *et al.*

"Confessions of Joe Manuel of the Raddio Patrol." See: Stroup, "Confessions . . ."

"Creole," *Encyclopaedia Britannica,* 11th ed. (1910), VII, 409.

*Curme, George O. *Syntax.* (Vol. III of *A Grammar of the English Language,* by George O. Curme and Hans Kurath.) New York: D. C. Heath and Company, 1931.

Currey, R. F. "English in the National Life," in *Coming of Age,* by Edgar H. Brookes, *et al.* (Cape Town, 1930), pp. 75-86.

"Da Terrific Probslem." See: Stroup, "Confessions . . . ," *Honolulu Star-Bulletin*, November 19, 1932.

Das, Upendra K. (comp.). "Terms Used on Hawaiian Plantations." Hawaii: Experiment Station, Agricultural Department, Hawaiian Sugar Planters' Association, 1930. (Mimeographed.)

A list of Hawaiian, Japanese, and Filipino words in use on the plantations of Hawaii, sent in by plantation men in reply to a circular letter.

*Davies, H. R. *Yün-nan: The Link between India and the Yangtze*. Cambridge: Cambridge University Press, 1909.

Discusses the bilingual tribes of Shans, etc., which are being assimilated to the Chinese culturally and linguistically.

*Dean, Arthur L. "Can We Teach 1000 Basic Words?" *The New Americans* (Honolulu), XIII, No. 1 (January, 1933), 5.

A splendid example of the man-in-the-street's muddled ideas of the language problem in Hawaii.

Delaisi, Francis. *Political Myths and Economic Realities*. New York: Viking Press, 1927.

See pp. 168-177 for the concept of a language of command.

*Department of Public Instruction. See: Hawaii. Public Instruction.

"Dialect," *Encyclopaedia Britannica*, 11th ed. (1910), VIII, 155-156.

Diary of Andrew Bloxam. See: Bloxam, Andrew.

*Dietrich, Adolphe. "Les parlers créoles des Mascareignes," *Romania*, XX (1891), 216-277.

Drewes, G. W. J. "The Influence of Western Civilisation on the Language of the East Indian Archipelago," in *The Effect of Western Influence on Native Civilisations in the Malay Archipelago*, edited by B. Schrieke (Batavia, Java: G. Wolff and Company, 1929), pp. 126-157.

†Elbert, Samuel H. "The Hawaiian Dictionaries, Past and Future," in *Sixty-Second Annual Report of the Hawaiian Historical Society for the Year 1953* (Honolulu, 1954), pp. 5-18.

†————, and Keala, Samuel A. *Conversational Hawaiian*. 5th ed. Honolulu: University of Hawaii Press, 1965.

Evans, Maurice S. *Black and White in South East Africa: A Study in Sociology*. London: Longmans, Green and Company, Ltd., 1916.

See especially pp. 51-52.

*Flacq, Jean Charlemagne. *The Evolution of French Canada*. New York: Macmillan Company, 1926.

See especially pp. 147-148 and 177.

†Franck, Harry A. *Roaming in Hawaii*. New York: Frederick A. Stokes Company, 1937.

*Gamio, Manuel. *Mexican Immigration to the United States: A Study of Human Migration and Adjustment.* Chicago: University of Chicago Press, 1930.

*Gilliéron Jules, and Edmont, E. *Atlas linguistique de la France.* Paris: Champion, 1902-1912.

Girvin, James W. *The Master Planter or Life in the Cane Fields of Hawaii.* Honolulu: Press of the Hawaiian Gazette Company, Ltd., 1910.

　　A formless piece of fiction containing a melange of material on early plantation life, apparently in the 1870's.

Graff, Willem L. *Language and Languages: An Introduction to Linguistics.* New York: D. Appleton and Company, 1932.

*Gulick, (Rev. and Mrs.) Orramel Hinckley. *The Pilgrims of Hawaii: Their Own Story of Their Pilgrimage from New England and Life Work in the Sandwich Islands, Now Known as Hawaii, with Explanatory and Illustrative Material Compiled and Verified from Original Sources.* New York: Fleming H. Revell Company, 1918.

Haarhoff, T. J. "Afrikaans in the National Life," in *Coming of Age,* by Edgar H. Brookes *et al.* (Cape Town, 1930), pp. 45-74.

†Hall, Robert A., Jr. *Pidgin and Creole Languages.* Ithaca, N. Y.: Cornell University Press, 1966.

Hamilton, Johanna. "Zur Sprachbeeinflussung in anderssprachiger Umgebung," *Sociologus,* IX, No. 4 (December, 1933), 427-439.

　　English synopsis, p. 439: "Along what lines a language of a minority in foreign linguistic surroundings is affected" is studied among the Germans in Ontario.

Handy, E. S. Craighill. *Cultural Revolution in Hawaii.* Honolulu: Institute of Pacific Relations, 1931.

　　An invaluable summary of the revolution in native culture which followed the advent of the Westerner.

Harada, Koichi Glenn. "A Survey of the Japanese Language Schools in Hawaii." Unpublished M.A. thesis, University of Hawaii, 1934.

†Haugen, Einar. *The Norwegian Language in America: A Study of Bilingual Behavior.* Philadelphia: University of Pennsylvania Press, 1953. 2 vols.

*Hawaii. Governor. Messages of the Governors of Hawaii to the Legislature of the Territory of Hawaii. *Message of Governor L. E. Pinkham to the Ninth Regular Session of the Legislature of the Territory of Hawaii, February 21, 1917,* pp. 22-24. *Message of Hon. C. J. McCarthy, Governor of Hawaii, to the Legislature, Territory of Hawaii, November 10, 1920, Special Session,* pp. 6-7. *Message of Hon. W. R. Farrington, Governor of Hawaii, to the Legislature, Territory of Hawaii, February 21, 1923, Twelfth Session,* pp. 12-14. *Message of Hon. Wallace R. Farrington, Governor of Hawaii, to the Legislature, Territory of Hawaii,*

February 18, 1925, Thirteenth Session, pp. 14-15. *Message of Hon. Wallace R. Farrington, Governor of Hawaii, to the Legislature, Territory of Hawaii, February 20, 1929, Fifteenth Session*, pp. 17-18.

————. *Report of the Governor of Hawaii to the Secretary of the Interior.* Washington: Government Printing Office, 1920-1934.

Reports of 1920, pp. 7-8, 57-62 [by Gov. McCarthy]; 1921, pp. 11-12 [by Gov. McCarthy]; 1922, pp. 5-6 (a brief history of the language schools), 63-65 [by Gov. Farrington]; 1923, pp. 5-9 [by Gov. Farrington]; 1924, p. 4 [by Gov. Farrington]; 1925, pp. 69-70 [by Gov. Farrington]; 1926, p. 69 [by Gov. Farrington]; 1927, pp. 79-80 [by Gov. Farrington]; 1928, pp. 83-84 [by Gov. Farrington]. See also Report of 1934 for figures on population.

Hawaii. Legislature. *Journal of the House of Representatives of the Legislature of the Territory of Hawaii*, 1900 to 1927.

————. *Senate Journal of the Legislature of the Territory of Hawaii*, 1900 to 1927.

*————. *Session Laws of the Territory of Hawaii.* Acts 30 and 36 of the Eleventh Legislature, Special Session of 1920. Act 216 of the Eleventh Legislature, Regular Session of 1921. Acts 171 and 182 of the Twelfth Legislature, Regular Session of 1923. Act 152 of the Thirteenth Legislature, Regular Session of 1925.

Hawaii. Public Instruction. *Census of the Hawaiian Islands, Taken December 27, 1884, under the Direction of the Board of Education.*

*————. *Course of Study in Primary Grades, Grades I to III.* Honolulu, September, 1924.

See section on language habits, pp. 20-21.

————. *Report of the General Superintendent of the Census, 1890.* Honolulu, 1891.

*————. *Report of the General Superintendent of the Census, 1896.* Honolulu, 1897.

*————. Reports of the Department of Public Instruction (biennial, from December 31 of even-numbered years).

The Report of December 31, 1912, contains a sketch of the "Japanese Schools, Territory of Hawaii," by S. Sheba, editor of a Japanese newspaper. The Report of December 31, 1920, contains a historical sketch of language schools in Hawaii, pp. 26-27. The Reports of 1921-22, pp. 3-6; of 1923-24, pp. 84-87; of 1925-26, pp. 123-125, contain some material on the part played by the Department of Public Instruction regarding the schools; while the Reports from 1921-22 on, give foreign language school enrollment. Scattered information on the earlier language schools can be found in Reports prior to 1912.

————. Reports of the state head of the school system, to the Legislature under the Kingdom and the Republic of Hawaii, to the Governor under the Territory. (The titles differ from year to year.) Quoted as *Report* of such and such a year. The dates are:

August 1, 1846.

April 29, 1847.

April 28, 1848.

April, 1850.

May 12, 1851.

April 14, 1852.

April 6, 1853.

April 8, 1854.

April 7, 1855.

April, 1856.

1858; 1860; 1862; 1864; 1866 (to the Legislature meeting in the respective years).

1868; 1870; 1872; 1874; 1876; 1878; 1880; 1882; 1884; 1886; 1888; 1890; 1892; 1894; 1896 (figures as of January 1 of each even-numbered year).

1897 (for the biennial period ending December 31, 1897).

1899 (for the biennial period ending December 31, 1899).

1900 (for the year ending December 31, 1900).

1902 (figures as of December 31; and so for the rest of the biennial reports).

1904; 1906; 1908; 1910; 1912; 1914; 1916; 1918; 1920; 1921-22; 1924; 1925-26; 1927-28; 1929-30; 1931-32.

————. *School Directory.* 1933-1934.

Hawaii. *Revised Laws of Hawaii, 1925,* Vol. I.

See Chapter 32, "Foreign Language Schools," Sections 390-399.

†Hawaii. University, Drama Department. *University of Hawaii Plays.* 1958-1962. Honolulu: University of Hawaii, 1963. 5 vols. (Typewritten.)

†Hawaii. University, English Department. *College Plays.* 1937-1956. Honolulu: University of Hawaii. 10 vols. (Typewritten.)

Hawaii Educational Review. Honolulu: Department of Public Instruction, Territory of Hawaii, 1913-[1954].

The organ of the Hawaii Educational Association. It contains some references (other than the articles cited) to the problem of teaching English—but surprisingly few, and those are valuable chiefly as showing the limitations of educational thought in Hawaii.

Hawaii Hochi. Japanese daily with English section; George W. Wright, English editor. See especially English editorials of September 18, 1925;

September 26, 1925; February 21, 1927; February 23, 1927. The *Hawaii Hochi* adopted an uncompromising attitude toward legislation directed against the language schools and was largely responsible for the victory of the schools.

*Hawaii Hōchi Sha Hakkō. *Hawaii no Nippon-gō-Gakkō ni Kansuru Shiso Oyobi Futai Jiken* (*The Test Case and Its Collateral Cases Relative to the Japanese Language Schools of the Territory*). Honolulu: n.d. [c. 1927].

Reprints of articles in the *Hawaii Hochi*, covering the language school controversy.

"Hawaii Journalism Ends Its First Century Today; Maui Paper Blazed Trail," *Honolulu Star-Bulletin*, February 14, 1934.

Hawaii Nenkan (*Hawaiian Japanese Annual and Directory*).

Published in Japanese by the *Hawaii Shinpo* from 1902 or 1903 to 1924 and by the *Nippu Jiji* from 1927 on. Contains statistics of the Japanese schools.

Hawaiian Almanac and Annual. See: *Hawaiian Annual.*

Hawaiian Annual, 1875–.

Commonly referred to as "Thrum's Annual." Contains many articles which throw indirect light on linguistic conditions in Hawaii.

Hawaiian Census of 1884. See: Hawaii. Public Instruction. *Census of the Hawaiian Islands . . .*

Hawaiian Census of 1890. See: Hawaii. Public Instruction. *Report of the General Superintendent of the Census . . .*

Hawaiian Census of 1896. See: Hawaii. Public Instruction. *Report of the General Superintendent of the Census . . .*

Hawaiian *House Journal.* See: Hawaii. Legislature. *Journal . . .*

Hawaiian Immigration Society. *Report of the Secretary, with a Map of the Hawaiian Islands.* Honolulu: Executive Committee of the Society, 1874.

Hawaiian Sugar Planters' Association. *Story of Sugar in Hawaii.* Honolulu: Hawaiian Sugar Planters' Association, 1926. (Rev. ed.: 1929.)

*Hayashida, Akiyoshi. "Japanese Moral Instruction as a Factor in the Americanization of Citizens of Japanese Ancestry." Unpublished M.A. thesis, University of Hawaii, 1933.

Holds that the language schools perform a moral rather than a linguistic function.

*Hintze, Hedwig. "Regionalism," *Encyclopaedia of the Social Sciences* (New York, 1930-1935), XIII (1934), 208-218.

Hiraiwa, Masa. "Life of Early Japanese Immigrant Laborers to Hawaii is Recounted," *Nippu Jiji,* October 3, 1934.

Hohman, Elmo P. *The American Whaleman: A Study of Life and Labor in the Whaling Industry.* New York: Longmans, Green and Company, 1928.

Honolulu Advertiser.

> Daily English language paper; published by Lorrin A. Thurston. Before the litigation of the language schools began, the *Advertiser* was critical of the language schools, but conciliatory toward the Japanese community; afterward, it became rather hostile toward the litigating schools.

Honolulu Directory. See: Polk-Husted Directory Co.

Honolulu Star-Bulletin.

> Daily English language paper; controlled by Wallace R. Farrington. Always hostile toward the Japanese language schools and toward the policies of the *Hawaii Hochi.*

Hörmann, Bernhard Lothar. "The Germans in Hawaii." Unpublished M.A. thesis, University of Hawaii, 1931.

†————. *Selected Bibliography on Social Research in Hawaii by Sources.* Romanzo Adams Social Research Laboratory, University of Hawaii, Report No. 37. May, 1963.

†Hymes, Dell (ed.). See: Reinecke, John E., "Trade Jargons. . . ."

Ichihashi, Yamato. *Japanese in the United States: A Critical Study of the Problems of the Japanese Immigrants and Their Children.* Stanford: Stanford University Press, 1932.

*Ifa, Fuyu. "The Fate of the Japanese Language in Hawaii," *Jitsugyō-no-Hawaii,* XVII, No. 11 (November 1, 1928), (?).

International Migrations. See: National Bureau of Economic Research, Inc.

*Japanese Educational Association of Hawaii. *A Brief Survey of the Foreign Language School Question.* Honolulu, February, 1923.

> A brief historical sketch; the thirteen appendices contain copies of important documents of the early stages of the controversy.

*"The Japanese Schools in Hawaii," *The Friend,* LXXIV, No. 7 (July, 1926), 147-148.

*"Jargon," *Encyclopaedia Britannica,* 11th ed. (1910), XV, 275.

"Jargon," *New English Dictionary* (i.e., *Oxford English Dictionary*).

Jarrett, Lorna H. *Hawaii and Its People.* Honolulu: Honolulu Star-Bulletin, Ltd., 1933.

> See especially pp. 187-190.

*Jespersen, Otto. *Growth and Structure of the English Language.* 4th ed. New York: D. Appleton and Company, 1929.

————. *Language: Its Nature, Development and Origin.* New York: Henry Holt and Company, 1921.

* ————. *A Modern English Grammar on Historical Principles,* Part II, Vol.

1: *Syntax.* Heidelberg: Carl Winters, 1922.

*Johnston, Sir Harry Hamilton. *Liberia.* New York: Dodd, Mead and Company, 1906. 2 vols.

Jones, Thomas Jesse (ed.). See: African Education Commission.

"Jose Bulatao 1st President," *Honolulu Star-Bulletin,* May 17, 1934.

*Judd, Laura Fish. *Honolulu.* Reprinted. Honolulu: Honolulu Star-Bulletin, Ltd., 1928.

Judd, Henry Pratt. "The Changes in the Hawaiian Language in the Last Hundred Years." Unpublished study. [Not able to verify its existence or to secure further details.]

Kahn, Morton C. *Djuka: The Bush Negroes of Dutch Guiana.* New York: Viking Press, 1931.

Kawakami, Kiyoshi Karl. *Asia at the Door: A Study of the Japanese Question in Continental United States, Hawaii and Canada.* New York and Chicago: Fleming H. Revell Company, 1914.

*————. *The Real Japanese Question.* New York: Macmillan Company, 1921.

*Keesing, Felix M. *The Changing Maori.* Memoirs of the Board of Maori Ethnological Research, Vol. 4. New Plymouth, N. Z.: Thomas Avery and Sons, Ltd., 1928.

A discussion of Maori problems of language and culture (pp. 61-62, 87-88, 105-106, 133-142, 173-175) which throws light on the change of language among the Hawaiians.

*————. "Language Change and Native Education in Samoa," *Mid-Pacific Magazine,* XLIV, No. 4 (October, 1932), 303-313.

Largely the same material as pp. 444-447 of *Modern Samoa* but expanded and more specifically devoted to linguistic problems; illuminating.

————. *Modern Samoa: Its Government and Changing Life.* London: George Allen and Unwin, Ltd., 1934.

Chapter X, "Educational Influences," especially pp. 437-439 on the results of learning English; p. 441 on the influence of the English-language motion-pictures; and pp. 444-447 on the processes of language development and the foundation of a language dualism in Samoa.

†Kess, Joseph. "English Influences in the Phonology of Japanese as Spoken in Hawaii." Unpublished M.A. thesis, University of Hawaii, 1965.

King, Myrtle (Chairman, Territorial Course of Study Committee in English Expression). "English Course of Study Questionnaire." Mimeographed materials presented to intermediate school teachers of Hawaii during the spring of 1934 and summarized during the first semester, 1934-1935.

Most teachers appeared unqualified to analyze the situation. On the basis of the data gathered, and supported by the Committee, Miss King, who has taught English abroad, is preparing a workbook based on Hawaiian needs. Her work represents the most realistic, analytical, wide-scale attempt made thus far to adapt the teaching of English so as to bring the speakers of the local dialect to use more nearly standard English.

*Klein, Henri F. "Dialect," *The Encyclopedia Americana* (1940), IX, 56-58.

†Knowlton, Edgar C., Jr. "Pidgin English and Portuguese," in *Proceedings of the Symposium on Historical, Archaeological and Linguistic Studies on Southern China, S. E. Asia and the Hong Kong Region,* edited by F. S. Drake (Hong Kong: Hong Kong University Press, 1967), pp. 228-237. Paper read at the Golden Jubilee Congress (Sept. 11-16, 1961), University of Hong Kong, Sept. 14, 1961.

†————. "Portuguese in Hawaii," *Kentucky Foreign Language Quarterly,* VII, No. 4 (December, 1960), 212-218.

†————. "The Portuguese Language Press of Hawaii," *Social Process in Hawaii,* XXIV (1960), 89-99.

*Kohn, Hans. *Nationalism in the Soviet Union.* Translated by E. W. Dickes from *Der Nationalismus in der Sowjetunion* (Frankfurt am Main: Societats-Verlag, 1932). London: George Routledge and Sons, Ltd., 1933.

See especially Chapter VI, "Language and Culture." Pp. 87-89 contrast the bourgeois nationalist and the communist ways of spreading their culture; pp. 91-93 contain a masterly and concise analysis of the function of speech in political nationalism.

Kono, Ayako. "Language as a Factor in the Achievement of American-Born Students of Japanese Ancestry." Unpublished M.A. thesis, University of Hawaii, 1934.

"There is every indication that the test performance of Japanese children is lowered by language handicap." A careful study.

Krapp, George Philip. *The English Language in America.* New York: Century Company, 1925. 2 vols.

————. *The Knowledge of English.* New York: Henry Holt and Company, 1927.

†Kuykendall, Ralph S. *The Hawaiian Kingdom, 1778-1854: Foundation and Transformation.* Honolulu: University of Hawaii Press, 1938.

†————. *The Hawaiian Kingdom, 1854-1874: Twenty Critical Years.* Honolulu: University of Hawaii Press, 1953.

————. *A History of Hawaii.* New York: Macmillan Company, 1926.

Prepared under the direction of the Historical Commission of the Territory of Hawaii. Though elementary, the best general history of

Hawaii [at the time], very valuable for reference, especially to some phases of social and economic history.

————, and Gill, Lorin Tarr. *Hawaii in the World War.* Honolulu: Historical Commission of the Territory of Hawaii, 1928.

Suppression of the German language and German schools during the World War, pp. 435-440.

†Lai, Kum Pui. "The Natural History of the Chinese Language School in Hawaii." Unpublished M.A. thesis, University of Hawaii, 1935.

*"Language," *Encyclopaedia Britannica*, 11th ed. (1910), XVI, 179.

*"Language," *Encyclopaedia Britannica*, 14th ed. (1929), XIII, 686-703.

Based almost verbatim on Jespersen's *Language.*

†Larry, Etta Cynthia. "A Study of the Sounds of the English Language as Spoken by Five Racial Groups in the Hawaiian Islands." Unpublished Ph.D. dissertation, Columbia University, 1942.

Lasker, Bruno. *Filipino Immigration to Continental United States and to Hawaii.* Chicago: University of Chicago Press for the American Council, Institute of Pacific Relations, 1931.

Valuable especially for Appendix B, "The Movement of Filipino Population to and from Hawaii," by Romanzo Adams, and Appendix C, "Provinces of Origin of Filipino Laborers Migrating from the Philippine Islands to Hawaii, 1916-1928."

Lenz, Rodolfo. *El papiamento, la lengua criolla de Curazao (la gramática más sencilla).* [Reprinted from *Anales de la Universidad de Chile* II.4.695-768, 1021-1090 (1926) and II.5.287-327, 365-412 (1927).] Santiago de Chile: Balcells and Cia., 1928.

The present writer used only an extract, pp. 31 ff.

Leroy-Beaulieu, Paul. *De la colonisation chez les peuples modernes.* 4th ed. Paris: Guillaumin et Cie., 1891.

Especially pp. 189-234.

Lind, Andrew W. "Occupational Trends among Immigrant Groups in Hawaii," *Social Forces*, VII, No. 2 (December, 1928), 290-299.

*"Lingua," *New English Dictionary* (i.e., *Oxford English Dictionary*).

*"Lingua Franca," *Encyclopaedia Britannica*, 14th ed. (1929), XIV, 163.

Littler, Robert M. C. *The Governance of Hawaii: A Study in Territorial Administration.* Stanford: Stanford University Press, 1929.

The language schools are discussed briefly on pp. 138-142.

*Loram, Charles T. *The Education of the South African Native.* London: Longmans, Green and Company, Ltd., 1927.

Lum, Kalfred D. "The Education of the Chinese in Hawaii," in *The Chinese of Hawaii,* (ed.) Overseas Penman Club (Honolulu, 1929), pp. 18-20.

A brief account of eleven Chinese language schools in Honolulu.

Lydecker, Robert C. (comp.). *Roster Legislatures of Hawaii 1841-1918. Constitutions of Monarchy and Republic. Speeches of Sovereigns and President.* Archives of Hawaii, Publication No. 1. Honolulu: Hawaiian Gazette Company, Ltd., 1918.

Lydgate, J. M. "The Hawaiian Contribution to English," in *Hawaiian Annual,* 1914, pp. 131-135.

*Macartney, C. A. *National States and National Minorities.* Oxford: Oxford University Press, 1934.

A very thorough survey of national minorities in Europe and the Near East, with much attention to linguistic problems.

Malinowski, Bronislaw. "The Problem of Meaning in Primitive Languages," in *The Meaning of Meaning,* by C. K. Ogden and I. A. Richards (London: Harcourt, Brace and Company, Inc., 1927), Supplement I.

†Matsuda, Mitsugu. *The Japanese in Hawaii, 1868-1967: A Bibliography of the First Hundred Years.* Hawaii Series, No. 1. Honolulu: Social Science Research Institute, University of Hawaii, 1968.

This is the first of a projected series of annotated bibliographies of Hawaii's people of Asian ancestry. The other three will cover the Koreans, the Chinese, and the Filipinos.

*Maunier, René. *Sociologie coloniale: Introduction à l'étude de contact des races.* Paris: Les éditions Domat-Montchrestien, F. Loviton et Cie., 1932.

Mead, Margaret. *Growing Up in New Guinea.* New York: Blue Ribbon Books, Inc., 1930.

See pp. 304-306 for a fine example of the limitations of Beach-la-mar pidgin when it must bear the weight of complex ideas of relationship and trade; also pp. 40-41 for how Melanesian children learn pidgin.

Mellen, George. "Chart Sui Arp" (Lau Yee Chai advertisement), *Honolulu Star-Bulletin,* April 14, 1933.

Mencken, Henry L. *The American Language.* 3rd ed. New York: Alfred A. Knopf, 1923.

This edition contains valuable examples of foreign mixed speech and an excellent bibliography.

*Messages of the Governors of Hawaii to the Legislature of the Territory of Hawaii. See: Hawaii. Governor. *Messages* . . .

*Miller, Herbert Adolphus. *Races, Nations and Classes.* Philadelphia: J. B. Lippincott Company, 1924.

See Chapter VI, "Language as a Symbol [of Nationality]."

————. *The School and the Immigrant.* Cleveland: Survey Committee of the Cleveland Foundation, 1916.

Millis, Harry Alvin. *The Japanese Problem in the United States: An Investigation for the Commission on Relations with Japan Appointed by the Federal Council of the Churches of Christ of America.* New York: Macmillan Company. 1915.

Moore, Golda Pauline. "Hawaii During the Whaling Era, 1820-1880." Unpublished M.A. thesis, University of Hawaii, 1934.

Mori, Masatoshi Gensen. *The Pronunciation of Japanese.* Tokyo: Herald-Sha, 1929.

*Mowat, Olive Day. *A Synopsis of English Sounds, with Corrective Exercises for Elementary, High, and Night Schools.* New York: Macmillan Company, 1926.

    A list of "Errors in Pronunciation Found in Schools of Hawaii and in Several Cities of the United States" is given on pp. 97-101. It represents seven years of observation.

†Murdoch, John. "Ethnological Results of the Point Barrow Expedition," in *Ninth Annual Report of the Bureau of Ethnology to the Secretary of the Smithsonian Institution, 1887-1888* (Washington, D. C., 1892), pp. 3-441.

National Bureau of Economic Research, Inc. *International Migrations.* Vol. I. Statistics compiled on behalf of the International Labour Office, Geneva, with Introduction and Notes by Imre Ferenczi and edited on behalf of the National Bureau of Economic Research by Walter F. Willcox. New York: National Bureau of Economic Research, Inc., 1929.

    Contains data relevant to migration to and from Hawaii.

"Naturalization of Tongues," *The Interpreter* (New York), VIII, No. 4 (April, 1928), 7-15.

†Navarro Tomás, Tomás. *El español en Puerto Rico: Contribución a la geografía lingüística.* Río Piedras: Universidad de Puerto Rico, 1948.

Nippu Jiji.

    Japanese daily with English section; Yasutaro Soga, editor. The editorials written in Japanese by Mr. Soga were for the most part translated for the English section of the following day. The *Nippu Jiji* usually took a middle-of-the-road attitude, opposing litigation of the language schools and the *Hawaii Hochi* on the one hand and the anti-Japanese views of the *Advertiser* and especially of the *Star-Bulletin* on the other. Its news reports of the foreign language school controversy are probably the fullest and least biased of any. Its editorials, though showing Mr. Soga's personal bias, reflect a considerable part of the Japanese public opinion.

Nordhoff, Charles. *Northern California, Oregon, and the Sandwich Islands.*

New York: Harper and Brothers, 1874.

✳†Nunes, Shiho. "The Hawaii English Project: Brave New Venture," *Hawaii Schools,* IV, No. 3 (November, 1967), 14-17.

N. W. *Ayer and Son's Directory of Newspapers and Periodicals.* (American Newspaper Annual and Directory.) Philadelphia: N. W. Ayer and Son, Inc., (annually).

This directory should be of great value in checking the circulation of the foreign language press in Hawaii.

Obookiah. See: Beecher and Harvey.

Odgers, George Allen. "Educational Legislation in Hawaii, 1845-1892." Unpublished M.A. thesis, University of Hawaii, 1932.

*Odum, Howard W., and Johnson, Guy B. *The Negro and His Songs.* Chapel Hill: University of North Carolina Press, 1925.

See especially pp. 10-11 and 292.

Ogden, C. K., and Richards, I. A. See: Malinowski.

*Okumura, Takie. "The Chain Schools," *The New Americans* (Honolulu), XIII, No. 6 (June, 1933), 1, 3-6.

Treats of the language classes conducted in the Honolulu public school buildings by the Japanese Language Education Association.

Opukahaia. See: Beecher and Harvey.

*Otremba, Frances M. "The English Placement Test as a Criterion of College Aptitude with Respect to the Prediction of Success in Freshman English Courses." Unpublished M. A. thesis, University of Hawaii, 1932.

Overseas Penman Club. See: Lum.

*Pankhurst, Estelle Sylvia. *Delphos: The Future of International Language.* New York: E. P. Dutton and Company, 1927.

†Pap, Leo. *Portuguese-American Speech: An Outline of Speech Conditions among Portuguese Immigrants in New England and Elswhere in the United States.* New York: King's Crown Press, 1949.

*Park, Robert E. *The Immigrant Press and Its Control.* New York and London: Harper and Brothers, 1922.

*————, and Burgess, Ernest W. *Introduction to the Science of Sociology.* 2nd ed. Chicago: University of Chicago Press, 1930.

See the following chapter-end bibliographies: "Language Frontiers and Nationality," pp. 274-275; "Dialects as a Factor in Isolation," pp. 275-276; "Slang, Argot, and Universes of Discourse," pp. 428-429; "Language Revivals and Nationalism," pp. 945-946; and the bibliography for the chapter on "Assimilation," pp. 775-782.

See also the following extracts: "The Analysis of Blended Cultures," by W. H. R. Rivers, pp. 746-750; "The Extension of Roman Culture in Gaul," by John H. Cornyn, pp. 751-754; "The Competition of the Cultural Languages," by E. H. Babbitt, pp. 754-756; "Language as a Means and a Product of Participation," from the *Memorandum on Americanization,* pp. 763-766.

Partridge, Eric. *Slang To-day and Yesterday; with a Short Historical Sketch and Vocabularies of English, American, and Australian Slang.* London: George Routledge and Sons, Ltd., 1933.

*"Patois," *Encyclopaedia Britannica,* 11th ed. (1910), XX, 930.

†Petersen, Robert O. H. "The Hilo Language Development Project," *Elementary English,* XLIV, No. 7 (November, 1967), 753-755 and 774.

"Pidgin-English," *Nouveau Larousse Illustré* (Paris, 1898-1904), VI, 875.

*Pillsbury, Walter B., and Meader, Clarence L. *The Psychology of Language.* New York and London: D. Appleton and Company, 1928.

Polk-Husted Directory Co. *Directory of City and County of Honolulu and the Territory of Hawaii.* Honolulu: Polk-Husted Directory Company.

> The directories of Honolulu and Hawaii, issued since about 1890, are valuable, especially since 1900, for lists of foreign language publications.

*Poyen-Bellisle, René de. *Les sons et les formes du créole dans les Antilles.* Baltimore: John Murphy and Company, 1894.

> The present writer used only an extract, p. 13.

*Prince, John Dyneley. "Surinam Negro-English," *American Speech,* IX, No. 3 (October, 1934), 181-186.

Psychological Bulletin, XXVI, No. 5 (May, 1929).

> "Special Language Number," containing résumés of articles dealing with the effect of bilingualism on subjects linguistically and in relation to their intelligence-test scoring. Pp. 248-252, 262, 266-267. Special reference to D. J. Saer, "The Effects of Bilingualism on Intelligence," *British Journal of Psychology,* XIV, Pt. 1 (July, 1923), 25-38.

†Pukui, Mary Kawena, and Elbert, Samuel H. *English-Hawaiian Dictionary.* Honolulu: University of Hawaii Press, 1964.

†————. *Hawaiian-English Dictionary.* 3rd ed. Honolulu: University of Hawaii Press, 1965.

†————. *Place Names of Hawaii.* Honolulu: University of Hawaii Press, 1966.

†Reinecke, John E. "Additional Notes on Personal Names in Hawaii," *American Speech,* XVIII, No. 1 (February, 1943), 69-70.

†————. "The Competition of Languages in Hawaii," *Social Process in Hawaii,* II (May, 1936), 7-10.

*————. "Hawaiian-Island English—An Unexplored Field," *The Mid-Pacific Magazine,* XLV, No. 3 (March, 1933), 273-277.
A preliminary statement of the questions in this field.

†————. "Language and Dialect in Hawaii." Unpublished M.A. thesis, University of Hawaii, 1935.

†————. "A List of Loanwords from the Hawaiian Language in Use in the English Speech of the Hawaiian Islands." Honolulu: University of Hawaii, August, 1938. (Mimeographed.)

†————. "Marginal Languages: A Sociological Survey of the Creole Languages and Trade Jargons." Unpublished Ph.D. dissertation, Yale University, 1937.

†————. "Personal Names in Hawaii," *American Speech,* XV, No. 4 (December, 1940), 345-352.

†————. "Pidgin English in Hawaii: A Local Study in the Sociology of Language," *The American Journal of Sociology,* XLIII, No. 5 (March, 1938), 778-789.

†————. "Trade Jargons and Creole Dialects as Marginal Languages," *Social Forces,* XVII, No. 1 (October, 1938), 107-118. (Reprinted in Dell Hymes [ed.], *Language in Culture and Society* [New York: Harper and Row, 1964], pp. 534-542.)

————. (Unpublished collection of Hawaiian loanwords in English.) [For mimeographed version, see: "A List of Loanwords. . . . For published version, see: Reinecke and Tsuzaki, "Hawaiian Loanwords. . . .]

————, and Tokimasa, Aiko. "The English Dialect of Hawaii," *American Speech,* IX, No. 1 (February, 1934), 48-58; IX, No. 2 (April, 1934), 122-131.
An amateurs' effort to analyze the dialect of Hawaii, but the pioneer study in this field. Partly sociological, but chiefly devoted to an analysis of the structure of the dialect.

†————, Phan thi Thuy-Nuong, and Ton-nu Kim-Chi. "Tây Boi: Preliminary Notes on the Pidgin French Spoken in Vietnam." Paper presented at the Conference on Pidginization and Creolization of Languages (April 9-12, 1968), University of the West Indies, Kingston, Jamaica, April 11, 1968.

†————, and Tsuzaki, Stanley M. *English in Hawaii.* See: Tsuzaki and Reinecke.

†————. "Hawaiian Loanwords in Hawaiian English of the 1930's." *Oceanic Linguistics,* VI, No. 2 (Winter, 1967), 80-115.

Report of the Governor of Hawaii to the Secretary of the Interior. See: Hawaii. Governor. *Report. . . .*

Report of the President of the Board of Education to the Hawaiian Legislature. See: Hawaii. Public Instruction. Reports of the state head of the school system . . . .

*Reports of the Commissioner of Labor on Hawaii. See: U. S. Bureau of Labor.

*Reports of the Department of Public Instruction. See: Hawaii. Public Instruction. Reports of the Department of Public Instruction.

*"The Resultant Language," *The Friend,* XLIV, No. 4 (April, 1886), 10.

The Hawaiian has already shaped the future colloquial English "by limiting the vocabulary of English words and by accommodating that language more to the idiom of his own language." "The colloquial English of Hawaii nei is even now sufficiently *sui generis* to be noticeable to strangers."

*Reuter, Edward B. "The Social Process with Special Reference to the Patterns of Personality among the Chinese in Hawaii," *Publication of the Sociological Society of America,* XXVI, No. 3 (August, 1932), 86-93.

Some reference to language as affecting cultural adaptation.

Revised Laws of Hawaii, 1925. See: Hawaii. *Revised Laws.* . . .

*Richmond, Ethal Blanche. "Oral English Errors of Ninth Grade Students in the Public Schools of Hawaii." Unpublished M.A. thesis, University of Hawaii, 1930.

Roberts, Helen H. *Ancient Hawaiian Music.* Bernice P. Bishop Museum, Bulletin 29. Honolulu: Bernice P. Bishop Museum, 1926.

Romano, Juan. "That Persisting Shyness" (in "Our Own Poets" column), *Honolulu Star-Bulletin,* October 6, 1934.

"Sabir," *Nouveau Larousse Illustré* (Paris, 1898-1904), VII, 439.

Sakamaki, Shunzo. "A History of the Japanese Press in Hawaii." Unpublished M. A. thesis, University of Hawaii, 1928.

A very thorough description of the Japanese press of 1927, with considerable attention to its sociological functions. On the historical side, it is slightly deficient.

*Sapir, Edward. "Communication," *Encyclopaedia of the Social Sciences* (New York, 1930-1935), IV (1931), 78-81.

————. "Dialect," *Encyclopaedia of the Social Sciences,* V (1931), 123-126.

* ————. "Language," *Encyclopaedia of the Social Sciences,* IX (1933), 155-169.

* ————. *Language: An Introduction to the Study of Speech.* New York: Harcourt, Brace and Company, 1921.

*Sheba, S. "Japanese Schools, Territory of Hawaii." See: Hawaii. Public Instruction. Reports of the Department of Public Instruction. (Annotation.)

School Directory. See: Hawaii. Public Instruction. *School Directory.*

Schrieke, B. See: Drewes.

*Schuchardt, Hugo. "Kreolische Studien. V. Über das Melaneso-Englische," *Sitzungsberichte der k.k. Akademie der Wissenschaften zu Wien (Philosophisch-historische Klasse)*, CV (1883), 131-161.

    [For the other studies in this series, see Hall, *Pidgin and Creole Languages* (Ithaca, N. Y., 1966), pp. 173-174.]

Schultze, Ernst. "Sklaven- und Dienersprachen (sogenannte Handelssprachen: Ein Beitrag zur Sprache- und Wanderungs-Soziologie," *Sociologus*, IX, No. 4 (December, 1933), 377-418.

    English synopsis, p. 418: "Slave and Servant Languages (So-called Trade Languages): A Contribution to the Sociology of Language and Migration."

Schwartz, Henry Butler. "A Study of the Effect of Attendance at Language Schools Upon Success in the McKinley High School," *Hawaii Educational Review*, XIV, No. 2 (October, 1925), 30-31, 40-41.

*Seabrook, W. B. *The Magic Island.* New York: Harcourt, Brace and Company, 1929.

    Contains valuable references to and examples of Haitian creole, especially pp. 285-288.

Session Laws of the Territory of Hawaii. See: Hawaii. Legislature. *Session Laws. . . .*

*Shaw, George C. *The Chinook Jargon and How to Use It: A Complete and Exhaustive Lexicon of the Oldest Trade Language of the American Continent.* Seattle: Rainier Printing Company, Inc., 1909.

    Draws on the earlier lexicons.

*Sheba, S. "Japanese Schools, Territory of Hawaii." See: Hawaii. Reports of the Department of Public Instruction. (Annotation.)

Smith, Madorah E. "A Study of Five Bilingual Children from the Same Family," *Child Development*, II, No. 3 (September, 1931), 184-187.

    A study of five Chinese children in Hawaii, from which the author concludes that there is "confusion in learning to talk on the part of the bilingual children."

Smith, William C. "Pidgin English in Hawaii," *American Speech*, VIII, No. 1 (February, 1933), 15-19.

    Smith was for some time at the University of Hawaii. This article is essentially a historical summary of Hawaiian Island "pidgin," with some examples as an aid in its analysis. It does not differentiate between the levels of "pidgin."

*Soga, Yasutaro. "The Japanese Press in Hawaii," *The Mid-Pacific Magazine*, XXIII, No. 1 (January, 1922), 39-41.

Very sketchy.

Spaulding, Thomas Marshall. "The Adoption of the Hawaiian Alphabet," in *Papers of the Hawaiian Historical Society*, No. 17 (Honolulu, 1930), pp. 28-33. (Paper read before the Society, September 30, 1930.)

†Stefánsson, V. "The Eskimo Trade Jargon of Herschel Island," *American Anthropologist*, XI, No. 2 (April-June, 1909), 217-232.

Story of Sugar in Hawaii. See: Hawaiian Sugar Planters' Association. *Story. . . .*

"The Story of the Prodigal Son" (as told by Mrs. Hattie Saffery Reinhardt), *Honolulu Advertiser*, May 11, 1924. Reprinted in part in W. C. Smith, "Pidgin English in Hawaii," *American Speech*, VIII, No. 1 (February, 1933), 16. [Now also reprinted in H. A. Franck, *Roaming in Hawaii* (New York, 1937), pp. 148-150.]

An example of pidgin with a strong Japanese coloring as used by a Part-Hawaiian to a Japanese audience.

Stratford, Jane. "Cross-Section of a High School Student's Life." Unpublished M.A. thesis, University of Hawaii, 1930.

Section 5 is on "quality of English spoken by parents" (pp. 26-47). Home languages are treated on pp. 57-58; attendance at language schools on pp. 59-60; reading habits of students on pp. 112-114. The cultural background, which has much to do with the linguistic habits of the students, is fully discussed.

Stroup, Harry. "Confessions of Joe Manuel of the Raddio Patrol," *Honolulu Star-Bulletin:* June 18, Oct. 8, Nov. 19, 26; Dec. 3, 10, 17, 24, and 31, 1932; Jan. 7, 14, and 21, 1933.

————. (?) "Evangelist Speak, Prodigal Son Get Too Muchee Nice Kind Luau," *Honolulu Star-Bulletin* (c. 1929).

*Sullivan, Helen. "Literacy and Illiteracy," *Encyclopaedia of the Social Sciences* (New York, 1930-1935), IX (1933), 511-523.

A Survey of Education in Hawaii or *Survey* of 1920. See: U. S. Department of the Interior, Bureau of Education.

*Sweet, Henry. *A New English Grammar Logical and Historical.* Oxford: Oxford University Press, 1900.

Symonds, Percival M. "The Effect of Attendance at Chinese Language

Schools on Ability with the English Language," *The Journal of Applied Psychology,* VIII, No. 4 (December, 1924), 411-423.

The effect was found not to be harmful; Chinese students attending language schools were slightly better in English than those not attending.

Taft, Donald R. *Two Portuguese Communities in New England.* New York: Longmans, Green and Company, 1923.

*Tempski, Armine von. *Hula: A Romance of Hawaii.* New York: A. L. Burt Company, 1927.

* ———. *Lava: A Saga of Hawaii.* New York: Frederick A. Stokes Company, 1930.

Thomas, William Isaac, and Znaniecki, Florian. *The Polish Peasant in Europe and America.* Chicago: University of Chicago Press, 1918-1920.

*Thompson, Edgar T. (Unpublished manuscript outlining a theory of the plantation and its natural history.)

See especially the chapter, "Plantation Activity and the Moral Order." Thompson's treatment of the creole language of the plantation owes something to the present writer's oral discussion of the subject, but Thompson's treatment is very much more clear.

"Tonga," *Encyclopaedia Britannica,* 11th ed. (1910), XXVII, 3-5.

†Tsuzaki, Stanley M., and Reinecke, John E. *English in Hawaii: An Annotated Bibliography.* Oceanic Linguistics Special Publication No. 1. Honolulu: Pacific and Asian Linguistics Institute, 1966.

*U. S. Bureau of Labor. (*First*) *Report of the Commissioner of Labor on Hawaii, 1901.* Washington: Government Printing Office, 1902.

This and succeeding reports give a valuable picture of labor conditions and the composition of the laboring population, together with valuable references to the social conditions generally.

* ———. (*Second*) *Report of the Commissioner of Labor on Hawaii, 1902.* Washington: Government Printing Office, 1903.

Summary of the history of the penal labor contract system, pp. 12-20.

* ———. *Third Report of the Commissioner of Labor on Hawaii, 1905.* Washington: Government Printing Office, 1906.

* ———. *Fourth Report of the Commissioner of Labor on Hawaii, 1910.* Washington: Government Printing Office, 1911.

See p. 736 for statistics of Japanese language schools.

*U. S. Census. See: U. S. Department of Commerce, Bureau of the Census.

U. S. Census of 1900-1930. See: U. S. Department of Commerce, Bureau of the Census.

U. S. Department of Commerce, Bureau of the Census. *Twelfth Census of the United States: 1900*, Vol. III. *Thirteenth Census of the United States: 1910*, Vol. III. *Fourteenth Census of the United States: 1920*, Vol. III. *Fifteenth Census of the United States: 1930. Population Second Series: Hawaii: Composition and Characteristics of the Population and Unemployment. Occupation Statistics: Hawaii.*

*U. S. Department of Labor. *Labor Conditions in Hawaii: Letter from the Secretary of Labor Transmitting the Fifth Annual Report of the Commissioner of Labor Statistics on Labor Conditions in the Territory of Hawaii for the Year 1915.* Washington: Government Printing Office, 1916.

    See pp. 60-61 for information on Japanese language schools.

U. S. Department of the Interior, Bureau of Education. *A Survey of Education in Hawaii.* Made under the direction of the Commissioner of Education. Department of Interior, Bureau of Education Bulletin, 1920, No. 16. Washington: Government Printing Office, 1920. (Quoted in the present study as *Survey.*)

    This survey reflects the attitude toward the language schools held by many influential Americans immediately after the World War, and in turn was of importance in molding public opinion on the language schools. It also helped secure some reforms in the government schools. See especially Chapter III, "The Foreign Language Schools," the appendices, and pp. 37-42.

U. S. Senate, Committee on Foreign Relations. *Hawaiian Islands. Report of the Committee on Foreign Relations, United States Senate, with Accompanying Testimony, and Executive Documents Transmitted to Congress from January 1, 1893, to March 10, 1894.* Washington: Government Printing Office, 1894. 2 vols. (The so-called Blount Report.)

    The testimony of the various people interviewed contains several references to the degree of Americanization of the Hawaiians and to the use of the English language.

†University of Hawaii. See: Hawaii. University.

†Vanderslice, Ralph, and Pierson, Laura Shun. "Prosodic Features of Hawaiian English," *The Quarterly Journal of Speech,* LIII, No. 2 (April, 1967), 156-166.

Vendryes, Joseph. *Language: A Linguistic Introduction to History.* Translated by Paul Radin from *Le language: Introduction linguistique à l'histoire* in the series "L'evolution de l'humanité." New York: Alfred A. Knopf, 1925.

The book was completed in July, 1914; printed in 1920; and revised in 1924. There is a foreword by Henri Berr.

*Vossler, Karl. *The Spirit of Language in Civilization.* Translated from the German by Oscar Oeser. International Library of Psychology, Philosophy and Scientific Method. London: Kegan Paul, Trench, Trubner and Company, Ltd., 1932.

See especially Chapter VII, "Language Communities," and more especially section (c), "Language and the Sense of Nationality."

†Walch, David B. "The Historical Development of the Hawaiian Alphabet," *The Journal of the Polynesian Society,* LXXVI, No. 3 (September, 1967), 353-366.

*Ware, Caroline F. "Foreign Language Press," *Encyclopaedia of the Social Sciences* (New York, 1930 1935), VI (1931), 378 382.

Waterman, T. T. "Insular English," *Hawaii Educational Review,* XVIII, No. 6 (February, 1930), 145-146, 161-165.

*————. "Sidelights on English," *Hawaii Educational Review,* XVIII, No. 10 (June, 1930), 258-259 and 277-279.

*Wessel, Bessie Bloom. *An Ethnic Survey of Woonsocket, Rhode Island.* Chicago: University of Chicago Press, 1931.

The statistics on language usage among children and parents (pp. 198-209) point the way to a similar study in Hawaii. Considerable attention is paid to the French Canadians, the largest group, who for a number of generations remain bilingual and bicultural; there is a good Canadian-French bibliography on pp. 220-228.

*Westerman, Diedrich. *The African Today.* Oxford: Oxford University Press for the International Institute of African Languages and Culture, 1934.

See especially Chapter XI, "Language and Education."

*Whitney, William Dwight. *Language and the Study of Language: Twelve Lectures on the Principles of Linguistic Science.* New York: Charles Scribner and Company, 1867.

*Wilkinson, Lupton A. "Gullah *versus* Grammar," *North American Review,* CCXXXVI, No. 6 (December, 1933), 539-542.

Wirth, Louis. *The Ghetto.* Chicago: University of Chicago Press, 1928.

See especially the last chapter, "The Sociological Significance of the Ghetto."

†Wise, Claude M., and Hervey, Wesley D. "The Evolution of Hawaiian Orthography," *The Quarterly Journal of Speech,* XXXVIII, No. 3 (October, 1952), 311-325.

†Wist, Benjamin O. *A Century of Public Education in Hawaii, 1840-1940.* Honolulu: Hawaii Educational Review, 1940.

Withington, Frederick Burnham. (Unpublished study on the influence of English on Hawaiian.) [Not able to verify its existence or to secure further details.]

Wolfe, George. "Notes on American Yiddish," *The American Mercury,* XXIX, No. 116 (August, 1933), 473-479.

*Wright, George W. "Pidgin English" (editorial), *Hawaii Hochi,* May 19, 1934.

*Wyld, Henry Cecil. *A History of Modern Colloquial English.* London: T. Fisher Unwin, Ltd., 1920.

    See especially pp. 1-7.

    ———. *The Historical Study of the Mother Tongue: An Introduction to Philological Method.* London: John Murray, 1906. (Reprinted: April, 1926.)

    The author's point of view is so sane that all teachers attempting to deal with Hawaiian Island English should read this book, especially chapters I, III, IV, V, and XV.

*Wyndham, H. A. *Native Education: Ceylon, Java, Formosa, the Philippines, French Indo-China, and British Malaya.* ("Problems of Imperial Trusteeship.") Oxford: Oxford University Press, 1933.

    Incidental information on language problems of education in these colonies.

COMMUNICATIONS

LETTERS

Dr. Romanzo Adams, 19 November, 1934.
Mr. Arthur C. Alexander, 1 May, 1934.
Mr. H. H. Brodie, 3 February, 1933.
Dr. Dai Yen Chang, 29 October, 1934.
Mr. Theodore Chinen, 23 September, 1933.
Mr. Chock Lun, 16 October, 23 October, and 21 November, 1934.
Mrs. George P. Cooke, 2 September, 1933.
Mr. Frank Cundall, Secretary, The Institute of Jamaica,
    16 November, 1934.
Mr. U. K. Das, 7 October, 1933.
Mr. Chester A. Doyle, 5 November, 1933.
Miss Frances Fox, 29 August, 1933.
Dr. E. S. C. Handy, 21 March, 1934.
Miss Bernice E. L. Hundley, 4 March, 1933. (Miss Hundley, Supervising
    Principal of Kauai, reported the views of teachers at a meeting at which
    she kindly introduced the subject of "pidgin English" for discussion.)
Rev. Henry P. Judd, 17 February, 1933.
Prof. R. S. Kuykendall, 24 February and 25 October, 1934.

Mr. Kum Pui Lai, 18 October, 1934.

Dr. K. C. Leebrick, 19 October, 1933.

Miss M. H. Lemon, Registrar General, Bureau of Vital Statistics, Territory of Hawaii, 28 August, 1934.

Dr. A. W. Lind, 7 January, 1932; 29 May, 1933; 1 October, 1933; 22 February, 1934.

Dr. Kalfred Dip Lum, 25 August, 1933.

Miss Esther Ann Manion, Librarian, National Geographic Society, 5 February, 1934.

Mrs. Olive Day Mowat, 22 April, 1933.

Miss Ella H. Paris, 20 February, 1934.

Mr. Gaston L. Porterie, Attorney General of Louisiana, 1 March, 1934.

Dr. E. V. Sayers, 16 October, 1933.

Dr. Madorah E. Smith, 20 September, 1932.

Mr. E. I. Spalding, 26 April, 1934.

Dr. J. Frank Stimson, 23 March, 1934.

Miss Bertha Ben Taylor, 15 June, 1933.

Mrs. Violet U. Tsugawa, 13 November, 1934.

Tungi, Premier of Tonga, 6 March, 1934.

Mr. Jean L. Urruty, Registrar of the Schools Department, Mauritius, 25 April, 1934.

Miss Elsie H. Wilcox, 8 March, 1934. (Miss Wilcox kindly assisted me at several times during the past two years, with my study of language problems.)

INTERVIEWS

Numerous persons have, in formal interviews or informal conversations, given the author information on the history of language in Hawaii or suggestions regarding linguistic processes. The more important interviews have been referred to in footnotes.

EXAMPLES OF HAWAIIAN ISLAND USAGES

Many of these have been obtained from the writer's students, and some from private letters, especially from a number lent by Mrs. George P. Cooke of Molokai.

INDEX